Acclaim for *Two Kisses for Maddy*

"Chronicling the year Matt Logelin spent raising his newborn preemie after becoming a new father and widower at once, TWO KISSES FOR MADDY is almost unparalleled as a raw and unapologetic portrait of grief. But Logelin has given us far more than a remarkable story of loss and healing. TWO KISSES FOR MADDY is a stunning testimony of the kind of love—fated, magnificent—that inspires novels. So vivid, so powerful and pitch-perfect, is Logelin's evocation of his beloved Liz, the woman he met at a gas station at eighteen, that I could hear her laughter and see her face for days after putting the book down."   —Claire Fontaine, national bestselling
coauthor of *Come Back*

"Triumphant...I devoured this poetic, charming, tearful, sometimes funny memoir...and loved it."   —Parenting.com

"No one wants to read a depressing book. But how can you possibly call *depressing* what is so filled with love and life and the unstoppable message of how lucky we are to have what we have? Read this book and put your life back in perspective."
—Brad Meltzer, *New York Times*
bestselling author of *Heroes for My Son*

"The thing that distinguishes this sad, sad story...is the sweet but not sappy credit Logelin pays to those who helped him along the way."   —*Library Journal*

Two Kisses for Maddy

A Memoir of Loss & Love

Matthew Logelin

GRAND CENTRAL
PUBLISHING

NEW YORK   BOSTON

Grand Central Publishing
Hachette Book Group
237 Park Avenue
New York, NY 10017

www.HachetteBookGroup.com

Printed in the United States of America

Originally published in hardcover by Grand Central Publishing.

First Trade Edition: April 2012
10 9 8 7 6 5 4 3 2

Grand Central Publishing is a division of Hachette Book Group, Inc.
The Grand Central Publishing name and logo is a trademark of Hachette Book Group, Inc.

The Hachette Speakers Bureau provides a wide range of authors for speaking events. To find out more, go to www.hachettespeakersbureau.com or call (866) 376-6591.

The publisher is not responsible for websites (or their content) that are not owned by the publisher.

The Library of Congress has cataloged the hardcover edition as follows:
Logelin, Matthew.
Two kisses for Maddy : a memoir of loss & love / Matthew Logelin. — 1st ed.
p. cm.
Summary: "Matt Logelin writes a courageous and searingly honest memoir about the first year of his life following the birth of his daughter and the death of his wife" —Provided by the publisher
ISBN 978-0-446-56430-4 (regular ed.)—ISBN 978-1-4555-0007-9 (large print ed.)
1. Logelin, Matthew. 2. Single fathers—United States—Biography.
3. Widowers—United States—Biography. 4. Logelin, Matthew—Marriage.
5. Logelin, Matthew—Family. 6. Spouses—Death—Psychological aspects—Case studies. 7. Mothers—Death—Psychological aspects—Case studies. 8. Loss (Psychology)—Case studies. 9. Infants—Care—United States—Case studies.
I. Title.
HQ759.915.L625 2011
155.9'37092—dc22
[B]
2010029881

ISBN 978-0-446-56429-8 (pbk)

for madeline.

Foreword

I am not a writer.

At least, I didn't think I was. But in your hands you hold a book that I wrote.

I wish I hadn't had a reason to write this thing. On the morning of March 25, 2008, my life was the best I ever imagined it could be; an instant later, everything would change. More on that soon, but first I want to share a couple of stories.

I've always been of the mind that great art can only come from a place of immense pain (mostly because I hate happy music), and that the resulting work is beautiful because it is motivated by the purest and most authentic of emotions: sadness. I've never believed so strongly in this axiom as I did in the two moments I'm about to describe...

September 2000. I was living in Chicago, working my way through the first year of graduate school. While reading Marx, Weber, and Durkheim for my sociological theory class, I discovered a song that, more than any other had so far, altered my perspective: "Come Pick Me Up" by Ryan Adams. It was the kind of song I wished I could write—it was sad, it was funny, and it included the word *fuck*. But I loved it mostly because it was sad. The words made me feel something I'd never felt before: hearing the swelling pain of that song made me yearn for the kind of heartache that would allow me to create something—anything—so amazing.

After listening exclusively to this song for a couple of days, I called my girlfriend to tell her about it. "I think I could probably write a song like this, but you've been way too good to me." Liz and I had been dating for just over four years at that point, and we had what I considered a nearly perfect relationship. She had never caused me the kind of agony that would allow me to tap into whatever creative side may have been hiding deep within me. And as much as I wanted to write The Next Great Depressing Song, I was glad that I hadn't had the ability—or the need—to do so.

May 2006. I was living in India for a work assignment, and half way through my stay, Liz came to visit. I took a few weeks off so we could travel the country and see things we never imagined we'd have a chance to see. I had a long list of places for us to visit, but Liz insisted we get to one site in particular: the Taj Mahal. Standing in front of one of the Seven Wonders of the World, we listened to our guide tell us the story of how it came to be. He explained that the Mughal emperor Shah Jahan had ordered its construction to fulfill a promise to his wife. Legend has it that on her deathbed—shortly after giving birth to their child—she asked her husband to build her a monument that would forever be known as the most beautiful in the world.

I rolled my eyes, wondering if the story was even true or if it was something the guides fabricated to make female tourists swoon, but Liz was feeling every word of it. She stared in awe at the mausoleum, her eyes welling with tears and her lips agape. Her sweaty hand squeezed mine tighter and tighter as our guide continued the story. When he finally finished, Liz turned to me and said, "You would never do something like this for me."

She was right—I can't build anything. I can barely hang a picture on the wall. But I never imagined a need to do such a thing.

As I began putting this book together, these two stories stuck in my head, and they swirled around and intertwined and coalesced while I wrote it and revised it. They were a huge spark. I hadn't forgotten about that song, and I hadn't forgotten about that trip, but before Liz died, I had forgotten exactly what they'd meant to me.

I know that this book is no "Come Pick Me Up" and it's most certainly no Taj Mahal, but it is my attempt to turn my sadness into something beautiful. It is mine. Mine for Liz. And no matter what, I know that she would be proud of me.

And I guess you could say that I am a writer now. But I really wish I wasn't.

Part I

Part

it seemed obvious
(though probably only to us),
that we'd
spend the rest of
our lives
together.

Chapter 1

I met my future wife, the future mother of my child, at a gas station. It was a Tuesday in late January 1996, and we were both eighteen years old. Though we lived fewer than two miles apart, this was only the second time we had met, as we went to different high schools and ran with different crowds. But that night, when she saw me just a few feet away, Liz Goodman waved and said, "Are you Matt Long-lin?" She mispronounced my name, but it was close enough. An awkward and shy teenager lacking a lot of self-confidence, I was shocked when this beautiful blonde girl started talking to me. It was weird at first—girls like Liz didn't talk to boys like me, so I figured she thought I worked at the gas station and she needed some help filling her tank. I responded with a confused look and sheepish

"Yeah. That's me," and continued filling my own tank. I was instantly captivated by Liz's gregariousness, her moxie, and, of course, her beauty. She stood at exactly four feet eleven inches tall, but carried herself like she was six feet one. Years later, she would tell me that I had impressed her by holding the door open for her when we walked into the little store to pay. I would counter with my surprise that an act as small as that could convince her to see past my unquestionably awkward looks.

We went on our first date that Friday, January 26. Three days later, standing in her parents' driveway, Liz let the L word slip from her lips. I responded with a smile, a kiss, and an "I love you, too," and we were both positive that this was it: we'd both found the person of our dreams. We were just a few months away from heading off to college in different states (I was staying put at St. John's in Minnesota, while Liz was off to Scripps in California), so we became almost inseparable, wanting to make the most of the short time we had left together in the same town.

During my spring break trip to Mexico, I purchased calling cards with money that ordinarily might have been used on beer and admission to clubs, and spent almost the entire trip talking to Liz from pay phones while my friends got drunk and made out with random girls. I'm pretty sure I was the only eighteen-year-old male in Mazatlán doing this on his spring break. A month after my return from the trip, Liz was off to Spain, spending three weeks living with a host family as part of a program designed to get high school seniors out of their comfort zones and into a new environment. While there, she used her dad's calling card to talk to me multiple times each day, running up a phone bill so enormous and so shocking that to this day her dad still remembers the amount, down to the penny. As fall approached and we prepared to head off to college, we promised each other that the distance would not come between us. Thanks to these short practice runs, we were confident that we'd be one of those rare high school couples that would make it all the way through our college years with our relationship—and sanity—intact.

In fact, the distance intensified our relationship—we had to work much harder than the couples we knew who weren't worrying about being apart. Phone and webcam communication became integral so that we could study "together." And no matter where we had been or how late we had been out, we exchanged e-mails nightly. During our four years in college, Liz only missed out on sending four of them compared to my six—a fact that she liked to throw in my face whenever I gave her shit about something later on. When we were able to be together in between our time apart, we truly appreciated it and showed it by walking arm-in-arm through the tree-lined sidewalks of Claremont. Liz spent the money she earned from her on-campus job along with the monthly stipend from her parents to fly me out to California every six to eight weeks. She figured that because she was paying, I should do the flying, and I knew better than to put up a fight. She did visit me enough times for us both to realize that we had more fun together in California anyway. During our summers home, we worked less than half a block apart, using our lunch breaks to make up for the time we had lost during the school year.

Our junior years, we both decided to study abroad for a semester, but knowing one would influence the other's decision, we agreed to discuss our chosen destinations only after the applications had been submitted. Even with a literal world of choices before us, we both picked London. It was incredible to be living in the same city at the same time, without our parents. We both truly felt like we were out in the world on our own for the first time in our lives, but we didn't spend every waking moment together for fear of seriously affecting the other's experience. I know that sounds strange, but we believed that we should continue on as if we were in different parts of the country so that we could both fully experience our semester abroad—but now, we were a forty-five-minute tube ride apart, rather than a four-hour flight. After we finished our studies in London, Liz took off with her friends, and I with mine, to travel around Western Europe. We made a plan to meet up after two weeks, ditch our friends, and travel alone, together. Our paths converged on the island of Corsica, and that was where things changed for both of us. We'd been alone with one another before, but never for two consecutive weeks. We went from Corsica to Italy to Switzerland to Germany, learning what it was like to live happily together as adults. The trip confirmed what we already suspected: ours was a lifelong love—a love that would transcend distance, time, petty disagreements, and any relationship turmoil.

As our college careers came to an end, we were faced with the opportunity to finally live together in the same city on a permanent basis. The only question was, where would we settle? After four years in Southern California, Liz was loath to leave the place, and she took a position with a small consulting firm in downtown Los Angeles. I decided that I wasn't ready to enter the working world quite yet and accepted a generous offer from a graduate school in Chicago, setting out to work toward a PhD in sociology.

These decisions forced us to renew our promise to not let the distance come between us. Against all odds, we had made it work for the past four years—what was a few more? Besides, thanks to her entrance into the real world of working adulthood, Liz would now be making enough money to fly me to Los Angeles more often, or herself to Chicago. Still, we were confident our relationship would last.

Some people would meet Liz and assume that she was all beauty and no brains, but nothing was further from the truth. With her job after college, she turned her sights on becoming a high-powered management consultant. She traveled the country dressed in business suits and high heels, meeting with executives from some of the largest domestic financial institutions. Within seconds of shaking their hands, she'd have them enchanted by her intelligence, poise, humor, and wit. She could astound you with her explanation of some esoteric economic theory, but she also studied the pages of *US Weekly* and *People* magazine and could tell you all about this season's hottest clothing trends and which celebrity was sleeping with his nanny. But whether she had met you an hour earlier or you had been lifelong pals, she was your friend.

Her smile invited people into her life, and her laughter made them stay. But if you deserved it, if you crossed a line and patronized her because of her size or the fact that she was a blonde woman, she could be tough. She once told an older male colleague who patted her on the head to fuck off. When we met someone new at a party and they asked what her job was, I would pipe in: "She fires low-level employees in order to raise stock prices by five cents for multi-billion-dollar banks and insurance companies." Always quick to correct me, she'd say, "I don't actually fire anyone. I recommend head-count reductions and leave the firing of employees to someone else." Four years at an all-women's college and her time as a management consultant only intensified the spitfire attitude she'd been cultivating since birth.

I loved her for that.

After two years, Liz and I independently came to the same obvious decision: it was time to live in the same city. Though used to the distance, we no longer wanted to deal with it.

When I called her one night and told her about my realization, we agreed that I would move to Los Angeles as soon as I finished up my classes and passed my master's exam—the PhD was put on hold.

I graduated at the end of January 2002, and less than a month later my things were packed and I was on a cross-country road trip to Los Angeles, set to move in with Liz. I arrived on her front step with a newly purchased, prized possession.

"What is that?" Liz said.

"It's an original drawing by Wesley Willis. It's the shoreline of Chicago and Wrigley Field."

"Well, it's not coming in the house."

"What? Why not?"

"Because it's huge and ugly. Wait. When did you buy that thing?"

I thought about lying, but I knew she'd see right through it, so I felt compelled to tell her the truth. "Uh, last week, just before I left Chicago. I wanted something to remind me of the city and I thought this was perfect."

Shaking her head, Liz asked, "How much did you pay for it?"

She knew that I had about three dollars in my bank account and a total of sixty-seven dollars of credit left on my Visa, because she'd had to pay for my U-Haul trailer and other moving supplies. Though I'd just told the truth, I used this opportunity for a little lie that I figured would keep me out of trouble. She was pissed that I'd bought this ugly-ass drawing, and she would have been even angrier if she knew how much I'd really paid for it.

"Uh, twenty dollars."

"You paid twenty dollars for a shitty ink drawing on a giant piece of tagboard? What the hell were you thinking?"

I have no idea why I lied. I mean, the thing actually cost me fifty dollars, so a thirty-dollar lie wasn't going to make a difference. What I didn't realize then was that the cost of the thing didn't really matter. It was the fact that I'd spent money when I didn't have any to spend, at a time when we were preparing to start our adult lives together as a couple. I was still living in the fantasy world of graduate school, where student loans were used for records and beer. I had no idea what it was like to be a financially responsible, unselfish adult.

My philosophy around that time was perfectly summed up by a T-shirt I saw on a homeless man on the street outside of our apartment during my first week in Los Angeles: The Working Man's a Sucker. I didn't have a car, so I'd drop Liz off downtown each morning to make some money for us, then I'd pick her up later that evening. Every day, her first question was "Did you find any interesting jobs today?" I had a new excuse each time, but I didn't really need to tell her what she already knew: I spent my first few months in Los Angeles actively trying to not be the sucker mentioned on that shirt by hanging out with my other unemployed friends and attending tapings of *The Price Is Right*.

In June of that year, after more than a few arguments about my motivation level, and a little over three months after my daily fake job search began, one of Liz's friends recommended me for a job at an Internet company in Pasadena. I interviewed, and in their desperation to get a warm body in front of a computer screen, they offered me the job. My grandmother was appalled when she learned I went to work in shorts and flip-flops, spent most of the week playing foosball, and that Friday afternoons were dedicated to drinking beer at my desk. If only she'd known that I was writing ads for breast enhancement supplements and penis enlargement pills...

There was no real hope of advancement at my job. It was an hourly position, and I sort of just showed up and found novel ways to occupy my time until I could clock out for the day, earning salary increases that barely kept up with yearly cost-of-living adjustments. I didn't hate what I was doing, but I didn't love it.

Meanwhile, Liz moved up at her company, gaining titles and invaluable experience, and making more and more money. She also spent a significant amount of time traveling on consulting assignments. Though we finally lived together, months would go by when we'd see each other only on the weekends. For many couples, this extreme amount of time apart would be a real blow to the relationship, but for us it was just par for the course. It actually made the transition to living together a lot easier—if Liz had been home full-time, she would have immediately realized just how much of a lazy slob I was and probably would have kicked me out.

a few weeks
here, a couple of
months there,
nothing more than
a few seconds
when viewed through
the lens
of forever.

Chapter 2

In early 2004 I received an e-mail from one of my college
roommates, Biraj Bista, inviting Liz and me to Kathmandu
for his wedding. I was excited. Going to Nepal had been high
on my list of things to do since I'd met Biraj, but I never
dreamed I'd actually have the money or the time to be able to
go. It took a little convincing to get Liz to agree to the trip because we didn't have a ton of money at the time, and she knew
that I would be unable to contribute a significant amount since
I made less than half of her salary. But thanks to all of the
frequent-flier miles she had racked up traveling for work over
the past four years, the flight would be free. She knew how important this trip was to me, and she told me we'd make it work
no matter what.

What Liz didn't know was that I planned on proposing to her a few days after our arrival in Nepal. I'm not exactly a traditionalist, so I wasn't going to ask her dad for permission or get down on one knee or hire a skywriter to write out my words with airplane exhaust. I always wanted our engagement to be different; I had hoped to surprise her with a ring in a foreign country with the idea that we'd someday make a special return trip there with our children, and this trip to Nepal came at the perfect time. We arranged to go on a short trek through the Annapurna region of the Himalayas. I pictured us hiking to the top of the mountain, at which time I'd whip out the ring and, crying, she'd scream, "Yes! Yes!"

But surprising Liz in any way was a tall order: our finances were closely intertwined, and marriage was a foregone conclusion for us. I'd saved almost no money, so my only hope for getting her the ring of her dreams was to take out a loan for the full amount. As soon as I'd secured it, I called A.J., my closest friend and my only friend who'd already taken the marriage plunge, to ask him where he bought the ring he gave to his wife. He put me in touch with a jeweler in Minnesota, an old friend of his parents who had designed pieces for his family. After eight years together and countless lectures about the "Four Cs," I knew exactly what Liz wanted, and A.J.'s jeweler was able to custom-make it to my specifications. I sent the guy a check, sight unseen. The ring arrived in the mail the day before we left for Kathmandu, and it was fucking gorgeous.

After a flight halfway around the world, we met up with Biraj and some of his friends, and as if we still were back in college, the beer began to flow. Liz lasted as long as she could that first night, but eventually her eyes began to close. I walked her to the hotel, put her to bed, and went back to drink with the guys. We talked of Biraj's upcoming wedding, and about the women in everyone else's lives. When the conversation turned in my direction, Biraj asked when Liz and I were going to tie the knot. Without thinking, I told him that I planned on asking her to marry me when we reached the summit of our trek. There were congratulations all around and, of course, enough beer to require me to close one eye to walk a semistraight line back to the hotel.

I woke up early the next morning with one of the worst hangovers I'd ever had, but we were in a new country and we had to explore it. I thought back to the night before. What had I told the guys? Did they understand that this whole thing was supposed to be a surprise? Shit. I was picturing them congratulating Liz at the dinner party we were to attend that night, thus ruining my dream of surprising her with the ring. I knew what I had to do. Today was the day; it was not the day I wanted, but it would work.

As we walked through town, my sweating had nothing to do with the fact that it was 100 degrees. I tried to get Liz to the spot I'd randomly chosen that morning from the map we were given at our hotel, but she insisted on stopping at every shop along the way. It was so her. I kept my hands in my pockets, trying to hide the fact they were shaking uncontrollably, my right hand clutching the ugly green and white marbled cardboard box that held my promise to Liz. We finally reached Durbar Square, an historic area in the middle of Kathmandu known for its Hindu temples and wondrous architecture. It was obvious Liz was hot and tired, mostly because she kept bitching about both, and her complaining was making me even more nervous. I saw the perfect spot to sit her down and give her the ring, and I suggested we climb the steep stairs up to a temple.

"It's way too hot and the steps are too big for my short legs," Liz said. "Besides, there are monkeys everywhere. I'm not going near those damn things." I pleaded with her to climb up with me, but there was no convincing her. She insisted that it was time to go back to our hotel. I started to panic.

"Liz..." I rarely began a sentence with her name, so she knew I was serious. "Can we please just sit down in the shade before heading back to the hotel!" I said this with the kind of frantic urgency usually reserved for demanding that some awful pop song playing in her car be turned off before my ears started bleeding. So she agreed.

We were now as alone as we could be in such a public place, and I had to do something to stop my hand from shaking. I pulled the box from my pocket, and without a word I handed it to Liz. She looked more surprised than I'd ever seen her, and without opening it she said, "Oh my God! You bought me earrings!"

I just shook my head. "Open it."

She lifted the top of the box and immediately started crying. And screaming. Her high-pitched screams attracted the attention of everyone within earshot, including a man sweeping the inside of the temple who poked his head out of a door to make sure everything was okay.

I smiled, knowing that I had succeeded in making her happy, and I was thrilled that my vision had mostly been realized. She couldn't have been more surprised if I'd told her I was a woman. I wasn't sure this was how Liz had pictured her engagement when she dreamed of it as a little girl. We were both unshowered, wearing white T-shirts (mine with yellow stains under the arms), and looking as jet-lagged as we felt, but for us it was the most perfect imperfect moment.

We decided to get married in our hometown of Minneapolis, Minnesota, so that our friends and family wouldn't have to travel to attend, and we set a date of August 13, 2005. I'm not a superstitious guy, but I suggested we choose a different date, reminding Liz that our anniversary would eventually fall on a Friday. But she said, "I checked out the *Farmer's Almanac*, and the thirteenth of August is historically the best Saturday of the month, weather-wise." Holy shit. I should have known. She had seriously examined the historical weather patterns to ensure perfection. She was a masterful planner, and for this wedding to be a success she had to be. We were living in Los Angeles, but for eight months leading up to the wedding, Liz was traveling each week to Connecticut for work, all while planning our wedding in a third state. To no one's surprise, and with very little help from me, she executed it perfectly. It was elegant, beautiful, and dreamlike, just like Liz.

Surrounded by more than two hundred of our favorite people, we put a label on the love we'd felt for each other from the first moment of our second meeting. I can still see the huge smile on her face, her body wrapped in a cloud of white, and her feet enveloped, making it appear as though she were floating. She commanded the attention of everyone in the room, and not simply because she was the bride. It was her presence and the radiant beauty that flowed forth from every pore in her body that had everyone watching her every move. I can still remember the scent of Stargazer lilies permeating every piece of fabric in the place, from Liz's dress to the linen napkin I used to dab the tears from my eyes as I thought once again that she could never be more beautiful than she was that night.

A few months after returning from our honeymoon in Greece, we sat down for dinner and a serious conversation. Liz told me that she was sick of traveling and that she wanted to find a different job that wouldn't require so much of it. When I questioned whether or not we could afford such a change, she told me that she didn't care if she had to take a pay cut—she wanted to be at home with me. She wanted us to be together.

She loved her job, but she was willing to give it all up to be with me.

I don't know if it was marriage, maturity, or possibly even fear, but just a month after Liz told me that she was quitting her job so we could be together, I volunteered to move to Bangalore, India, for a major six-month-long work project. It was a temporary reassignment, but if I did well, it could have led to much larger responsibilities. When I told Liz, she was thrilled—I knew she would be. She saw me taking initiative at work, and she knew what this would mean for us. Though it wasn't ideal, delaying our time together by six months would bring us closer to fulfilling the dreams we had for the future: a house in Los Angeles and, soon after, a baby.

I left for Bangalore on a Sunday in March 2006—the day before Liz was to start her new job at Disney. It would be three months before we saw each other, which was the longest we would have been apart since we'd started dating. In May she came to Bangalore and I took a couple of weeks off so we could travel through South India before heading north to visit the Golden Triangle area and, most important to Liz, the Taj Mahal. We had the time of our lives seeing sights together that we had only dreamed of, but before we knew it we were back to the routine we knew so well: daily phone calls, nightly e-mails, and the occasional video chat.

I arrived home from India a few days before our first wedding anniversary and promised Liz that I would never leave her again. But after two months back at work, I was asked to return to India to help get a new team up and running. The assignment would mean a huge increase in pay, a salaried position with a well-defined career path, and, finally, a challenge. It was a tremendous step forward for me, but I had just promised to never, ever, leave Liz again. When I talked to her about what was going on, she cried, but mostly out of excitement. There was something in her reaction this time, a slight look of disappointment that made me think she didn't want me to leave her, though. She had already given up so much for me, and I had just returned from six months abroad and was now preparing to leave her again, but we both knew I needed to take this job.

By December, I was back in Bangalore. Liz came out to see me toward the end of the month, and for the first time for either of us, we spent Christmas away from our families. It was an emotional visit. We had obviously missed each other terribly, but finally we were truly in a place that would make possible a home and a family and our happily-ever-after. I decided that this was what it felt like to be an adult.

When I returned to Los Angeles a few months later, Liz must have picked up on my newly achieved sense of adulthood. She told me that she wanted to buy a house before the year was over. I knew what that really meant: she wanted to be pregnant before the year was over. She didn't have to convince me—I was ready, really ready, to become a father. I felt like together we would be fucking amazing parents. In May we found the house of our dreams, a house we couldn't ever have had in Minnesota, complete with lemon, grapefruit, and orange trees in the yard.

And four months later we found out we were going to be parents.

together during
the worst of times
is better than
being alone at
the best of times.

Chapter 3

Early on in Liz's pregnancy, there were concerns about the health of our child. She had awful morning sickness. I mean *awful*. I called it "morning, noon, and night" sickness. It was so bad that her obstetrician, Dr. Sharon Nelson, prescribed her Zofran, which is usually given to people undergoing chemotherapy to help them control the nausea. Liz was worried about taking the medication, but Dr. Nelson assured us that it wouldn't harm the fetus. Though it did little to actually help her feel better, she took it for almost her entire pregnancy.

More often than not, the nausea led to vomiting, and with the vomiting came a significant loss of nutrients to Liz and to our baby. The nausea also ruined Liz's appetite, so she ended up losing weight, and as a result our baby was not gaining the expected amount of weight at each gestational age. To assess the situation, Dr. Nelson suggested we see an ultrasound doctor, Dr. Greggory DeVore.

Dr. DeVore's primary concern was the health of the fetus. That's not to say that he didn't care about the health of the mother, but we were warned by some parents in the area that Dr. DeVore had a bedside manner that made him seem rather cold. More than one of these people referred to him as Dr. Doom because of his proclivity to present the worst-case scenario. When we arrived at his office, I immediately felt that his waiting room was one of the most depressing places I had ever visited. On the walls there were photos of Dr. DeVore surrounded by his large brood, giving me the feeling that the photos were there to provide reassurance that the babies in his care would turn out as healthy as his own kids had—apparently, if the recommendation of your ob-gyn along with this guy's copious certifications, published works, and awards didn't make you believe that this guy knew what he was doing, then these photos would. It wasn't just the decor, though. The waiting room was filled with expectant couples. Yeah, families. Unlike every trip I'd made with Liz to Dr. Nelson's office, there were actually men in this waiting room. Maybe the seriousness of these tests convinced them that they should be there to hold their wives' hands, but I found the presence of these men most disconcerting.

Many of these families were here because an earlier test had indicated something of concern. Others, like us, were there preemptively, hoping to rule out their worst fears. But everyone in the room had the same sullen and pale look, and it was obvious that they were wondering the exact same thing that we were: were they about to hear that their unborn child would be the one out of every thirty-three babies born with birth defects? I still remember the words from Dr. DeVore's website that followed that shitty statistic—that these birth defects are the "leading cause of infant death and childhood disability." We hoped this visit would rule out the unnerving possibility that our baby would wind up dead or disabled, and we saw firsthand how quickly that hope could disappear. More than once we watched as a woman, held tightly by her partner, was led through the doors in tears. We knew exactly what that meant, and each time Liz squeezed my hand a little tighter.

The door opened and a nurse popped her head through, calling Liz in. As she lay down on the exam table, I sat down next to her and grabbed her hand, aiming to give her the kind of reassurance that only the report of a completely healthy baby could provide. Within minutes, Dr. DeVore entered the room, sat down at Liz's side, and with very few words began to perform the ultrasound.

I know that Liz had a thousand questions for the doctor; she *always* had a thousand questions, and I can't think of a time in our twelve years together when she bit her tongue. But here, she was intimidated into silence by Dr. DeVore, and she let him do his work in the quiet. He did speak a couple of times—not to us, but to the nurse in the room, who was taking notes. Even if he had been speaking to us, there's no way we would have understood his medical jargon. Just a few minutes later, he was pulling off his rubber gloves and walking toward the counter near the door, still without a word to us. Liz was practically jumping off the table, waiting for any sort of information.

Finally he spoke: "Liz, your amniotic fluid level is low, your baby is very underweight for the gestational age, and the umbilical cord is wrapped around its neck. You're going to have to go on bed rest for the next three weeks, beginning by lying on your right side. When you can no longer handle lying on your right side, then switch to your left side. When you can no longer handle that, switch back to your right side. You'll come back in three weeks so I can check you out again."

And with that, he was out the door. Liz immediately started crying, and I felt as though I'd been punched in the stomach.

"What the fuck?" I said to Liz.

The nurse tried to calm us down with an explanation of what the doctor had said so tersely. "It's just a precaution. The low amniotic fluid is a concern, because a normal amniotic fluid level is like a shock absorber. It offers the fetus some protection from being jostled around as you carry on your normal daily activities. If you spend the next three weeks lying on your side, there's a much lower risk of causing damage to the fetus, and the hope is that all of the calories you'd normally expend walking through your office or around your house will go directly to the baby, which will help her gain weight."

It made perfect sense, but we were both thinking the same thing: how was Liz going to lie still for three straight weeks?

"What about the umbilical cord around her neck?" Liz asked.

"That oftentimes corrects itself," answered the nurse.

There were a few more questions from Liz and a few more answers from the nurse, but I really wasn't paying attention. I was too distracted wondering if our child was going to become a statistic.

And so just like that, Liz stopped working and followed the doctor's orders. No more constant trips to public restrooms to vomit or lunch hours spent catching up on sleep in the car. Liz completed her three weeks of bed rest, complaining far less than I thought she might. I did everything I could to make her life easier when I was around, and when I had to leave the house, I only wished I could be at home with her.

When we found ourselves back in Dr. DeVore's office, he said, "Things don't look any better. You need to go to the hos-

pital immediately. You'll be there until your baby is born."
Fuck.

Liz was devastated. For some reason we had both been under the clearly mistaken impression that the three weeks of
strict bed rest would be the magic cure for all of the problems
Dr. DeVore had previously diagnosed. Obviously not. Then I
realized our daughter wasn't due for another nine weeks, and I
had a physical reaction to my fear. I've never been so scared in
my life—my entire body was shaking. I tried my best to sup-
press it in an attempt to be strong for Liz, but I was holding
her hand and she could feel it.

"Immediately?" Did this mean that our baby was in some
sort of grave danger? Now it was me who had a thousand questions, but I sensed that there wasn't time for any of them; we
needed to get to the hospital. Luckily, the nearest one was less
than half a mile from Dr. DeVore's office. We jumped in my
car, and a few minutes later Liz was filling out admission papers. While we were checking in, a group of expectant parents
and a hospital staff member walked past us on a tour of the maternity ward. We never got the chance to take that tour. Nor
did we take any birthing classes. I realized then just how useless I'd be to Liz when it finally came time for her to give birth.

This new hospital setup required us both to adjust, and neither
of us found it that easy. There were all sorts of medical ma-
chinery, scheduled tests, a ton of staff in and out of the room,
and little comfort or privacy. We had to make our own enter-
tainment. For the duration of her stay, Liz was required to wear
leg cuffs that helped circulate the blood in her calves to keep
potential blood clots at bay. She hated how hot they made her
feel, and one afternoon she decided to remove them. Not long
after, a nurse entered the room and noticed the cuffs dangling
from the end of the bed.

"What are you doing?" she screamed like a mother who had just busted her teenage son with a stack of porn. "You must keep these on! Not wearing them can kill you! It's happened before and it will happen again!"

Liz just nodded as the nurse put the cuffs back on her lower legs, but as soon as the door closed behind her, Liz lost it.

"Fuck her! I mean, I know she's right, but she didn't have to yell at me like that. How scary! God! What a bitch."

I let out an uneasy laugh as the words came from her mouth, and then I agreed with her. "Yeah, that nurse is a bitch." But that was the last time Liz ever removed those leg cuffs without consulting a nurse. No matter how painful the procedure, no matter how awful and uncomfortable she felt, she knew she had to endure it—and she wanted to, because her only concern was delivering a healthy baby as close to full-term as possible. She made it her job, and once it became her job, it was her singular focus. That was just Liz. Once her mind was set on something, she not only had to complete the task but she had to do it as well as she possibly could.

Even though we lived closer than a ten-minute drive to the hospital, I refused to let Liz spend even one night by herself. I was there as much as I humanly had time to be; this pregnancy was bringing us so much closer, and I just couldn't let her do it alone. I slept on an extremely uncomfortable foldout chair, waking up at least once every hour when some random alarm would go off, or when Liz woke me up to tell me to cover my ears so she could use the bedpan. (I have a passionate, lifelong hatred for the sound of anyone peeing.) My schedule was the same every day: I left the hospital before six o'clock each morning, to avoid the daily parking charge, and headed home to take a shower and change my clothes. I spent most of my days at work thinking about our soon-to-be-delivered baby while replying to e-mails from Liz:

Watching *Titanic*. You're sooooo lucky you're at work.
Meatballs sound so good tonight. Can you pick some
    up before you come up here?
I just had the BEST mani/pedi in my hospital room,
    thanks to Mari.
I'm watching midget madness on *Jerry Springer*...
    AAAAHH!
Good massage, onto my bath... Ah, the life of luxury I
    lead...

I would leave my office after eight hours of being too distracted
to accomplish anything, and stop home just long enough to
grab our mail, pick grapefruit from our tree for the nurses, and
gather flowers from our yard for Liz. I would pick up meatballs,
mint chocolate chip ice cream from Baskin Robbins or whatever she was craving at the moment, and deliver it to her hospital room. We ate together, watched shitty television, listened
to the music I thought she should hear, entertained guests during visiting hours, and talked on the phone to friends and
family about how we were doing.

Liz was often not up to taking visitors, sometimes because
she felt nauseous, other times because she thought she didn't
look cute enough. Instead of telling them not to visit,
though, she insisted that I was happy to entertain them, usually just outside of our room, in the lobby of the hospital, or
in the cafeteria. When the phone calls became too much for
Liz to handle and I grew unwilling to repeat the same mundane story to friends and family all over the world, I decided
that I'd update my blog each evening so that everyone had a
central source of information whenever they had a question
or wanted to know how our baby was doing. It was a website that I'd had for years but rarely posted to—nobody but
my mother checked it. Liz thought this was a good alterna-

tive to answering the endless stream of calls that flooded our evenings, but she insisted that I not post any photos of her lying in a hospital bed.

As much as I complained at the time, I was happy to be there with Liz, especially learning things about her that I didn't yet know. For example, I never knew that her lucky number was seven, or that she considered herself Catholic even though she wasn't religious. In retrospect, it feels strange that we had never discussed these things before, but in the hospital we had nothing to do but talk. When we were apart, we hadn't had the luxury of discussing mundane details, as we were in different parts of the world, where conversations were either expensive or difficult to conduct due to the constraints posed by different time zones. And these simple conversations were not urgent; we were looking forward to a long life together during which such details would eventually emerge.

During our waking hours, when Liz was most worried, I put on a smile, used a confident tone, and assured her that everything would be okay as I sat next to her in her hospital bed, softly stroking her IV-free arm. "Our baby will be perfect...she has you as a mother." That always brought a smile to her face. When she'd finally fall asleep, I'd sit on that back-ruining foldout chair and worry about how things would turn out. Yeah, she was going to have Liz as a mother, but she was going to have me as a father, and that couldn't be good. I'd felt fairly sure of myself over the last seven months, but now that our child was closer to being born, I was far less certain that I'd be a good parent. More worrisome for our baby in the short term, however, was the unknown: her health. We had no idea what was really going on inside Liz's womb, and this early in the pregnancy we didn't want to know—really knowing could only come after delivery and it was too early.

Liz had seemed so confident of the health of our child,

but after she entered the hospital her entire outlook changed. She was visibly worried, looking ashen and sad when we were alone. It was quite a reversal of roles for us. I had always been the pessimist in our relationship while Liz was the optimist. But a lot of the concerns she had early in her pregnancy were no longer the stuff of ob-gyn warnings; now they were very real possibilities.

While in the hospital, she had been reading a book about premature babies. One night she was so fed up with the negativity spewing forth from its pages that she sat up straight in her hospital bed and threw it to the other end of the room. "Fuck this piece of shit!" I looked up from my computer screen as the words left her lips and the book hit the whiteboard listing the names of her nurse and personal care attendant for the day.

"That was one hell of a throw," I said, and turned to see her shaking as though she'd just been retrieved from beneath the surface of a frozen lake. Clearly this was no time for one of my jokes. I picked the book up from the floor and crawled into bed with her, doing everything I could to hug the pain away. After she calmed down, I opened the book and flipped straight to the copyright page. "Liz, this book was published in 1978," I said. "I guarantee things have advanced in the field of premature babies in the last thirty years." That was enough to coax a small chuckle from her, and for one more day I felt like I had done my best work, supporting my wife and best friend.

At night, when it got late and the visits from hospital staff became less frequent, Liz and I would fantasize about our future with our daughter. Liz talked of traveling the world, shopping for shoes and purses, mother-daughter spa trips for manis, pedis, and massages, and high tea at the ever-so-elegant Huntington Library. I talked of autumn nights at Dodger Stadium, shopping for records, father-daughter fishing trips to Alaska with her uncle Nick, and beers and Shirley Temples at the Polish restaurant down the street from our house.

As soon as we could possibly find out the sex of our baby, we did. Well, that wasn't my choice. I had this very romantic belief that giving birth should be one of the great surprises in our life, but Liz disagreed.

"How am I supposed to have a baby shower without knowing the sex of our child?" Liz asked.

"I don't know. How about doing what Neolithic humans did?" I responded.

"What's that?"

"Register for gender-neutral gifts."

At this, she rolled her eyes, which she often did in response to my sorry-ass attempts at humor. Deep down I knew that this was an argument I'd never win, because one of Liz's finest traits was to obtain all available data so that she could have every last detail planned out. I knew it was important to Liz, so I followed her lead.

When Dr. Nelson asked us if we were ready to learn the sex of our baby, Liz brought her hands together just under her chin, clapping expeditiously, the way she always did when she was excited, and let out a squeal that indicated she was indeed ready. With a few swipes of the transducer probe and a couple of tilts of the resulting photograph, Dr. Nelson said, "It's a girl!"

A girl.

I used to scowl at the little girls at the baseball stadium, covered head to toe in pink Dodgers gear, jumping up and down in the aisles, waving pom-poms and screaming at the top of their lungs even when the ball wasn't in play.

"Little boys don't do this kind of shit," I'd say. "Can't these girls just shut the hell up and watch the game?"

"You'll think it's so cute when we have a little girl and she does it," Liz would answer.

"Maybe, but I think that's what *you* want."

We both started crying as soon as we heard Dr. Nelson's words. To be honest, it wasn't just Liz who wanted a girl. I have no idea what the hell it was, but something in me changed the day we learned she was pregnant, and from that moment on I only pictured us with a girl in our lives. But it didn't mean I wasn't without fear.

Liz envisioned a mini-Liz, which I was actively trying to avoid for a couple of reasons. First, I knew having two strong-willed women in my house would make it hard for me to get my way. Second, I wanted to turn our daughter into a tomboy to keep the boys away from her as she got older. Liz wasn't exactly thrilled with this plan, but I told her it was better than my first thought.

"What was that?" she asked.

"Well, if she looks anything like you, we're doomed, so I think we should consider giving her a nifty little ear-to-ear scar."

"Jesus, Matt. That's not funny."

"I know," I said. "It's not a joke."

Of course, it was a joke, and I knew she knew it was, because she gave me that slight look of disapproval I saw whenever I made a crass comment. But that was my role in our relationship. I had to do something to lighten the mood, because as we lay there night after night, trying to ignore the hum of the heart monitor and other hospital equipment, the future we dreamed of seemed so far away.

How the fuck did this happen to us?

baby's heart rate dropped around 3:30 a.m.
everyone was concerned.
dr. stopped by in the morning.
and said that it may be best
to have madeline come out and play.

Chapter 4

I always sort of imagined something out of a '50s television show: Liz would shoot out of bed in the middle of the night, shake me awake, and yell at me to get her overnight bag and the keys to the car because the baby was coming. I'd say, "Are you sure? How far apart are the contractions?" and she'd say, "Trust me. This is gonna happen tonight." I'd be nervous, trying to remember the breathing exercises we'd learned in those birthing classes. I'd put on an unmatched pair of shoes and trip on a few things on the way out the door like some slapstick comedian. I'd get her in the car and realize I had forgotten her overnight bag in the house. We'd rush to the hospital, get pulled over for speeding, and then, after shouting at the cop in my exasperated voice, "My wife is having a baby!" we'd get a police escort the rest of the way there. I'd pace the halls of the hospital with Liz's father, my father, and my stepfather, waiting for the doctor to come out and announce that we had a healthy baby girl. "Ten toes and ten fingers!" the doctor would say, and we'd all shake hands, slap backs, and smoke cigars. And then? Happily ever after, of course.

Early on a Monday morning before I'd left the hospital for work, an alarm went off in the nurses' station, just outside of room #7. Liz's room. Her lucky #7. A nurse came in and told us the news: our baby's heart rate had once again experienced a significant drop, which meant that today was the day we'd finally meet our child. Many factors went into the decision, but the doctors simply believed it was time. With Liz's amniotic fluid level still low and our growing baby taking up more and more space in her womb, the possibility of damage to our daughter became a serious concern. In addition, as she got bigger, the umbilical cord got tighter around her neck, so if her heart rate showed a sustained drop it indicated a possible lack of oxygen getting to her brain and other parts of her body. They determined that our daughter would be better off out in the world than in Liz's womb. We experienced a mix of excitement and fear; we were definitely ready to hold our baby, but she was still seven weeks early, and we were terrified that she might be too young to survive.

While one of the nurses was talking to Liz, I called our parents and told them to get on the next flight to Los Angeles because their granddaughter would be making her first appearance sometime before noon. Liz's parents and my mom all said they'd be in Los Angeles before the day was over. My stepfather was unable to make it due to a work conflict, and my dad and stepmother were in Florida on vacation, but they promised to come out in a couple of weeks for the trip they'd already booked to coincide with our baby's scheduled due date. I called

Anya, Liz's best friend, and told her to ditch work and come to the hospital because Liz wanted her in the recovery room after the C-section.

I posted something on the blog for the rest of our friends and family. It was a simple photo of the whiteboard in Liz's hospital room. Preprinted on the board were the words, "Today is..." Underneath, I wrote, "March 24, 2008—and Madeline will be here in about 1 hour." It was the first time I had ever written out my daughter's name. Seeing it there on that board, in my handwriting, and knowing that today was the day we would finally meet her, made my heart feel like it was going to burst.

As soon as we had learned that Liz was pregnant, we began our search for the perfect name. She kept a book of baby names on her bedside table, and we started at the beginning, taking turns thumbing through a new letter each night, calling out names to the one not holding the book. We had pretty simple criteria for choosing our child's name: it couldn't rhyme with anything terrible, it couldn't be the name of any girl/woman from our past who was in any way insufferable, and it couldn't be the name of any of my ex-girlfriends. I suggested names of women in my favorite songs and books, and Liz suggested names of strong females throughout history. Each of us rejected the other's idea for one of the reasons mentioned above.

It was on the thirteenth night that Liz called out a name that neither one of us objected to. "What do you think of Madeline?" she asked.

"I love it."

And that was the last time we opened the book.

Choosing a middle name was a bit more difficult. We hadn't even considered one until Liz's very first delivery scare. One of the nurses asked us to fill out some paperwork, and when she got to the spot for middle name, she paused.

"We need to come up with a middle name for Madeline."

It hadn't occurred to either of us.

A few days later, we still didn't have any ideas. I was walking through the halls of the maternity ward and I stopped at the window of the nursery. I looked from baby to baby, hoping that when ours was born, she would be as big and as healthy as they all appeared, when it came to me: Madeline's middle name should be Elizabeth.

I ran back to the room, excited to share the news with Liz.

"No way," she said. "It's way too narcissistic."

"What? I think it's cute. Think about it: Maddy is similar to my name, and with your name as her middle name, she'd sort of be named after both of us."

She digested my point of view for a few seconds, and then her contemplative look gave in to that huge smile that meant she was thrilled.

"I don't hate it," she said playfully.

As the nurses came in and prepared Liz for her delivery, I made a mental note of all the things I needed for the big moment. Still camera: check. Video camera: check. I had no intention of photographing or recording any parts of the birthing process, mainly because the thought of watching it had me hyperventilating; I simply planned on taking some abstract shots of the delivery room and possibly a shot of our daughter, but only after the doctors and nurses removed all the nasty birthing goo from her. I brought the video camera to record Liz's trip to and from the delivery room, capturing our moments together just before and just after our child was born. That was it. No breathing exercises to remember, no overnight bag to forget at home—just some electronic equipment.

We heard a knock and then saw Anya's head peek through a crack in the doorway. Liz's face lit up immediately and the tears began to flow. She had this sadly beautiful way of crying when she felt an overwhelming sense of relief: her lower lip would quiver, her eyes would open wide, and her head would tilt slightly to the left. Despite the uncertainty of the situation she was about to face, she instantly felt better when her best friend arrived. Anya and Liz went to college together at Scripps and had been almost inseparable since they had met, becoming even closer after the rest of their group of friends moved away from Southern California. They were always there for one another, but more important, Anya was always there for me, indulging Liz's shopping fantasies when I didn't feel like watching her try on twenty-five different outfits or listening to her drone on and on about some idea she had for redecorating the house. I never heard Liz laugh as loud or as hard as she did when she was with her best friend. Liz was always at her happiest in Anya's company, and I was a very, very close second. Aside from the big reason that Anya was at the hospital, this day was no different than any other time they got together. They were laughing hysterically and I was rolling my eyes at their inside jokes.

A few minutes later, we heard another knock on the door. This time it was Dr. Nelson. She entered the room with a huge smile, bringing Liz even more tears of relief. Dr. Nelson shared with us information about the delivery, answered some last-minute questions, and reassured us that things were going to go great. Liz asked again if our baby would be okay if she came out today.

"Yes," the doctor replied. "At this point it's safer for her to be outside the womb than inside." To illustrate the point, she unfolded the long printout, a pink and white grid with a black line representing our baby's heart rate over the past several hours. Liz and I had become uncertified experts in reading these over the past three weeks. When Dr. Nelson without so much as a word pointed to a dramatic dip in the line, indicating a significant and prolonged drop in our baby's heart rate, it was obvious to us that she had to come out. And soon. "Don't worry," Dr. Nelson continued, sensing our growing anxiety. "I'm an expert in getting them out. But I have no idea what to do with them after that. That's going to be up to you and Matt."

I had gotten to know Dr. Nelson quite well during the previous seven months, meeting her monthly during Liz's checkups. She was just the kind of doctor I pictured taking care of my wife: confident, intelligent, and funny. Almost more important than being an amazing and highly skilled physician was the fact that she seemed better able to read people than most doctors. She always knew exactly what to say to Liz to make her feel better, no matter the situation. During one appointment, Liz was crushed to learn that she had not gained the expected amount of weight for someone at her pregnancy stage. I'm not sure if Dr. Nelson could sense the fear in Liz's questions or if she saw the tears welling up in her eyes, but she said, "Nicole Richie just gave birth to a healthy baby girl, and she couldn't have weighed more than eighty pounds during the final days of her pregnancy. Liz, your baby's going to be just fine." With that, Liz looked up from her lap. It took a special doctor to know that there was nothing like a pop-culture reference to make Liz feel better about her own situation.

Now, Dr. Nelson left the room, and I could tell that Liz was getting more and more nervous as the time to deliver approached. I went to her bed and held her hands. As I rubbed her palm with my thumb, I kissed her on the cheek then whispered in her ear, telling her just how excited I was to finally see the daughter we had created. I'll never forget how beautiful she looked at that moment. She was pale, but this ethereal glow emanated from her. The pain she felt clouded the room, yet her eyes had an incredible gleam, like she knew that this hard-fought battle was almost over and that everything was going to work out just as we had hoped it would.

When the time arrived to wheel Liz to her first meeting with our baby, I grabbed the cameras and followed behind. With a nurse at Liz's head pushing her bed down the hallway and Anya by her side holding her hand, I filmed the entire ride from room number #7 to the delivery room. Once we entered a sterile hallway through a set of double doors, the nurse informed me that they had to do a bit of prep work before Liz's C-section, and told me to wait outside the delivery room until someone called me in. "I'll see you in a few minutes. I love you so much" is what I said to Liz as she was wheeled away.

After I changed into operating room gear—a daddy suit, as the nurses called it—and Anya headed back to the waiting room, I was alone for the first time in a few hours. I nervously paced up and down the hallway, taking a few photos of the hospital equipment along the walls of the corridor, and worrying now not about our baby, but about my wife.

Soon, a nurse opened one of the doors to the delivery room and beckoned me in. My anxiousness suddenly multiplied a million times, and I started to sweat. My eyes were immediately drawn to the big blue paper sheet hanging at the crest of the mountain that was Liz's pregnant belly. I wouldn't be seeing anything I didn't want to see, but suddenly I didn't give a shit what I saw. I realized at that moment just how ridiculous my earlier neuroses about the delivery actually were. As long as everything worked out fine, I'd be happy to watch ten full-grown adults and a bear pop from her vagina, high-fiving each of them on the way out. I was brought back to reality by a nurse instructing me to wash my hands and arms up to my elbows.

As I stepped on the foot pump to start the water running, I heard Liz's voice. I couldn't really make out her words, but a louder, male voice said, "Your wife has been given some pain medication. She's conscious, but she's not totally lucid." I was directed to a chair next to her hospital bed, and I sat down to her right, our heads parallel. I whispered to her, "I love you." She said, "I love you, too. And I love my, uh, ana, ana, uh, anesthesi...whatever." I craned my neck toward Liz's new best friend, the anesthesiologist. Smiling behind my face mask, I thanked him for taking care of her.

I reached for Liz's hand and looked around the room, seeing, in addition to the anesthesiologist, a couple of nurses and a doctor. A few seconds later, Dr. Nelson walked in and said that they were ready to get started. "We'll have your baby out in fewer than thirty minutes."

That's it? I only have to wait half an hour to meet the daughter of my dreams? Awesome.

Soon the sound of hospital instruments got louder, and the unmistakable nonsmell of sterility and surgery permeated the stale air in the room. I continued to hold Liz's hand, and I realized at a certain point that I might have squeezed it a little too hard when the sound of the doctor's tools made a loud noise. A few minutes into the delivery, my eyes fixated on the clear plastic tube that stretched from behind the blue sheet, transporting way more blood than I ever would have imagined across the room and into a big, enclosed, cylindrical device. I suddenly felt like I was going to pass out. Fuck. This was exactly what I was worried about when I told Liz I couldn't be in the delivery room. I felt the sweat soaking into my hospital-issued hat, and my chest tightening as I thought about fainting. I knew it was all in my head, yet the more I tried to get over it, the closer I got to these thoughts actually manifesting themselves into actions—actions that would result in diverting the attention of the hospital staff in my direction, away from my wife and daughter.

I felt like such a failure as a partner. I knew that I couldn't do that to Liz, so I quickly talked myself into pulling my shit together. I stared down at the hospital identification bracelet hanging loosely around her wrist, straining my eyes to read the tiny print. I started to feel the way I felt after drinking a bottle and a half of red wine, like I was circling the drain of some giant bathtub. I needed something else, another point of focus.

I looked to my left and found Liz. I stared at her face, studying each pore, every freckle. I admired the extraordinary vividness of her blue eyes glinting beneath the hot lights of the delivery room, and with my own eyes I smoothed out every hint of a wrinkle on her face. Wrinkles barely visible even at this close distance; wrinkles that would inevitably deepen as we grew old together.

As I stared, I realized that I had never seen her face this closely. I couldn't believe how different she was from the Liz I'd been looking at for a little more than twelve years. She was even more gorgeous than I remembered, and right then I felt like the luckiest motherfucker in the world. It was the beauty of her face that brought me out of my stupor and into the place I needed to be for her and for our baby.

madeline met mom.
mom met madeline.
i cried a little.
cleaned up my act.
cut the cord.
and took a nice close-up of baby.
madeline took a little trip to the nicu.
mom took a nap.
i paced.

Chapter 5

All of a sudden I heard a baby screaming. Then I had a moment of clarity. Holy shit! That's not *a* baby! That's *our* baby! A few weeks ago, we had been worried about our daughter's lungs being fully developed. A nurse told us that if she came out screaming, it was a good indication that she was doing well. I started crying immediately upon hearing that little scream. Liz, on the other hand, panicked. "Is she okay? Is she okay?"

"Yes, Liz, she's doing great! Don't you hear her screaming?" I squeezed my wife's hand as hard as I could, in an attempt to calm her down, to let her know that all of the pain, all of her hard work, had paid off.

From behind the blue shield came Dr. Nelson's voice. "Guys, she looks great. She is absolutely beautiful."

I looked at the clock hanging high on the wall. The red, interconnected vertical and horizontal lines formed by a series of LED lights came together to indicate the exact minute our lives changed—11:56 a.m.

Before I knew it there was a nurse at my side, directing me toward the sink. Standing nearby was another nurse, holding my daughter in a generic blue, pink, and white striped blanket. My first glimpse of her took my breath away. Yes, there was a small amount of goo stuck to her face and in her hair, but wow! She had hair! I could see it around her ears, sticking out from underneath the little knit hat that was already on her head. And her nose! It's beautiful, and her cheeks are full, and she has the same chin as me! And her eyes! Her eyes are closed, but I bet they look just like Liz's eyes! Wait! How tall is she? How much does she weigh? No one counted her fingers and toes! Are there ten of each? My mind was racing. The thrill I felt upon seeing my daughter was unlike anything I'd ever felt before. It was like our wedding day, a new Neutral Milk Hotel record, and a trip to Nepal, all wrapped into one tiny screaming bundle of joy.

I was jolted from my thoughts by one of the nurses, who asked if I would like to cut the umbilical cord. Of course, I thought. Then another thought: Holy shit! That must be the longest umbilical cord of all time. I mean, I had no idea how this usually goes, but I didn't know the thing could stretch from Liz's womb all the way to the sink on the other side of the room. I soon realized that my cutting of the cord was a mostly symbolic gesture, because when the nurse lifted the blanket and uncovered our baby, I saw that she was already untethered from Liz—there was just a small, one-and-a-half-inch piece of cord pinched off by a little plastic clip. I grabbed the scissors from the nurse and struggled to get the two blades to slice through the sinuous, rubberlike thing that had kept our child well fed for the last thirty-three weeks.

Suddenly, I heard Liz's voice; she sounded far more alert than she had during the delivery. "Can I see my baby?" I turned toward her as she strained to see the child she'd dreamed about all her life. The nurse walked toward her with our daughter, and I asked if I could take a photo. She responded, "Make it fast—we have to get your baby to the NICU." I grabbed my camera and snapped a couple of photos of Liz getting her first look at our daughter, Madeline Elizabeth Logelin.

In the commotion, however, I failed to immediately process the words spoken by the nurse. NICU? What the fuck? I thought our baby was doing great. The thrill I felt was replaced by equal parts dread and fear. Dr. Nelson stepped in to explain: "Madeline looks great, but we need to get her to the NICU to confirm."

I tried to remain calm for Liz. She was just coming down from the high of the pain medication, and the last thing she needed was to have me in a panic. While the nurse wheeled her to the recovery room, I went to get Anya from the waiting room. I knew that Liz would need us both.

When we arrived, Liz was in good spirits but was still reeling from the drugs. She was calmer than I expected. I held her hand as she and Anya talked, but I don't remember a word of what they said. I was anxious to see our baby and to confirm that she was okay, but I couldn't leave Liz. It was impossible to reconcile those feelings. Where do my loyalties lie? I thought. And where *should* they lie? With the woman of my dreams and the mother of my child, or with the child to whom she just gave birth, the child who was born seven weeks early? I'd never felt a pull this strong. The only thing even kind of similar was when I had to decide whom to cheer for when the Los Angeles Dodgers played the Minnesota Twins in interleague play—and I assure you, that didn't come close.

"Liz, I'm gonna go check on Maddy," I blurted out.

"I see how it is," she said. "I'm already number two."

Shit. I felt awful, but then she gave me a smile to show that she was just fucking with me. I grabbed my camera and calmly walked out the door. As soon as it closed behind me I started running—I just had to get to our daughter. I stopped in front of the window with all the babies, and only then did I realize that I had no idea where the Neonatal Intensive Care Unit was. I had walked by the regular nursery every single day and that was where I had expected to see Madeline, but things hadn't really happened the way they were supposed to. I knocked and someone buzzed me in; I stuck my head just inside the door.

"Can I help you?"

"Can you tell me where the NICU is?"

"Down the hall to the right."

Without so much as a thanks, I bolted down the hallway and made my way inside. A nurse stopped me. "Sir. Are you Madeline's dad?"

"Yes I am." Madeline's dad. Wow. I understood then that I would forever be defined by my relationship to my child. It felt amazing.

Pointing at the window in front of her desk she said, "Madeline's in here. You need to remove your ring and wash your hands and arms up to your elbows for at least two minutes before going in." I did exactly as I was told. I didn't want to be responsible for ruining the health of someone else's baby—or of my own—because I had cookie crumbs or bacon grease on my hands.

I stepped inside and was stopped by a male doctor who introduced himself and immediately started telling me about Madeline. "She's doing great, considering how early she was born." He told me that she was in an incubator to help regulate her temperature, and she had a tube covering her nose to deliver her oxygen. He said that this was merely a precaution and he thought they'd be able to remove it in the next couple of hours since she appeared to be breathing just fine on her own. He then explained that she had a feeding tube in her mouth, running directly into her stomach because at her gestational age, she had yet to develop the ability to suck and swallow. I was so concerned about my baby's health that I couldn't even laugh at the double entendre.

"Let's go see her," he said, walking me into the room. There was a see-through plastic box and a small, handwritten sign with her name—Madeline Elizabeth—and the words Welcome Baby Girl.

Inside was our baby, on top of the same blue, pink, and white striped blanket that had covered her when she left the delivery room. She was now loosely covered by another blanket, this one with multicolored hearts. I tensed up at the sight of my daughter's face covered in an oxygen mask, tubes and wires peeking out from under her blanket, running through to the monitors next to her box.

The sounds of the machines humming and beeping put me into a trancelike state. Those few minutes with my daughter seemed like hours. There she was: out of the womb and into our world. I couldn't help but think how fragile she looked—she had seemed more robust just seconds after delivery. Our baby. I watched her chest. Was it moving? Yes. Up and down, however slightly. I relaxed a bit. As scary as things looked with the oxygen tube and all the wires, and as unsure as I was about the situation, I reminded myself that she was being taken care of by an amazing group of doctors and nurses. For the first time since Liz had gone on bed rest, I felt oddly content that everything was going to be okay.

"Would you like to touch her?"

The words that brought me out of my thoughts. Touch her? I thought. Why can't I hold her? Wasn't she supposed to be in Liz's arms by now, just finishing up her first breast-feeding, then being lulled to sleep by Liz's rendition of "Twinkle, Twinkle, Little Star" while I filmed the whole thing? I guess I hadn't thought of the logistics. With all of the wires and tubes, there was no way she could be in my arms. Then I wondered how long she'd be in that box. Liz was a rather impatient person, and I knew that she'd want to hold Madeline right away and take her home as soon as possible.

"Please," I answered. The doctor unlocked the hinged plastic that covered the armholes, then stepped out of the way and nodded at the box.

I moved toward it and reached both of my hands inside, careful not to disturb any of the wires. Madeline was lying on her right side. I reached my left hand underneath the oxygen tube so I could touch her head, and I slowly rubbed the small patch of skin not covered by the straps that secured it to her head. It felt so soft. I studied every last bit of her, starting from the top down. With her hat now off, I could see that she had a covering of light blonde hair. I touched it, feeling a few strands between my thumb and my forefinger. They felt like tiny threads of silk. Her skin was light pink in color, and it almost appeared to be gently coated in white velvet. Her eyes were still closed. I wondered if they stayed closed for a few days, like a baby raccoon or something. I had heard that babies have very pliable heads, and I was seriously concerned that the straps securing the oxygen tube to her face would leave a permanent imprint on her head and cheeks. On her left arm was a little pink splint that appeared to hold the IV in place.

Just then I wondered about her fingers and toes again. Were there really ten of each? I gently lifted her arm and felt her fingers, in my head counting each one as I touched them. Good news: five on her left hand. I grabbed her right hand. Once again I touched and counted five fingers. I lifted the

blanket covering the lower half of her body and went straight
for her toes. I noticed an electrode on the bottom of her left
foot, but paid little attention to it as I counted off her toes.
Five on each foot. The ultimate indication that your child is
perfect, right?

I didn't want to leave Madeline, but I knew I had to report
back to Liz before she jumped out of bed and made her way
down here by herself. I snapped a couple of photos before giving my daughter's shoulder a few more strokes, and then I
closed the doors to both of the armholes and headed for the
door. Before walking out of the room, I paused and turned back
toward the doctor. "Can you tell me how big she is?"

He looked down at the chart on the desk in front of him.
"Three pounds, thirteen and a half ounces, and seventeen and a
quarter inches long." Statistics I'll never forget.

Back down in the recovery room, I gave Liz and Anya the run-
down, relaying everything the doctor told me and emphasizing
the part about Madeline doing great, considering how early she
was born. They both seemed relieved.

Liz's eyes lit up with excitement when I offered to show her
photos of our baby. I pulled up what I had taken in the delivery room, followed by the ones I had just taken in the NICU.
"Oh my God! Is she okay?" I could hear the panic in her voice
and immediately realized that I should've withheld the photos
of Madeline in the box, wires protruding, her face covered by
the oxygen tube. I reassured her that our baby was going to be
okay, as the doctor had done for me.

The nurse in the room piped in, as if to take some of the
pressure off me. "The doctor told me that you'll be able to see
your daughter in twenty-four hours."

That didn't help as much as any of us hoped, though. "I
want to see her now. How can we make this happen?" Liz was

a great deal maker, but this was one negotiation she wasn't going to win, and the nurse told her so.

Soon after, we said good-bye to Anya, and Liz was wheeled into her postdelivery room. It was different from the one she had been in for the previous three weeks, but all our things had already been moved for us, including the uncomfortable armchair on which I'd been sleeping. We settled in and I made phone calls to our parents, telling them the good news. My mom and Liz's parents had found flights and would arrive in Los Angeles that evening. Liz napped. I listened to some new music and updated the blog:

> madeline was born
> at 11:56 am (march 24, 2008)
> at a bruising 3 pounds, 13.5 ounces.
> 17.25 inches long (almost as tall as her mom at age
>   30).
> kidding of course, but liz is really short
> and baby is really long.
> we've been joking over the past few days...
> if madeline gets daddy's height and mommy's looks,
> everything will be okay.
> if it goes the other way, she's in trouble.
> thankfully she's long...
> and beautiful.

Eventually a doctor entered the room, waking Liz to tell her the same things about Madeline that I had already shared, and to confirm what she had been told earlier: she had to remain in the hospital bed for twenty-four hours before she could get up to see, feed, or touch Madeline. He informed us of our daughter's schedule: "She'll be fed every three hours through the tube in her mouth. Matt, you can come in and feed her anytime.

You'll also be able to change her diapers." For the first time in my life, the idea of changing a diaper sounded like the greatest thing in the world.

By the time the doctor left, Liz's whole demeanor had changed. I think she felt better hearing the information from a real doctor rather than just from me, but she was still extremely disappointed that she couldn't be with Madeline immediately. "She's not even going to know her mom! She'll already be so attached to you by the time I get to see her."

I assured her that would not be the case, and added, "You've been waiting seven and half months for this moment. What's another twenty-four hours?" She smiled at me, and I felt like I had successfully deflected her concerns. We had spent thirty-three weeks worrying about nothing but the health of our daughter, and here was another doctor telling us that she was doing well. And soon, Liz would hold our baby.

For the rest of the afternoon and into the evening, I shuttled between the NICU and Liz's hospital room. I found it hilarious, but Liz had a serious fear that our child would be ugly, though deep down I think she knew Madeline would be gorgeous. Nonetheless, each time I came back from visiting Madeline, Liz insisted on seeing the latest photos and asked me if she was beautiful. I promised that she was, and I showed her the photos, sharing details about each of my successive trips. I told her about using a syringe to slowly push what the doctor called a "baby cheeseburger," a high-fat liquid formula, through the feeding tube directly into her stomach, and I teased her mercilessly that I was one, two, three diaper changes ahead of her and that she would have to catch up when we all finally made it home.

When our expected company arrived at the hospital, they came in and hugged Liz, talking to her for a short time. It was obvious who the grandparents were really there to see, so we left Liz alone and I walked them down the hall. Because of NICU visitor restrictions, I had to accompany each of them, one at a time, to see and touch their grandchild, while the other two looked in at us through the window. Sometime between my last visit and this one, the oxygen tube had been removed from Madeline's face and the tube in her mouth had been moved to her nose. Much to my relief, the straps had left no visible indents on her head or her cheeks.

We went back to say good night to Liz before I walked her parents, Tom and Candee, and my mom to the rooms they had booked in the hotel attached to the hospital. I stopped in to check on Madeline one last time on her first day of existence before heading to Liz's room to sleep. I knew there would be a lot of late nights coming up, so I decided to take advantage of the NICU nurses, telling them that I wouldn't be coming in for any of the overnight feedings. March 24 had been a big day. I needed some rest.

the proud parents will continue to update
everyone on our beautiful baby.
look forward to even more good news.
(i know we will).

Chapter 6

I woke up before Liz early the next morning and sneaked out to go see our baby. When I arrived, the nurse asked if I would like to hold her this time.

I couldn't believe I was going to be able to hold Madeline. I hadn't asked, but I had assumed I wouldn't be able to do so for a few weeks. She still had the wires attached to her body, and the feeding tube was still present. "Yes, but how?" I said.

"Very carefully," the nurse replied. I watched as she opened up the side of the Madeline's incubator and slid the wires and feeding tube through the openings at its bottom end.

I sat down in a blue rocking chair, and for the first time in my life I held my daughter. I was surprised by my reaction. I'm generally not very emotional, and if ever I felt the urge to cry in public before, I certainly would have suppressed it. But when I held Madeline, I just let the tears fall. I suddenly recognized the feeling that overcame me—it was the same wave of contentment and relief that hit me when she had come out screaming the day before. With her temporarily out of that incubator and in my arms, I knew she was going to be fine. And I couldn't wait to tell Liz.

I finished up Maddy's feeding and headed back to Liz's hospital room. She was awake when I got there. "How is she doing?" she asked, eyes wide with the kind of anticipation she usually reserved for the moment the dessert menu was recited to her at her favorite restaurant.

"I got to hold her," I said, smiling wide enough to show my teeth (something I rarely did).

She immediately sat up, wincing a bit from the pain she felt coming from the incision in her abdomen. "You did? I'm superjealous! Tell me all about it!" For the next few minutes I sat next to her in bed, and as the room filled with sunlight I told my wife all about holding our healthy baby girl in my arms.

We spent the morning doing all of the mundane things that new parents do the day after their child is born: We chatted with family members. We filled out insurance and hospital paperwork. We applied for Madeline's Social Security number and birth certificate. We debated whether we should rent or buy a breast pump. We decided which day to attend the recommended baby CPR class. We discussed what it would be like at home, just the two of us with Madeline, with no help from the nurses and doctors.

The sense of relief I felt about having our baby out in the world overwhelmed me, but now I felt a new nervousness at the tasks that lay ahead. We were now responsible for this kid's life. Unlike some of the other major events in our lives, I planned to take an extremely active role in raising our daughter, but I sort of felt that as a man, I didn't have that motherly instinct. I knew I had a lot to learn, but I was confident that Liz was ready and prepared, and that she'd be able to lead the way. Together, the two of us would be able to handle any challenge.

Midday, my mom called and asked me if I was ready to go to Tiffany's to pick out a gift for Liz. She knew that I had planned on surprising Liz with a piece of "thank you for enduring this hellish pregnancy" jewelry, but that I hadn't yet had a chance to get anything. I thought that jewelry would be the absolute best way to show her that I cared, that I appreciated her, and that we were creating new memories to cherish for the rest of our lives. I also owed her a couple of pieces.

A few months earlier, just after we had learned that our baby was a girl, we decided to paint the nursery green. We chose a lovely, light, bright green partly because we liked the color, and partly because the idea of too much pink made me ill. And if our next kid was a boy, well, the room would still be gender-appropriate.

We wanted to make painting a family affair, so we waited until Tom, Candee, and Liz's sister, Deb, were in town, and we invited them to join us. The evening after they arrived, we were standing on our porch, having just come back from dinner, excited to begin coating the bare white walls with broad strokes of Corn Husk Green. I was fumbling to find my keys when I realized that something about our house felt . . . wrong. Through the sheer fabric of the curtain in the living room, I could see that some things were out of place. The television and the stand upon which it sat were away from their usual spot against the wall, and the floor looked more cluttered than we had left it. My first thought was an earthquake.

Had I been thinking rationally, I would have wondered why every light was on, and I would have noticed the unfamiliar car parked directly in front of my house—unusual on our nearly empty street.

"Stay outside," I said to Liz and the assorted Goodmans. At that point, Liz was a little over five months pregnant, and I didn't want her stress level to increase, so I planned to do a quick cleanup before she entered the house. As soon as I pushed the door open, it was clear that the mess was not a result of any tremors. In the middle of the living room floor was one of Liz's suitcases, opened wide and half filled with electronic items. The door to our office was open, and so were all of the desk drawers, the contents spilled out everywhere. Right behind me was Tom, his eyes huge and his eyebrows nearly touching his receded hairline.

"What's going on?" he shouted from the living room.

"Fuck! Fuck! Fuck! My camera!" I yelled. Actually, four cameras were missing, including the one I had purchased just a few months earlier to replace one that had been ripped out of my hand by a thief on a motorcycle in Ho Chi Minh City. "We've been burglarized!" So much for the whole not-wanting-to-stress-Liz-out thing.

"Just stay outside!" I didn't know how bad the rest of the house was going to look.

I walked into the hallway and saw the door to Madeline's future room wide open. I could feel the cool air of the Los Angeles winter evening blowing down the hallway. Our bedroom looked like something out of a bad TV movie: the drawers were pulled from the dressers and everything had been dumped out. I looked toward the open French doors at the back of our bedroom, the white curtains billowing inward. I was in a daze.

"Matt! Come here!"

Liz was at the porch railing looking through the grapevine that runs up the trellis attached to our house. With her hand on her hips like any good mother about to scold her child, I heard her yell, "Excuse me! Excuse me!" A little blonde woman, not quite five feet tall and more than halfway through her pregnancy, standing there yelling at the two men who had just ransacked our home.

Since we had surprised them mid-burgle, they easily went out through the back door. But they exited into our fenced-in yard, which appeared to be a problem for them, since their getaway car was parked directly in front of our house—their only route to freedom was through our side yard, right past the spot where Liz was standing. I think we were all a little surprised by their nonchalance as they strolled around the house.

"Get the fuck in the house!" I shouted at Liz. My fear evaporated and I bolted into action, running down the stairs and using my BlackBerry to type out their license plate number while Tom called 911. The dispatcher assured us that the police were on their way, so we went inside to figure out exactly what was missing. There were some obvious things: my cameras, Liz's laptop, and a few other small electronic items. They had been out in the open and easy to grab. As I dug through the mess in our office, I heard Liz's voice from the bedroom. "They got all of my jewelry."

My chin hit my chest and a wave of sickness came over me. I swallowed hard to keep the vomit from coming up, and I walked toward my wife. She was sitting on the edge of the bed, looking at the pile of clothes on the floor. All of the jewelry I'd purchased for her piece by piece for nearly every holiday since we'd been together—twelve years' worth of memories—was now gone.

"Babe, I'm so sorry. I'll replace it all, even if it takes me another twelve years. I promise."

"It's okay. It's not the jewelry. It's the reminders of the times and places."

"We'll always have those, but I'll still replace everything."

The LAPD arrived, and the officer in charge busied himself with his investigation. "We'll send someone out to fingerprint the house in the morning," he told us. "Try not to touch anything."

"What are the chances you'll catch these guys?" All I could think about was Liz's jewelry. Sure, I might enjoy replacing those cameras, but to Liz, the missing pieces were not about precious metal and stones.

"We'll do our best, but Los Angeles is a big city and there's a lot of crime."

In other words: Forget about your shit. It's gone forever.

"Fuck, I can't believe this," I yelled, as the officer drove off in the same direction the burglars had gone just an hour earlier. Liz was standing next to me on the sidewalk, her shirt slightly pulled up and exposing a couple of inches of skin, her hands on her lower back, holding the pain of her pregnancy.

"Matt. It's only stuff. None of us were hurt. We should be thankful."

I knew she was right, but I was still seething. I walked her up the stairs and into the house, and we called a cab to take her family back to their hotel.

"Sorry, guys. I guess we'll have to paint the baby's room tomorrow."

As is the case in most home invasions, I felt violated. Not because the asshole burglars had made off with our shit. And not because they poured the contents of our underwear drawers onto the floor while trying to find whatever treasures may have been hidden inside. No. I felt violated because the burglars had entered the house through my future baby's bedroom. I was scared and angry just thinking about what would have happened if we had been burglarized when she was in there. At that moment I felt like getting the hell out of Los Angeles.

Liz was exhausted and went to bed.

"I'll be in in a little bit," I said, lying to her. I knew that there was no way I could sleep that night, but I didn't want to tell Liz why. What if they came back? I wanted to be prepared for them if they did. I was in full alpha-male mode, ready to protect my family.

Problematically, I didn't have any real weapons that would effectively hold off a gun-wielding revenge seeker. I did have a baseball bat, a couple of kitchen knives, and a belt with a heavy buckle that I could whip at them if they walked through the front door. I brought my arsenal with me into the living room, just in case, and stayed awake all night on the couch, staring out the picture window toward the street.

It wasn't until the sun came up that I realized how ridiculous I was acting. This was not a movie, and the burglars were not going to come back for retribution. I put my weapons away and crawled into bed with Liz. "Glad you could make it," she mumbled without moving, and then fell back asleep.

Less than an hour later, I woke up to her phone ringing. I pulled a pillow over my head and tried to go back to sleep, but she smacked me on my back, so I rolled over. With the phone still up to her ear, she hit the mute button and said, "They caught the guys and they have our stuff at the police station!" We were both ecstatic. I listened as she finished up the phone call, telling the officer on the other end that we were on our way to the station.

When we got there, we were introduced to an extremely friendly burglary detective.

"I used to live on your street, just up the road from your house," he said. "It's a pretty safe neighborhood."

I don't know why, but his statement made me feel better. He directed us to a couple of tables set up in the middle of the room.

"On these tables are things we've recovered from several burglaries. Do you recognize anything as yours?"

Liz glossed over the items then looked up at the detective and said, "You didn't happen to recover any jewelry, did you?"

"No, we didn't. What are you missing?"

"Several necklaces from Tiffany's and some gold bangles that my husband bought for me in India and Nepal."

"We'll let you know if we find anything."

I felt sick again. The police had almost everything else, including a deck of cards we picked up at the King Tut exhibit at LACMA a few years earlier, and a plastic case filled with gold-foil stickers used to seal thank-you cards. But no jewelry. I grabbed Liz's hand.

"I'll replace everything," I told her again.

She just looked up at me and smiled.

Sitting at the edge of my wife's hospital bed just a day after she had brought our child into the world, it seemed obvious to me that now was the perfect time to begin her collection of new memories. I felt that I should go, right now, and fulfill this promise I had made to her. But as soon as I ended the call with my mother, Liz said, "You're not leaving me." She was stern.

"But Liz, I need to get some lunch. I haven't eaten in more than twenty-four hours and I'm fucking starving!"

Trying to plan a surprise for this woman hadn't gotten any easier. I knew I'd be gone for less than an hour, and I figured that she would be asleep while I was out anyway, so what would it matter?

Liz's eyes widened, and I could hear her breathing through her nose the way she always did when she was trying to control her anger toward me—this was also a pretty good indication that she was about to let me have it. "Matt. Don't you dare leave me here alone! What if the nurses are ready to take me to see Madeline and you're not here?"

Shit. I really wanted to do something nice for her, but as she yelled at me I realized that my plan really couldn't have been more thoughtless. Here was my wife, about to stand up for the first time in five weeks, about to hold our baby for the first time ever, and I wanted to go buy her something to make her think I was the perfect husband. But to be the perfect husband, I really just needed to be there with her. She could always make me see what was truly important, even if it took me a little while to get there. I called my mom back and told her that I was going to stay with Liz instead. "Lunch" would have to wait until tomorrow.

When I hung up the phone, Liz was calmer, her tone soft. "Thank you for staying. I just don't want to be alone right now."

"I know. I hope you know I didn't want to leave you. I just really needed something to eat," I said, still trying to preserve the secret plan I would execute the next day. "Please don't be mad at me." I knew she wasn't mad at me. In fact, it was obvious just how happy my small gesture had made her. I realized that the best gift I could have given her was being there with her and being there for her. And that was the only thing she wanted at that moment, and every moment before and after it.

"I just really want you to be here when I first hold Madeline," she said.

how?
why?
two questions
that mean nothing.
how will
we
survive without
you?
that's the question
i will repeat to
myself until the
day i die.

Chapter 7

"Is she awake yet?" Pat, Liz's favorite personal care attendant (PCA), stuck her head in the room.

We looked at my sleeping wife.

"Not yet," I said.

"Okay, I'll be back."

It was the second time she had checked in. Liz had been clock-watching all morning, longing for 11:56 a.m., when the prescribed waiting time of twenty-four hours would be up. She was so eager that just when it was time, she fell back asleep, still exhausted from the big events of the day before.

With Liz resting, I sat up on the foldout armchair, shopping online for baby gear. We had only purchased a few things in anticipation of Madeline's arrival—a couple of books, ten or fifteen outfits, a crib, and a manly diaper bag for me. We hadn't gotten around to any of the other necessary items, since we figured we had at least another month and half to do so.

While I shopped, I listened to the new WHY? album for the thirty-fifth time that week through my earphones. I don't usually fixate on one album like that, but there was just something about it. Some of the lines were hitting me in ways that few songs had in the past year. I attributed most of this to timing; after all, I wasn't just listening to background music right now. I was hearing the music, really hearing it, during one of the most intensely difficult and important weeks of my life. One line in particular stayed in my head: "I'm lucky to be under / This same sky that held / The exhale from your first breath." It described the feelings I had about the birth of our child better and more eloquently than I ever could have.

Over the next few hours, Pat stuck her head inside the room twice more to see if Liz was ready to go see Madeline, but each time Liz was still sleeping contently. I'd smile and wave to Pat from my chair, and she'd playfully put her left index finger up to her mouth to indicate that she was going to stay quiet and let Liz continue to sleep. I nodded in agreement, knowing that my wife really needed the rest.

Around two thirty, she finally woke up to the sound of the door opening. She knew precisely what Pat's presence meant, and she was thrilled to see her. Liz sat straight up in her bed, waiting for the words she'd been longing to hear since yesterday, or perhaps since the moment she learned she was pregnant. I also knew what her presence meant, so I paused "By Torpedo or Crohn's" by WHY? two minutes and fifty-eight seconds into the song, removed my earphones, closed my laptop, and set it on the floor between the bed and my chair.

Looking right at Liz, Pat, in a thick accent I'd been unable to place, asked if she was ready to go. At that moment, all of the pain, all of the anguish of the past seven and a half months was gone, replaced with the kind of elation I'd last seen on our wedding day.

"Yes!" she screamed.

"Well, okay, then. I'll be right back."

While Pat searched for one of her colleagues, I thought about calling our parents so they could meet us at the NICU and watch through the window as Liz held our baby for the first time. But I didn't. I decided that this should be our moment: just the two of us. Then just the three of us.

"I'm so excited to finally hold her," Liz said. "I've been waiting all my life for this."

Pat arrived with another PCA, and they walked in to help Liz up. One of them swung her legs to the side of the bed, while the other stood near the head. I watched from the foot, waiting for instructions. Pat looked at me and said, "She needs to get her legs back. Would you like to walk with her?" Grinning, I moved toward Liz, her smiling face following me the entire way to her side. As Pat held her left arm, I grabbed onto her right, and we worked together to lower her to the ground.

It was the first time Liz's feet had touched a floor in almost three weeks, and it was apparent. She stood there for a few seconds, wobbling a bit, as if these were the first steps she was ever taking. I could feel her determination in the grip she had on my arm, and so could Pat, who slowly let go of Liz, leaving me as her only means of support. She took one step, and then another, and then another. She moved tentatively, careful not to take on too much too soon. Slightly hunched at the back, Liz looked down at her feet, letting her eyes control each step. She held her left hand close to the spot from which Madeline had emerged, as if that could keep the contents of her stomach from spilling out in case they suddenly began to do so. The way she was moving made me feel as though we had been transported fifty years into the future: my old lady and me, our feet slowly shuffling on the sidewalk as we strolled down a tree-lined boulevard on a Sunday afternoon, holding hands, both of us silently reflecting on a lifetime of happiness.

Squeezing her hand, I said, "Hey, remember that time you were on bed rest and I waited on you hand and foot? Well, when we get home I'm just gonna lie in bed and ask you to bring me random shit." I kept going: "Remember all of those times you made me bring you your toothbrush and the spittoon and how disgusted I was when your toothpaste and spit would end up on my hand? I'm gonna do the same thing to you."

She smiled, knowing I was only kind of kidding. "Of course," she said. To drive the point home a little further, I added, "Seriously. Remember when I had to empty your bedpan? Well, payback's hell, and you'll get yours." She started laughing at this. She knew it had been difficult for me to attend to these personal needs, and I made the jokes, knowing it had been equally uncomfortable for her to have to rely on me for such things.

We rounded the corner of her bed and made our way to the window. She stopped at the sink to check out the mirror, seeing her face for the first time in a few days. "Jesus. My hair looks like shit."

I laughed at her. "Liz, it looks great."

Still staring into the mirror, she ran her fingers through her part, and said, "Look at my roots!"

"Okay. You've got a point with the roots. But what the fuck do you expect? You've been on bed rest for five weeks."

"I've gotta see Jeannette and Jennifer as soon as I get outta here," she said, referring to the team of sisters who cut and colored her hair.

"Perfect," I responded. "That means I'll get more alone

time with Maddy. We are gonna have such a tight bond. She's gonna like me way better than you."

Liz suddenly looked away from the mirror and directly at me. "Jerk," she said in the way she always did, mimicking how my little brother used to say it when he was ten.

The second PCA left the room, and Pat stood in the doorway holding a wheelchair. I was thankful that Liz was going to get a ride to the NICU, because at the rate she was moving, it would have taken us the rest of the day to get there. "Take one more lap and then we'll go," Pat said. We made our way back to the head of Liz's bed, then toward the door. We reached it, and Liz turned her back to the wheelchair. Still holding my arm, she started to lower herself into the chair. Just before she sat down, she uttered: "I feel light-headed."

With those words, Liz went completely limp and slumped toward the floor, and with all of my strength I tried to keep her from hitting it. Pat frantically pulled the wheelchair out into the hall and yelled for a colleague. Liz couldn't have weighed more than 130 pounds during her pregnancy, and now she was probably closer to her prepregnancy weight of 110. I'm not the strongest guy in the world, but I'd lifted her many times, and I kept thinking that I shouldn't have had that much trouble holding her up. Rather than fight it, I decided to lower her to the floor until I could get some help. Holding onto both her wrists, I set her body on the ground, putting her head on my left foot and creating a pillow with my shoe. Both PCAs were now in the room, and they tried to help me lift Liz from the floor.

I looked at Pat, my eyes saying what my mouth couldn't: What the fuck is going on here?

"This is completely normal," she said. "This happens all the time to women on bed rest."

And I believed her. I mean, what else could it be? Even

with three of us, the struggle was mighty. I felt a small bit of relief when we finally got her into the bed. At least now she can't hurt herself, I thought. I backed away from my wife, knowing that I would only be in the way. I watched as they shook her, slapping her face, yelling her name, telling her to wake up. I watched as she convulsed, her eyes rolling back in her head. I heard her gasping, saw her whole body shaking as if it was struggling to get the last bit of oxygen out of the air. It suddenly became very obvious that there was nothing normal about this situation.

Fuck. Of course it's normal. They just told me that it happens all the time. I saw Pat hit a button on the wall above Liz's bed. Then over the loudspeakers in the ceiling, I heard a cryptic hospital code, but even after the past few weeks there, I still had no idea what the fuck any of them referred to. I didn't immediately connect the two events. That code couldn't be for Liz, could it? No way. Despite what reality was telling me, I held on to Pat's words. *Normal. Normal. Normal,* I thought over and over.

Suddenly, a bunch of hospital staff rushed into Liz's room, one of whom instructed me to get out. I complied with the orders and stood just outside the doorway, trying to make some sense of the situation. Wait. Why am I being ushered out? More and more people brushed past me. It seemed like hundreds of people were in that room, but I knew that Liz was still behind them. They were all shouting, but I couldn't understand a thing. As I stood in the hall, the rational part of my brain kept trying to tell me that something was seriously wrong, but my illogical thoughts kept repeating, *Normal. Normal. Normal.*

A short woman, maybe in her midfifties, appeared by my side and introduced herself, but I wasn't paying attention. We'd been in this hospital for three weeks, and I felt like I knew most of the staff at this point, but I had never seen this woman before. "Mr. Logelin. I think you need to sit down."

I thought, Who the fuck are you and why the fuck are you telling me to sit down? "Why?" I asked.

"Please, sir, sit down. I don't want you to faint."

Faint? I thought. "I feel fine. Can you please tell me what's going on?"

"Sir, I don't know. They're working on your wife."

My mind was racing. What the hell was that supposed to mean? I saw someone run into the room with those heart paddles they use in the movies. I guess they have to use them on her. Fuck. I bet that means that she has to stay in the hospital for a few extra days to recover. Shit. Does that mean I'm going to have to go home alone with Madeline? I don't know if I can handle that.

The crazy thing was that the rational part of my brain knew exactly what those paddles were used for, but with only movies and television shows as a reference point, it was difficult for me to fully grasp the gravity of the situation. I tried to get the attention of everyone who ran past me—I needed to know what was going on with my wife—but the only person speaking to me was that damn woman I didn't recognize, and she was speaking in euphemisms I couldn't comprehend. I just wanted some straight answers. My questions were simple enough: How long until I can see her again? When can I tell her about the commotion she caused? When can she hold her baby?

She was still talking. "Mr. Logelin. Please sit down."

I swear I'm gonna punch her in the face if she says that to me again. Rather than giving her the fist I thought she deserved, I sat down against the wall just so she would leave me the hell alone. The woman walked away victorious, and I sat there with my knees pulled up to my chest, my arms holding them in place, my head shaking away the awful thoughts rationality was trying to get me to come to terms with.

A doctor in a white coat walked out of Liz's room and in my direction. She had dark hair, looked friendly, and was pretty like the doctors on television. I stood up, still leaning against the wall. I asked, "Who is that short lady who keeps telling me to sit down?"

"She's a grief counselor."

A grief counselor. Why the fuck do I need to talk to a grief counselor? "Can you tell me what's going on?"

Though we'd never met, she didn't have to ask who I was. She said, "It doesn't look good."

Well, that was the most direct language anyone had used yet. *Normal. Normal. Normal.* turned into *Fuck. Fuck. Fuck.* Then I asked, "What does that mean?"

"We think she may have had a pulmonary embolism," the doctor said. "A blood clot." She placed her hand on my shoulder and said, "We're doing everything we can."

She rushed off down the hall, leaving me alone. I started pacing. I found an empty corner in the hallway next to a stretcher and started talking out loud to myself—to Liz. "You can do this. You're tough. You're gonna make it." As the words came from my mouth, I remembered all the times I used to tell her that she wasn't tough. I was feeling like an asshole, and then all of a sudden it hit me: She was going to die, today, here in this hospital. And she was never going to hold her baby.

I had to see Liz. I had to hold her. The feeling overwhelmed me, and I was drawn back toward her room, getting as far as the nurses' station. Standing there was Olivia, Liz's favorite nurse. A tall, African-American woman, she had been a constant source of support to Liz during her time in the hospital. She reached out and gave me a hug, not saying a word. It seemed that she had come to the same conclusion I had.

As we stood there hugging, someone interrupted. "Excuse me." It was the grief counselor, and with her was a man in a black robe and a white clerical collar. A priest. In the movies, the priest shows up when someone is about to die.

I looked at the counselor and asked, "What the fuck is he doing here?"

She gave me a stunned look, but before she could answer, the priest said, "I understand that Liz is Catholic. Do you mind if we say a prayer?"

Now, I had been with Liz for over twelve years. Yes, she was born a Catholic, and I know that she believed in God, but she definitely wasn't religious. She simply chose to write "Catholic" on the admission documents she was given when we arrived at the hospital, as if it had been a question about her blood type. Looking furiously at the short woman and pointing at the priest, I said, "Get him the fuck out of here. I know what this means. I don't want to pray. I don't want to talk to you. I want to see my wife."

Looking more stunned than the counselor, the priest placed his hand on her shoulder and they both walked away. I instantly felt awful about the way I had treated them, but I just wasn't ready to hear confirmation of what I knew was inevitable. Not from them.

As they walked away, I turned the corner toward Liz's room and saw Dr. Nelson running down the hall. I'll never forget the look on her face when she passed me: panic, mind-numbing fear, profound sadness, and helplessness. We were mirror images of one another at that moment. She ran into Liz's room and I stood outside, leaning against the wall, once more not sitting simply to spite the grief counselor, though almost positive that I was, in fact, going to pass out.

My thoughts continued: This is it. It *is* happening. But this can't be happening. It's 2008. Healthy women don't die in hospitals after something as routine as having a baby. Certainly not women like Liz; she is young and in great shape. Where the fuck is our family?

I reached into my pocket and grabbed my phone. I called

Liz's mom, then her dad, and then my mom. No one answered. I called Anya's cell phone. She was at work, but picked up immediately. "Is everything okay?"

"No. Can you get to the hospital right now? I don't think she's gonna make it."

"Madeline?" she questioned.

"No. Liz."

"What?" she screamed, her voice cracking.

"Anya. Just get here. Please."

I hung up before she could say anything else. I tried Liz's mom again. This time she answered. "Candee. You guys need to get here right away. It's not good."

Like Anya, her response was "What?"

This time I gave a more specific answer. "Liz. There's something wrong. Things are not looking good." I heard her screaming "No, no, no!" as I hung up my phone.

I called my mom again. She answered. "Hi, honey." This was my third call, and my words were even more direct this time. "Mom, come to Liz's room right now. I don't think she's gonna make it." I knew that she'd have a thousand questions, so I hung up on her, too. I felt like I was being overly dramatic with these calls, but panic started to grip me as I tried once again to deny what I knew I was about to find out.

A couple of minutes later, Pat and the other PCA walked out of Liz's room, arms around each other's shoulders, backs to me. I didn't need to see their faces to know.

Liz was dead.

dead.
i can't fucking
believe that
dead follows
the words,
liz
is.

Chapter 8

Nothing could be done to bring her back. There was no one to blame. Shitty luck and, most likely, a pulmonary embolism brought about the saddest, most horrific moment of my life.

My back slid down the wall until my ass hit the ground. I started crying harder than I'd ever cried. An intense heat was emanating from my body, but I was freezing. I trembled so violently that I thought I was having a seizure. I felt like I was going to vomit and keep vomiting for the rest of my life. I thought I had gone deaf, because all I could hear was nothing. The only fact I could comprehend was that my heart was beating and Liz's wasn't. I wanted to feel something—I ached to feel some sense of detachment, some feeling of denial. I wanted

even for just a few seconds to believe that everything was okay
and that Liz was still alive. But I knew. I knew she was dead.

It had happened only a moment ago, and I was already conscious of it. And then my thoughts went straight to Madeline,
alone in that NICU, completely unaware of how drastically our
lives had just changed.

Liz's parents and my mom came running around the corner
to the nurses' station, eyes wide, unsure of what was happening. I pulled myself together enough to stand up, but I didn't
need to say anything.

Candee started bawling. I grabbed her and hugged her as
hard as I could. Behind her stood Tom, his face showing disbelief. He seemed to be watching an awful Greek tragedy as it
unfolded on a dark and distant stage—I don't think he could
fully grasp what had happened. Seeing my mom next to him,
trying to comprehend, made me cry even more as the reality of
Liz's death grew larger. I felt terrible that they hadn't gotten
there before she'd died, but what had they missed? The result
was the same no matter when they arrived.

I let go of Candee as Dr. Nelson came toward me, crying
with outstretched arms. "Matt, I'm so sorry. I'm so sorry." I
couldn't figure out why she was apologizing. She hugged Tom,
Candee, and my mom, and apologized to each of them, too.
Yes, it was by far the worst fucking thing that ever had or ever
would happen to us, but I knew that it was not her fault and
she did not need to apologize. The human body is a complicated machine, I thought, and sometimes shit happens. This
time it happened to Liz, and to all of us. It was no one's fault.
It couldn't be. She was just gone.

We held each other in the hallway for a few seconds, while
most of the hospital staff streamed out of Liz's room. All of
them had their eyes fixed on the ground before them, unwilling to make eye contact with two parents who just lost a child,

a woman who lost a daughter-in-law, and the man they knew would now be alone in raising a newborn baby. One of them closed the door to Liz's room on the way out.

"Do you know what it was?" I asked Dr. Nelson.

"We're pretty sure it was a blood clot that went from her leg into her lungs. We'll do some tests to confirm." She squeezed me again, looked mournfully at all of us and then walked away.

Even though my family was with me, I felt alone. Like I needed the wall to hold me up.

I thought about my fear of dead bodies. I'd seen a few of them, mostly at funerals and three times while in India, lying in the middle of the road after being hit by vehicles. I always avoided looking—nothing like the immediacy of a newly dead body to force a confrontation with your own mortality. But with Liz it was different. I wanted to—had to—see her, touch her, hold her hands one last time.

The grief counselor reappeared. I heard her hurling platitudes from some 1970s social work textbook at Tom, Candee, and my mom, all of whom accepted them with grace. But I ignored her, knowing that if we talked at that moment, my family would hear me say some things I'd regret. I heard her tell them that Liz was being cleaned up and that we could go in to see her soon. Jesus. This process is so fucking clinical. As if having her cleaned up was going to make this any easier. I hated the counselor, and I made a mental note to complain about her when I finally got my shit together. That was not something I normally would have done, but I thought about how Liz would have handled the situation, and I can guarantee it would not have been pretty.

Anya was walking toward us just as that awful woman finished talking. Fuck. She had no idea what I was about to tell her. As soon as I got the words out, she broke down. I held her, letting her cry on me. My family came to us and held us. We all just stood in the hallway together, unable to comfort each other in any other way.

A few minutes later, the door to Liz's room was opened and someone told me I could go inside. I took a deep breath as I walked through the doorway alone. I stared at her, my eyes dry for the first time in a while.

There she was, and there she wasn't. Eyes closed, skin pale. There was a tube in her mouth with some vomit stuck inside of it. Fuck. She looked awful. So much for cleaning her up.

I got closer and sat on the edge of her bed. I ran my hand over her head, brushing back her hair like I did when she was sick. It felt coarse and dry, like straw. It felt dead. Liz's hair never felt like that—it was the softest hair I'd ever felt. I touched her forehead, and all I could think was that I'd never before touched anyone or anything that cold. Fuck. Just a little while ago she was up and walking around, soft hair, warm skin, big smile, all the excitement of a new mother, but now...How could this be?

I grabbed her right hand, the same hand I had held as I walked her around the room not even an hour ago, and squeezed it the way I did when I was trying to secretly convey something to her when we were in public. I ran my thumb up and down her hand like I did when we watched movies on our couch. The tears came again. How could I get this image out of my mind? I did not want this to be my last memory of my wife. But there wouldn't be any more memories. This was it.

I closed my eyes as hard as I could, trying to erase what I'd just seen. I tried to remember her smile as she was about to go see Madeline. I tried to remember how her skin felt when I walked her around this room. I tried to remember how beautiful she looked. Holding her hand there on her bed, I kept repeating, "I'm sorry, I'm sorry." I knew it wasn't my fault, just like it wasn't anybody else's fault. But I wasn't apologizing for her death. I was apologizing for what could have been, what should have been, and for what she was going to miss as our daughter grew up.

I didn't want to leave her side, but sitting there in that room, my emotions flattened: I no longer felt love. I no longer felt hate. I felt nothing. It made me even sicker to my stomach than I already was.

That nothingness scared the shit out of me. I needed to go to Madeline, to hold her, to be with her, to know that my world hadn't totally imploded. To feel love again. To know that I was capable of doing so. If anyone could revive these emotions, it was going to be Madeline. The need to see her was sudden. I didn't think about it; I was compelled to go to her, because in that moment I knew that she was all I had, and I knew that if I was going to survive this day or any of the days that followed, she was going to be the reason.

When I walked out of the room, I saw the grief counselor again, but I no longer had the urge to knock her teeth out. Even my anger toward her had simply disappeared. "Matt," she began, "I need you to complete an inventory of the things Liz had with her in her hospital room." I followed her across the hall. I could see Liz from where I was, and I could see her mom and dad in there with her, but I turned my head away to keep from losing it again. I scanned the inventory list. Clothes, laptop, jewelry. I stopped. I hadn't seen Liz's rings in weeks. "Where are her fucking rings?" I yelled to anyone who would listen. This sudden outburst was a revival of my emotions, but not the one I wanted. I was scared. I started to sweat. They meant the world to her.

Liz loved her rings. Of course they were symbolic of our unending relationship, but she also admired them for the sheer beauty they possessed. She was as proud of them as I was of the fact that I'd actually figured out how to pay for them without her help. She knew how difficult it had been for me to afford them, which made her appreciate them more than if I'd been rich enough to put the Hope Diamond on her finger, and she treated them with the kind of care practiced by a chemist mixing potentially volatile chemicals. Liz took them to a jeweler at least monthly to have them cleaned, and she cleaned them at home almost weekly. She'd call me every time a barista or client complimented her on the brilliantly sparkling rocks that made the rings so gorgeous. "I always tell them that I have an amazing husband," she'd say.

At that moment, the only thing I cared about was finding the rings. I started tearing through everything in the room, frantically looking for Liz's prized possessions. While searching, my thoughts went to her funeral for the first time. The rings were a symbol of our lifelong commitment to one another, and that didn't end with death—I was certain that she needed to be buried with them. But then I thought about what Liz would really want. She would tell me that they were too pretty to bury, and that burying them would be a supreme waste of money. And she would be right—I was still making payments on the loan I took out to pay for them. Besides, some crooked funeral director would probably steal them after we left the funeral home anyway. But more than anything, I thought about our daughter and how much her mother's rings would mean to her someday. Though we promised to wear them forever, I couldn't bury them with Liz. They belonged to Madeline now, and I knew that Liz would agree with my decision.

After a few minutes of frenzied and fruitless searching, I saw Anya standing in the doorway. "Do you have any idea where Liz's rings could be? Maybe she told you where she put them or something?"

"Matt," Anya said gently, "I put them in her purse."

I found Liz's giant black leather purse buried under a pile of her clothes. I rifled through it, finding an old package of gum, a couple of pens, two airplane barf bags, a packet of Zofran, and whole bunch of other stuff, but no rings. I thought to myself what I always said to Liz when she asked me to get something from her purse: how the hell do you find anything in here? Anya said, "They're in the inside pocket." I acknowledged her with a glance, and then fumbled with the zipper for a second or two. I fished around the pocket, finally finding her engagement ring with the big square diamond on top and the much smaller wedding band, too.

I pulled them from the bag and held one between the thumb and forefinger of each hand. I rubbed my fingers together, feeling the cold platinum bands, watching the diamonds sparkle as the white light dispersed through them. My fear was abated, knowing that they weren't lost somewhere in her hospital room, but I didn't know what to do with them. Do I put them back in her purse? Do I give them to my mom or her parents to hold until I am ready to put them in a safe place? The only way I could ensure their safety was to keep them on me. I placed them on the pinky finger of my left hand, the same way that Liz did: first the wedding band, then the engagement ring.

Now that I had them safely on my finger, I no longer gave a shit about completing the inventory. I looked at my mom and then at the grief counselor. "Can you please take care of this for me? I'm going to feed Madeline."

I walked down the hall, trying not to acknowledge the looks of pity cast in my direction by the nurses I passed on my way. I knew what they must have been thinking, because it was the same thing I was thinking: *That poor guy. There is no way he is going to be able to get through this and raise that baby properly.*

They're both fucked. When I reached the NICU, a nurse greeted me. "I'm so sorry to hear about your wife," she said.

It was the first time I had heard those words, and they stung worse than the weekly allergy shots I had gotten as a child. My entire body tensed up. I knew that I'd be hearing that same phrase, getting that same reminder, for the rest of my life. I had been slapped with the label of widower, and it would be impossible to shake. I went to wash my hands, realizing that like my wedding band, Liz's rings would have to come off my finger. I removed them, placing them on the safety pin clipped to my belt loop that had been given to me by a nurse the first time I visited the NICU. I could feel everyone's stares as I walked to the room where my daughter was. Another nurse came to me and gently rubbed my shoulder. "I am so, so sorry." She looked up at me and into my eyes, coming face-to-face with a different kind of anguish than she normally dealt with. "Let me get your baby for you."

I stared at Madeline lying there in that plastic box, surrounded by tubes and cords. The relief I had felt just a day earlier was replaced by dread and crippling fear. Yesterday I had been absolutely certain that Madeline's health would be fine and that Liz and I would be the best parents there ever were. But without her . . . I didn't think I could do this without her, and I didn't *want* to do this without her. Where was the optimism? Where was the happiness? Where was the future? These things had died along with Liz. I felt so helpless, so vulnerable, and that was exactly how Madeline looked to me now. In reality, she was doing better than expected and had made great progress so far, but knowing that we had both lost the most important person in our lives, I wasn't sure that either one of us would survive.

I watched as the nurse maneuvered the cords and tubes so she could pull Madeline from the incubator. Sitting in the same rocking chair I sat in yesterday when I first held our child, I couldn't help but think how different everything was. I looked down at the T-shirt I was wearing, white, with the image of nineteen faceless women dressed in aerobics gear, the words Broken Social Scene underneath. A few hours ago it had simply been a reminder of a great show I'd been to, but now and forever it would be something else. It would be a reminder of the night I bought it—a night when a pregnant Liz was feeling too ill to join me. I went by myself, unwilling to miss a show I'd been anticipating for months. It was fucked up that I left her alone that night, and now this T-shirt would forever be a reminder of what a selfish asshole I was. Smudged with the mascara of a woman who had just lost her daughter-in-law and soaked in the tears of a mother who had just lost her firstborn, it would also be a reminder of something else.

The nurse placed Madeline in my arms. I bawled as I stared at her, worried that I was going to fail her as a parent. Not only in general; I really had no idea what to do with a baby girl. I grew up with five brothers, and I knew the kind of trouble boys would inevitably get themselves into. At least I wouldn't have to discipline our daughter for a mailbox bombing or a grass fire started with a gasoline-soaked, fire-engulfed soccer ball. I had a stepsister, but she was a lot older, so I never got to listen through the door, snickering as someone explained all the things that girls need to know as they grow up. My thoughts fast-forwarded twelve years into the future. When is it okay for her to start dating? Never, if she ends up looking anything like Liz. How am I going to explain a menstrual cycle with the delicateness of a mother? I won't be able to do it without making inappropriate jokes. How am I going to take her shopping for a training bra and not look like a total pervert? Wait...I should probably figure out what the fuck a training bra is first.

Madeline squirmed a bit in my arms, drawing me back into

reality. Though I knew there would be plenty, it was probably
too soon to start counting my fatherly failures. Holding her, I
knew that I was going to have to figure things out for her sake.
But I was going to need help. I looked at Madeline and said
out loud, "I don't care what you do when you're fourteen or fifteen, but for the next few years, you better be the best fucking
baby ever." The NICU nurse must have thought I was insane,
but at that moment, I *was* insane: my wife was dead, and I had
no clue how I was going to live without her.

I spent about twenty minutes with my child before heading
back toward Liz's room. As I walked the hallways, I noticed
they were devoid of hospital staff. Through an open door I
found the missing nurses, some sitting, some standing, most
crying. I recognized nearly all of them. I saw the grief counselor inside as well, and I knew for sure why they were there. I
stuck my head in and asked if I could join them.

I don't know why, but I felt compelled to say something to
the nurses and PCAs. I thanked them for everything they had
done to keep Liz comfortable during her time in the hospital,
and for everything they had done to get Madeline safely into
the world, too. And for everything they had done to try to save
my wife's life.

There was no reaction; just stunned silence as I exited the
room. Back in the hallway, I saw a man pushing a stretcher
with a large, white cardboard box on it. I didn't immediately
realize that inside that box was Liz's body. I stood there alone,
watching as the man took a left and pushed the stretcher—and
the only woman I had ever loved—away from me.

in the chair,
you in my arms,
it's almost
as if the rest
was nothing but
a nightmare.
i just wish we
could both
wake up.

Chapter 9

Word began to spread about Liz's death, and my phone was constantly ringing with people calling to say nothing. Each conversation was another chance to try to comfort the person on the other end of the phone, but it was weird to have to play that role for everyone else. I knew that our friends and family meant well, but what the hell were they really going to tell me? The circumstances were unimaginable to everyone; finding the right words was impossible. Some spoke of Liz in the present tense, acting as if she was on vacation, while others focused on Madeline, asking questions and telling me that they were looking forward to watching her grow up. But all of them used euphemisms that kept them from truly having to face my reality: Liz had passed on, passed away, or was in a better place.

None of them wanted to acknowledge the finality of her death, but I didn't have that luxury. I watched her die, I held her lifeless hand, I saw her body wheeled from the hospital, and now I was facing life as a widowed father to a newborn.

With an endless stream of people coming to cry with us, the hospital converted one of the maternity waiting rooms into a grieving room. I spent that evening lying on the floor, staring at a room full of mostly silent friends and family, everyone waiting for someone to say the right thing. But there was no right thing to say. There was simply no way to sugarcoat this situation: it just fucking sucked, but I was the only one willing to acknowledge that.

When anyone did finally speak up, I didn't hear a word. I was so deep in my own head that I may as well have been left alone in that room to talk to the walls. But I couldn't tell anyone that things were going to be all right, that I was going to get through this, that I would survive without Liz. And I didn't need to tell them how much I loved her, or how much I was going to miss her, because they all knew that. I just kept repeating the same thoughts: What the fuck am I gonna do without her? She was my life. I can't go on without her.

Sitting there, I felt that dying might be the only way to truly take away the pain, but I knew that suicide would never be an option. I just couldn't leave Madeline alone. The thought of our child as an orphan turned my stomach, and I hated myself for even thinking something so selfish. Besides, Liz would fucking kill me if I did something like that. Just hours after my wife had died, I became determined to make Madeline my reason for living. She would be my source of hope and happiness in every bleak moment I encountered. She would be the one to pull me out of the dark moments I knew I'd inevitably face. She would be my constant reminder of Liz, and no matter what happened during the coming days, weeks, months, and years, I would rely on her to make sure I was happy so I could be the best father possible for her.

After everyone but my mom and Liz's parents left the hospital that night, I realized just how alone I was. Our friends were headed home with their wives, their girlfriends, their husbands, their boyfriends, all probably saying the same thing: *I love you, and I'm so glad that it wasn't us.* Me? I had no idea what to do, nowhere to go. There was no possible way I could go back to our house. Not tonight. In fact, I felt then that I might never be able to step through our front door again. I headed to the attached hotel with my mom.

I lay on my back, staring at the ceiling. In one arm I clutched the red travel pillow that Liz had carried with her almost everywhere. In the other, her favorite pink pashmina, a gift I had picked up for her on one of my trips to India. Though I thought I had no tears left, they once again started to flow as I brought the pillow and the shawl up to my face, taking in her scent. Her perfume was so deeply embedded in both objects, I swore I wouldn't let them go until I'd sniffed every last bit of her from them. It was remarkable how the smell filled me with hope—hope that I'd be able to sleep through the night, hope that there'd be a dream during which Liz was still alive in my mind. I ached for just one moment in which this wasn't my reality. As I drifted off, I hoped I'd wake up the next morning realizing that this had all been an awful nightmare. Sleep was an escape. Plus I was so fucking exhausted that I couldn't have kept my eyes open even if I'd wanted to.

Sometime around 2:00 a.m., I woke up to my phone ringing.

"Is this Mr. Logelin?"

"Yeah. Who is this?"

It was a woman from an organ donation organization. "Mr. Logelin, we're so sorry to hear about your loss. We'd like to talk to you about organ and tissue donation."

This was not how I wanted to wake up: not only was I robbed of that one hopeful dream, but it was by a woman looking to exploit my worst nightmare for someone else's gain. It was an awful thing to think, and I knew it then, but I couldn't help it. I was a little out of my mind.

"How soon does this need to be done?" I asked.

"Procurement needs to take place within twenty-four hours," she replied.

Twenty-four hours? "Ma'am. My wife hasn't even been dead twelve hours. Is there any way we can talk about this in the morning?"

"Sure. We'll call you back at nine a.m."

I was pissed off and hung up the phone. "Twenty-four hours?" I asked out loud, waking my mom.

"What, honey?"

"Nothing, Mom. Go back to sleep."

I understood the time sensitivity, but all I could think about was the lack of sensitivity shown to me. A more spiteful person would have told them to fuck off, but as I tried to get back to sleep, I thought about what Liz would want in this situation. We had never talked about organ donation, but she had a donor sticker on her driver's license and had encouraged me to place one on mine as well. I knew what I had to do, and before I passed out again, I took a little comfort in knowing that Liz's death might actually help others live.

My phone rang again the next morning at nine o'clock on the dot, and I knew who it was. To spare Liz's parents the pain of having to listen to one side of the negotiation for their daughter's organs and tissue, I excused myself from the breakfast table and took the call in the lobby of the hospital.

I slumped down in a chair near the information desk and started answering the woman's questions. No, Liz didn't have any tattoos. Yes, we had traveled extensively, including to countries with plenty of blood-borne illnesses and mad cow disease. No, she was not an intravenous drug user. Yes, we'd had unprotected sex in the last year, pointing out the fact that she died the day after giving birth. No, she didn't have hepatitis, AIDS, or any other diseases. Yes, I'd be willing to donate any organs or tissue deemed usable. With each question and subsequent answer came another wave of nausea. This was exactly why I wasn't eating.

I watched as nurses and doctors walked through the lobby on their way to whatever part of the hospital they worked in; I was paying special attention to the female employees. I kept thinking, *I need to marry her.* This wasn't about needing a second income, love, or sex. And it certainly wasn't about replacing Liz. It was a reaction to my fear of raising a premature baby on my own, and my inability to be a good dad—and now mom, too—to my daughter. It wasn't really even about me; I was convinced that Madeline needed a woman in her life as soon as possible so she didn't grow up with only the parental influence of her derelict father. In my estimation, my mind was worth roughly half of what Liz's was. Shit. Madeline has one quarter of a parent.

The bad thing about the Internet is that word travels fast. So fast, in fact, that the day after Liz died, my phone didn't stop ringing, and the red light on my BlackBerry blinked almost constantly. Of course, the great thing about the Internet is that word travels fast, which meant my support system was suddenly enormous and stretched across the globe. I heard from high school friends I hadn't spoken to in twelve years telling me they remembered meeting Liz once and how they never forgot her smile. My friends from college contacted me, all shocked, in disbelief that someone as lively and vivacious as Liz could be dead. Biraj called from South Korea in tears, unable to say anything. My graduate school roommate listened to me cry into the phone for at least thirty minutes. Family members I hadn't heard from since the previous Christmas called to share memories of Liz. I heard from colleagues and friends in India and the Philippines, most of whom had never met Liz, calling and writing to tell me that they remembered the way my face lit up when I talked about her.

Standing outside the hospital, the sunshine of a beautiful Southern California morning unable to divert my attention from the darkest moment of my life, I talked on the phone to one of my oldest friends, Alex. I'd known Alex since he was the new kid in our third-grade classroom. We had the low-maintenance kind of friendship that was sustained by a call or an e-mail once or twice a year. I hadn't even gotten around to telling him that Liz was pregnant, so I was more than surprised to hear from him. He told me that he was away on business, but that he would catch a flight to Los Angeles as soon as he possibly could. I hadn't even considered that my friends from out of town would come to Liz's funeral. "I'm not even sure when or where the funeral is going to be, but I guess on Saturday? That's the day that funerals usually happen, right?" Neither of us really knew; we were too young to have ever thought about such things. Well, at least Alex was. I had aged over forty years in fewer than twenty-four hours.

As we continued to talk, a taxi pulled into the driveway of the hospital, stopping right in front of me. The door opened, and there was my best friend, A.J., and his wife, Sonja. I hung up with Alex and started crying all over again. They had been on a ski vacation in Colorado with A.J.'s family, and I hadn't spoken to them since Madeline's birth. I hadn't expected people to show up, but if anyone was going to, it would be A.J. and Sonja. I had gone to high school with both of them, and they were one of the few couples Liz and I knew who had been together longer than we had. I was in their wedding, and A.J. was in ours. They were the kind of couple other couples envied but didn't hate. And they were by far the nicest, kindest human beings in the world.

One night in the hospital, Liz had said to me, "I know we agreed that we don't want to baptize Madeline, but I really like the idea of her having godparents. Can A.J. and Sonja be Madeline's 'not-godparents'? You know, in case we die in a car crash or something, I'd want them to take care of Madeline." I thought about this conversation as I reached out to A.J., hugging him for what would normally have been an uncomfortable amount of time, weeping into his black fleece ski vest.

"What are you guys doing here?" I said, asking the dumbest question of the day. "You're supposed to be on vacation!" I needed them, and they knew it, so they came to me as fast as they could, even though I hadn't asked them to do so. I wiped the tears from my eyes, threw my arm around A.J.'s shoulder and said, "Come on. Let's go see the most goddamn beautiful baby in the world."

This scene played out multiple times over the next few days. Liz's sister, Deb, flew in from San Francisco, and her expression was something I hope I never see again. My dad and his wife came from their vacation in Florida, both still thinking that this was some awful joke we were playing on them. My brothers David and Nick; my stepbrother, Adam; my stepfather, Rodney; my cousin Josh; one of my college roommates, Nate; Liz's family; and her friends from high school and college—people streamed in from around the country, all coming to cry with our families and me.

Each time someone else arrived at the hospital, I promptly took him or her to the window of the NICU to catch a glimpse of Madeline. At one point I arrived to find Madeline's bassinette moved up against the window. The nurse told me she was drawing such a crowd that they wanted to move her to where everyone could see her. Liz would have loved the idea of her daughter being the star of the NICU, but I found it a bit awkward to be sitting in a chair, holding my baby and crying while our friends and family watched from the other side of the glass. Even more awkward was watching their lips move and not being able to make out the words. I was pretty sure I knew exactly what they were saying to one another, though. *That poor son of a bitch. How is he gonna do this without Liz? I'm so glad it wasn't my husband/wife.*

On Thursday afternoon, I went with Liz's parents, my mom and stepdad, my dad and stepmom, and Anya to a funeral home a few miles from the hospital. I'd driven up and down the street it was on thousands of times, but I'd never noticed it before. I didn't know how this particular place had been chosen, and frankly, I didn't give a shit. We walked inside and were greeted by a tall old man who introduced himself as the funeral director. No introductions were really necessary—I mean, he had the appearance of every funeral director I'd ever seen on TV, and the look in my eyes must have been the one he'd seen on ten thousand other widowers.

He led us into a room with a huge wooden table outfitted with tissue boxes and bottles of water. It reminded me of the hatchet rooms set up at my office when employees were laid off. He seated himself at the head and delivered us a well-prepared message about how sorry he was and how death is part of life, even when it happens at such a young age. Then his speech took an abrupt turn: "So, are we looking at caskets or are we looking at urns?" I appreciated his ability to get down to business, but I couldn't help feeling a little repulsed by the question. My wife had been dead fewer than two days, and here was a guy treating the question of how to deal with her remains with the kind of attitude usually reserved for de-termining what type of breakfast meat to have with one's eggs. But this choice wasn't as easy as saying, "Bacon, of course." In our more than twelve years together, Liz and I had never talked about what should be done if one of us were to die, and we were too young even to begin thinking about drafting a will that would have answered the question for me. I looked around the table, searching the faces of everyone in the room. Their teary eyes were staring back, waiting for *my* response.

But I didn't know how to make these choices. Liz handled the tough decisions in our life. And before that, my parents had made them for me. I didn't know if I should even be the one to answer the question at all. Maybe it should be up to the people who birthed and raised her? I peered up at them once again, and still their faces told me that I had to decide.

I was transported back to our 2004 trip to Kathmandu. During a break in Biraj's wedding festivities, he suggested we visit Pashupatinath, the holiest Hindu temple in Nepal. A tour guide led us around the grounds, finally stopping on a bridge overlooking the Bagmati River. He pointed to the smoke ris-ing from the banks of the river, the smoke that we had been breathing in. "If you look closely, you will see funeral pyres and cremations taking place down below," he told us. Our faces in-stantly went from inquisitive to disgusted, and we did our best to stop inhaling the smoke that was all around us. The sight and smell of a body on fire was too much to deal with, so our tour ended there.

Then I thought about when I was in Kathmandu in 2006, this time by myself. I was compelled to go back to Pashupati-nath, and to sit on the banks of the Bagmati River, watching the entire cremation ceremony. I witnessed body after body, each wrapped in white linen, brought to the cremation ghats on stretchers made of bamboo, then put onto the ground while a series of rituals were performed. The bodies were then placed on the funeral pyre, covered with wood, and lit while a man with a big stick stoked the fire. I watched as the wood and body were transformed into ash, and finally pushed into the river, thus bringing to an end the physical body. That day I realized that it was not the burning body or the smoke that rose from it that had alarmed us on that first trip; it was that we feared our own mortality. And to me, someone who doesn't believe in an afterlife, as I sat there on the banks of the Bagmati River that day in 2006, finally came some peace with the idea of death.

This insight was a huge contrast to the mostly Catholic funerals I had attended growing up. I found a funeral with an open casket to be a bit macabre, and always felt that burial didn't bring about any sense of finality. But cremation—the process of actually destroying the physical being once the brain stopped working and the heart stopped beating—well, that seemed like the only way to really say good-bye.

"We're looking at urns." It wasn't my answer that surprised me as much as it was the certainty with which I stated it. I looked around the room once more, waiting for someone to object. No one did. The funeral director stood up and led us to a hallway in the back of the funeral home where a bunch of urns were lined up on shelves along the wall. I quickly scanned them, finding every single one unacceptable. There was no way in hell I was going to place Liz's ashes into an urn with an image of an American flag and a crying bald eagle.

As I searched the wall for at least one possible option, the funeral director, perhaps sensing my disapproval, started talking again. "You don't necessarily need an urn. You can also have her remains stored inside a plastic bag and then placed inside a cardboard box."

I had no idea what to say. He continued, "And you can

either come pick her up, or we can mail her to your house." I was stunned. I was completely unprepared for this.

"Uh...no. I am not picking her up, and there is no way in hell you're mailing her to my house. Are there any other options?" He gave me some speech about state law prohibiting funeral homes from holding remains after some predetermined amount of time.

I was becoming visibly agitated. I was still in shock. Was I really standing here making funeral plans for Liz? My mom noticed my growing unease and stepped in. "Matt, I'll make a few phone calls and see if my funeral director friend in Minnesota can hold on to her until you're ready to make a decision." I was sick of making choices, and was desperate for someone to do so for me. I was so thankful to have help at that moment—it was exactly what I needed.

We all headed back into the front room so I could sign the necessary paperwork and make the rest of the arrangements. We agreed that the service would be held in the chapel at the funeral home on Saturday in order to give as many people as possible the opportunity to attend. I insisted that religion be left out because I wanted the focus to remain on Liz, rather than on the not-shared belief that God had taken her to a better place.

I thought the questions were over until the funeral director asked how many death certificates I wanted.

"None. I don't want any death certificates. I know she's dead," I replied. Really. The last thing I needed was another reminder that my wife was never going to hold her baby.

"Mr. Logelin, you'll need at least a few copies in order to settle her estate issues."

Estate issues? I hadn't even begun to think about her bank accounts, credit cards, and the countless other issues I was going to have to deal with over the next few weeks. This was most definitely not my area of expertise. Tom stepped in. "Matt, why don't we order ten copies so you have extras, just in case you need them." Once again, it was wonderful to have someone else make a decision for me. These were simple questions requiring simple answers, but to me, they were questions I never imagined I would have to answer. Especially not at age thirty.

When we headed back to the hospital, I went straight for Madeline. I saw her lying in her incubator and the tears immediately started to flow. But these tears were different from the ones I'd been crying for the past few days; these were tears of relief. Right then, watching Madeline's little chest move up and down as she breathed, I knew I wouldn't be able to deal with any of this without her. Just two days old and she was already saving me in a way that none of my friends and family could.

inside, where you
used to be,
though filled with
your things,
it's as empty
as it was the
day we moved in.

Chapter 10

Early Friday morning, I finally arrived back at my house. In the same way that I couldn't let Liz spend a night alone when she was on bed rest, I couldn't let Maddy be alone at the hospital, either, so I'd been sleeping at the attached hotel and planned to do so until she was ready to come home.

Behind me on the porch was a small army of friends and family there to support me as I entered our home for the first time since Liz died; I was not looking forward to this. I unlocked the door and rushed inside alone to deactivate the alarm. I walked through the kitchen and straight into our bedroom. It was exactly as it had been the day Liz was admitted to the hospital three weeks earlier.

While I scanned our bedroom, everyone gave me the space

they thought I needed. There on Liz's nightstand was a nearly empty water bottle, reminding me of all the times I gave her shit for her inability to finish one off. Next to it was a packet of her nausea medication, the foil sticking up from all but two of the pill slots, reminding me how difficult her pregnancy had been. Toward the back was her alarm clock, bringing me back to the day she had unplugged it to put an end to the awful interference buzzing it made when she received an e-mail on her BlackBerry. In the middle was the book of names we had pored over, where we found a name for our child.

At that moment, the last few lines of "I Remember Me" by the Silver Jews started playing in my head:

> I remember her
> And I remember him
> I remember them
> I remember then
> I'm just rememberin'
> I'm just rememberin'
> Just rememberin'
> I'm just rememberin'

The words repeated over and over again in my head as I rushed out of the room and into our office.

I sat down on the floor in front of my wall of music and began furiously grabbing CDs and records from the shelves. It probably was the last thing I should have been worried about then, but I had an overwhelming compulsion to gather songs for Liz's funeral. I couldn't bear the thought of hearing all the usual depressing funeral music—"On Eagle's Wings" and all the other bullshit songs that you're supposed to play when someone dies. I was suddenly determined to create the greatest funeral playlist that there had ever been, and it was a more difficult task than I had imagined. Liz and I had way different tastes in music. She was into the kind of pop music that made me want to gag—you know, Beyoncé, Justin Timberlake, and anything else played over and over again on the local Top 40 radio station—while I listened to indie rock and jazz that rarely made it to commercial radio at all. I tried to think of the best way to honor her memory, but there was no way I was going to be responsible for turning her funeral into a dance party. Luckily, most of the music I listened to was rather mournful, so I couldn't really go wrong with that. The only real requirement was that the songs meant something to both of us.

But the first song I wanted to add violated my only requirement, and was in fact hated by Liz because it was the one song I asked her to play if I died: "Dress Sexy at My Funeral" by Smog. The title alone indicates that it's completely inappropriate for an actual funeral, but I always hoped that mine would have a few moments of laughter, and I thought Liz's should be the same way. A.J. came into my office and sat down on the floor next to me, immediately joining me in scanning my music shelves. I didn't tell him what I was up to, but he figured it out. He knew what an important part music played in my life, and he understood just how cathartic the playlist creation process would be for me.

Without looking at him I said, "Dude. The first song is gonna be 'Dress Sexy at My Funeral.'"

A.J. shared my music taste, but had a better ear for the appropriate. "I don't know about that," he said, looking at me as if I'd truly lost my mind.

"Oh, come on. No one's gonna be listening to the lyrics. You and I will be the only people who'll know just how screwed up the song is." I added it to the playlist and continued digging through mine and Liz's musical past, running ideas past A.J., and listening to his suggestions.

He proposed "Une Année sans Lumiére" by Arcade Fire,

"Last Tide" by Sun Kil Moon, "Falling Slowly" by the Frames, and a few others.

"I've got to include that Bee Gees song that Feist covered, you know, the one we played at our wedding? 'Inside and Out.' And 'Tennessee' by the Silver Jews. Oh. And anything off of *In the Aeroplane over the Sea*." An hour later I had my playlist.

A.J. worked on extracting the files from the CDs and creating the perfect play order while I moved on to the next important task: culling through over twelve years of photos of Liz. I had a few favorites, but I wanted the funeral home to be wallpapered with pictures of her. I didn't want her death to define her, or to be the only thing that people remembered about her. If they could see her smiling in front of Machu Picchu, the Acropolis, the Taj Mahal, or any of the other wondrous places we visited around the world, at the very least they'd feel confident that she lived an incredibly full life in her short thirty years on this planet. But I was looking at each photo hoping these memories would help remove from my brain that final image of Liz lying dead in her hospital bed.

The rest of my friends and family took care of the things I was unable to think about yet. Tom and Candee worked with some of Liz's more astute and money-savvy friends to help set up a financial plan for me and to make a list of all of the things I would need to handle in the wake of her death. Sonja came up with the idea of creating a memorial fund to help us make up for Liz's lost income, and she worked with my cousin Josh to get a bank account set up. My mom and stepmom helped clean up my house, and my dad, stepdad, brothers, and one of Liz's uncles teamed up to tackle some long-neglected home improvement projects.

When A.J. and I finally emerged from the office, I walked into the kitchen to hear Candee talking to the *Los Angeles Times* about placing an obituary in the paper.

"Okay. We'll get something to you within the hour." Looking at me, Candee said, "Honey, would you like to write something for Lizzie's obituary?"

Oh.

She went on. "I don't want to put pressure on you, but they told me we have an hour to get something to them in order to make the deadline for the Friday newspaper."

I glanced at her with the helpless look I'd been wearing since Tuesday. "I'm not sure I can right now."

Sonja was standing nearby and offered to write it. "Take a look at it when I'm done and let me know what you think," she said.

While Sonja put pen to paper to encapsulate Liz's life in fewer than 220 words, I went outside and sat on the bottom stair of my front porch, staring at the houses on the hill in front of me. I breathed in the scent of the grapefruit blossoms in our yard and I did the math in my head. Madeline was born at 11:56 a.m., and Liz died the next day at 3:11 p.m. Twenty-seven hours. In twenty-seven hours I witnessed the only two things guaranteed to every single human being: birth and death. To experience the emotions associated with both events, the highest of highs and the lowest of lows, in a little more than one day, well, it was ruinous.

I tried to shake away the tears as I sat there thinking about how close to perfect those twenty-seven hours were. Our love, our jobs, our travels, our house in Los Angeles, our fruit trees, and finally, our beautiful baby girl; these were the things we'd been working toward, and we had finally achieved them all the moment Madeline was born. Twenty-seven hours of pure happiness. I felt so fucking lucky to have had even that short amount of time, and I was positive that Liz died confident that we had achieved all we had set out to. But I couldn't help thinking that we were robbed of a lifetime of true happiness. Twenty-seven hours wasn't enough—but really, forever wouldn't have been, either.

I jumped up and raced back up the steps and into my kitchen. I grabbed a pen and a notebook, and wrote the following:

life and death.
from the happiest moment of
our lives
to the saddest.
all
of it.
in a 27-hour period.
the pain is unbearable.
devastated
doesn't describe
the
loss
we're all feeling.
family and friends
from around the world
have
come to our home,
called.
e-mailed,
cried.
everyone died
a lot
when liz left us.
she
loved everyone
more than we can imagine.
she
left us
with the greatest gift she could

have.
a baby girl
who looks soooo much like
momma.
she'd be the first
to say it would all be
ok.
please try not to cry
(says the husband who can't
stop).
instead
think of liz.
remember
that laugh.
that smile.
that love.
i know i will.

I tore the sheet of paper from the notebook, handed it to Sonja who accepted it with no reaction, and walked out of the room. I had never written anything like this before. Sure, I wrote term papers in college and graduate school, and I wrote a couple of record reviews for a music magazine, but I had never shared my feelings in such an explicitly personal way. Getting those words down left me with an incredible sense of peace. They would end up on the back of Liz's funeral program.

That afternoon I found myself sitting back in the common room of the hospital's hotel. Though not reserved for us, it had become our de facto property based on the sheer number of family and friends who camped out there in the days following Liz's death. We had outgrown the waiting room in the maternity ward. Tables, countertops, and even portions of the floor were blanketed with fruit baskets, boxes of cold pizza, cookie platters, and all of the other offerings brought in by well-wishers hoping to keep my family and friends fed.

It had been three days since Liz died, and I still hadn't eaten anything, despite everyone's insistence. I was so sick of the questions about my food intake that I started lying to everyone who asked. No one seemed to understand that an empty stomach meant only dry heaves, and at this point I preferred dry heaves to the feeling of vomit burning through my throat and nostrils.

I sat there on the floor, working with our friends and family to sort through the five hundred plus photos of Liz that I'd printed, arranging them thematically on the photo boards to be displayed at her funeral. There was one with photos of the Goodmans; one with photos of her extended family; two with photos of her friends; three with photos of the two of us; and one with random images of Liz all by herself. Most of us found comfort in revisiting the moments captured in the photos, but Candee and Deb couldn't bear to see the images, so instead they sequestered themselves in their room. Just a few days removed from the worst day of our lives, we were all reeling, but Liz's death was hitting us differently; witnessing Candee's and Deb's reactions in this situation indicated to me that we weren't all going to deal with Liz's death in the same way.

I was still in a haze, but I knew that I couldn't lock myself in a room, nor could I be alone—I had to be around people. Though surrounded by those I loved, I found myself watching everyone somberly search the corners of our room for anything but the eye contact of another human being. The whole scene made me feel as though I was going insane, so I left the room in search of something that I knew would make me smile. I went to see my daughter several times that night, sometimes between feedings. Even asleep, she was the best distraction there was.

i'm not standing here,
at the front of
this room,
looking out at
these people,
trying to think of
something to say.
no.
i'm standing on a mountain in the himalayas.
i'm taking in the beauty of the taj mahal.
i'm staring into the ocean near santorini.
i'm floating through space.
and you,
you are here with me.

Chapter 11

I never really imagined my life without Liz, and we had both assumed that I'd die first. My triglycerides were dangerously high. I didn't exercise. I didn't sleep. I ate nothing but red meat and candy, and I'd been known to overindulge when it came to booze. If you'd been around us long enough, you would have heard Liz lecture me about my diet at least a thousand times: "You have to be healthy; you want to be around to see our kids grow up, don't you?" I always promised I'd eat better tomorrow, figuring I had years to turn my act around. People don't die until they're at least eighty years old, right? After all, I was eighteen or twenty-five or thirty. Whatever. I felt young.

But Liz was the picture of health.

"Why the fuck am I the one still alive?" I asked out loud,

as Alex stood behind me, looking over my head and into the mirror, trying to get my pink tie with the white polka dots to lie just right.

Adjusting the Windsor knot and creating the perfect dimple below it, he said, "The question I have for you is, how the hell did you make it through thirty years of life without learning how to tie a fucking tie?"

"Shut up, asshole. It's one of my proudest accomplishments. Not too many people my age can say such a thing."

He rolled his eyes and nodded in agreement. It was only the second time I was wearing this tie; the first had been my wedding day. The suit I had on—the only suit I'd ever owned—had been purchased specifically for our rehearsal dinner. Now, fewer than three years after that night in August, I was headed to Liz's funeral in it.

We arrived at the funeral home about an hour before the service, and as we approached the door, I saw at least forty flower displays lined up outside the place. Inside, there had to be ten thousand dollars' worth of flowers and plants—this must be why obituaries often say *in lieu of flowers*, I thought. We all looked around in amazement, our eyes finally settling on a display just to the left of the entrance that was so immense it rendered us motionless. Written on the ivory-colored ribbon woven through it were the words *From your friends at Blush*.

Confusion settled in and everyone's brows furrowed, but I started laughing and answered their unspoken question: "Blush is the salon where Liz got her hair done." She would have been so happy to see that.

Just as I'd hoped, the photo boards lined the hallway outside of the chapel, showing off a smiling Liz enjoying life to the fullest. There were a couple of hidden gems in the mix, pictures I'd chosen specifically to give people a good laugh. There was one of her standing next to the measuring stick at a ride at Disneyland, the implication being that she had just managed to meet the height requirement to go on it; one of her reliving an exasperated moment she'd had in North India when the temperatures reached 118 degrees; and one of her standing next to a clown-shaped garbage can at the Minnesota state fair, mimicking the open mouth it used to collect everyone's trash.

I walked into the chapel with A.J. and was immediately assaulted by the sounds of "On Eagle's Wings." "Fucking hell. We need to get this music turned off before I kill someone."

I found a man in a suit I didn't recognize and figured he must be one of the sons referenced on the sign outside of the funeral home. "Hey. I have a couple of CDs with music I want to have playing during the service. Can you take us to your sound system?" A few minutes later I was humming along to "Dress Sexy at My Funeral."

People started to stream in, stopping to share a hug and their condolences with every familiar face they encountered. I mostly ignored them, waving from time to time as I paced, trying to figure out what the hell I was going to say at my wife's funeral. I had decided that two of Liz's uncles would emcee the event, and that I would do the bulk of the speaking—that is, if I could find the words. There would be no prayers and no Bible verses while I was at the podium, just stories, but I hadn't really thought about how I was going to pull it off. I'd always been terrified of public speaking; I sort of possessed the confidence of a twelve-year-old girl in the early stages of puberty when standing in front of a crowd. This felt different, though.

The time came and I took my place at the front of the room. Liz's uncles said a few words for the God-fearing folks in the room before relinquishing the microphone to me. I stood there, clutching the sides of the wooden podium, staring down at nothing, and after a few seconds I looked up. All of the pews were filled, and people were sitting on the floor in the aisles, standing in the hallway, spilling out the door and into the parking lot. Our friends, family, coworkers, nurses from the hospital, total strangers—so many people had come, and for the first time in a public-speaking situation, I felt the power of confidence. I guess you could call it a supreme disregard for the feelings of others, but at that moment the only feelings that mattered were mine. Not one person or their opinion could challenge my grief, and it would be impossible for anyone to make me feel worse than I already did. I breathed in the scent of thousands of flowers, their combination creating the kind of amalgam that is present only at flower shops, weddings, and funerals.

"I'm just gonna say what all of you are thinking: this fucking sucks."

After spitting out that first thought, I felt totally at ease. The words flowed from me as if they were the only words I knew: I talked about the way Liz's smile lit up every room she entered, the way she looked at me with her coruscating blue eyes, and the way she didn't take shit from anyone. I talked about our amazing travels together, including the trips to Peru, India, Nepal, Greece, and Mexico. I told everyone about the great sense of accomplishment we felt when we had purchased our first house together just ten months earlier, and the excitement we felt about bringing Madeline into the world. I talked about my fears of raising our daughter alone. Mostly I just talked about how much I would miss having Liz in my life. As I spoke, everyone stared at me, seemingly holding their breath, waiting for me to stop talking before they exhaled. At one point I broke down in tears, and was joined at the front of the room by my brothers, dad, and stepdad. They passed the microphone around, telling their own favorite stories about Liz and giving me a break from baring my soul.

My brother David was the last to speak. "Matt and I are ten years apart, and since I was a little kid I've only known Matt and Liz, Liz and Matt. She was as much my sister as Matt is my brother." He paused for a second. "I've dated a lot of girls in my life, and not one of them has been half as great as Liz. I hope that someday I can find the kind of love that these two shared."

From the crowd, someone shouted out, "What's your number?" It was Annie, one of Liz's friends from college, making me laugh as she always managed to do. I'm sure there were some who found her words inappropriate, but they were exactly what I needed to hear. I'll forever be thankful to her for doubling me over in laughter during one of the most difficult moments of my life.

After that, I invited Liz's friends and family to join me at the front of the room to share their memories of her, too. It seemed like the service had been going on for five minutes, but when I looked at my watch—the watch Liz had given to me as a wedding gift, a watch I rarely wore—I realized I had been standing there, talking, listening, crying, and laughing, for over an hour. I had always felt that funerals, like weddings, should be short affairs, so after a few more words, I thanked everyone and invited them back to my house for a celebration. Before leaving, I made my way to one of the photo boards, grabbed a picture of a pregnant Liz happily pointing at her round belly in our backyard, and tucked it in the inside pocket of my suit coat.

Fifteen minutes later I stood in front of my house, watching people walk through our yard holding paper plates sagging under the weight of the food and red plastic cups filled with beer and wine. I couldn't help but think that Liz would be proud if she could see this, as one of the big reasons we bought this house was because she wanted to entertain and throw dinner parties in our yard. Here we were, my family, her family, and our friends from all around the country having a huge party in honor of Liz, but it made me sick to my stomach to know that she was missing from the event. I made my way from person to person, giving and receiving hugs, and patting my stomach to indicate that I was full each time someone tried to make me eat something. Day five with persistent nausea, day five without food. I felt like I might never be able to eat again, but I was okay with that because I had lost enough weight to make my suit fit for the first time in over a year.

I was thankful that so many people stopped by the house, but the only person I really wanted to be with—who I *could* be with—was Madeline. I hated that she had missed her own mother's funeral, but there was no other option. She was not ready to come home from the hospital and, according to the doctors, might not be for another seven weeks. I grew more and more anxious to see her as the crowd began to disperse. I pulled A.J. aside. "I've got to go see Madeline." I took him up on his offer to drive me back to the hospital, sneaking away from the people drinking in my back yard.

Still in my suit and tie, I walked through the hospital to the NICU. A few minutes later I was sitting in the now-familiar blue chair, staring at Madeline's yet unopened eyelids. I rocked back and forth, soothing myself as much as I soothed her. The nursery shades were open, and through the window I saw a few friends who had stopped by the hospital on their way out of town. I let them snap some photos before I asked one of the nurses to close the shades for me. "I'd like a few minutes alone with Madeline," I said.

With as much privacy as we could get in a room full of nurses and sick babies, I whispered to Madeline some of the stories I had shared at the funeral. While she fell asleep in my arms, I told her how much her mom loved her and promised to give her the best life I possibly could. I held her for a few minutes before returning her to her incubator, thanked the nurse, and made my way to the door.

As I reached to push it open, I remembered the photo in the pocket of my suit. I turned back toward Madeline, stopping at the doctor's desk to get a piece of tape. I opened up the incubator's arm holes and reached in to tape the photo of Liz inside. I pulled my hand out, then kissed the tips of my fingers two times, reached back in, and gently touched Madeline on the forehead. "One kiss from me, and one from your mother."

Part II

excitement.
fear.
happiness.
sadness.
dread.
confidence.
i felt all of that
when we walked up the stairs
to our house.

Chapter 12

It must have looked odd, a grown man sitting in a wheelchair, a newborn baby in a car seat on his lap, being wheeled out of the hospital. A woman, presumably the mother, walks ahead of them, snapping photos. I'd been spending all of my time, awake and asleep, at the hospital for over five weeks at this point, and I'd seen countless new moms in the exact same position I was in.

"Did you see the nasty look that old lady just gave me?"

"I did," Anya said, laughing.

"She must think I'm the biggest asshole in the world."

I hadn't given it much thought, but I always assumed that the wheelchair exit had something to do with the new mother's inability to walk out of the hospital on her own. What I couldn't figure out is why *I* had to be pushed out of the hospital.

"What's with the wheelchair?" I asked the NICU nurse, as I complied with her directions and sat down.

She explained that it was done for liability reasons. Apparently the safest way for a baby to leave the hospital was in someone's lap in a wheelchair. I had to laugh. The hospital staff didn't trust me to walk out of the building, but they were going to let me take my daughter home? Sitting there, I wondered if this was the same wheelchair that should have delivered Liz safely to our baby exactly two weeks ago today.

After saying good-bye to the NICU staff, I asked the nurse to push me around the hospital so I could show Madeline off to all of the friends I'd made during my time here. We stopped by the high-risk ward to say good-bye to Liz's nurses and went to the cafeteria and coffee shop to thank the staff for taking such good care of my family.

My dad pulled my car up to the entrance of the hospital just as the sliding glass doors opened. After she pushed us through the doors and onto the sidewalk, the nurse patted me on the back, making it apparent that I had been granted the freedom to walk and carry my baby. I stood up, both hands squeezing the handle on the car seat as if loosening my grip meant that my daughter would somehow disappear from my world. My eyes adjusted to the sunlight and I looked up at the sky. I pulled the shade of the car seat over Madeline, knowing that Liz would have been concerned about the sun hitting our baby's bright white skin for the first time. I turned around, said good-bye to the nurse, and walked toward my car to secure Madeline into it for the first time. I was worried that I had installed it incorrectly, so I gave the car seat a few gentle wiggles before feeling fully satisfied that I'd successfully gotten the thing in, and went around to the driver's side. Dad and Anya would follow us home in their own cars.

This day had come much more quickly than I had anticipated. Even though I spent a ton of time learning how to feed, burp, change, and even perform CPR on Madeline, I didn't even feel close to ready to bring her home. Since the day she had been born, I'd been told that Maddy might end up staying in the hospital until her actual due date—seven weeks later. Now she was coming home after only fourteen days, barely bigger than she'd been at birth: just over four pounds.

Sure, I was looking forward to bringing her home with me and getting her out of the hospital, but I needed more time to get ready for her arrival. When the NICU doctor told me that she was being discharged, I presented the hospital staff with every excuse I could think of to delay the inevitable.

She doesn't have any diapers at home.
I don't have a car seat for her.
My dad is painting my house.
I don't have any smoke detectors in the house.
Are you sure she's ready?
Are you sure I'm ready?

These weren't actually excuses; they were truths. Well, the ones about the car seat and the smoke detector weren't really true, but I thought they were the best shot I had at buying a few more days.

"All new parents have doubts," one of the NICU nurses reassured me, which of course, I knew. But my doubts were a little more pronounced than most. The nurse knew about Liz's death, but she failed to realize that I wasn't emotionally stable enough to grieve for my wife *and* take care of our newborn. Still, she insisted that Madeline would be going home with me that day.

I took my appeal to the NICU doctor on call. "There's no medically necessary reason to keep her here," he explained. "The sooner you can get her home, the better. The most dangerous place for a baby is in the hospital, but if you really think you need it, I can buy you one more day."

The most dangerous place for a baby is in the hospital? I could think of several places that had to be more dangerous than a hospital: a lion's den, Skid Row, the middle of the 110 freeway, and my not-yet-baby-proofed house.

I left the jokes in my head, figuring that this was not the time to demonstrate that I still had a sense of humor. I had hoped that by the time Madeline was ready to come home I would have the confidence and knowledge to deal with everything that came along with her. Two weeks in the hospital with the aid of doctors and nurses had taught me a lot, but I knew that one more day wasn't going to give me all of the answers. Hell, one more year wasn't going to get me where I hoped I'd be. When Liz was alive, I never doubted the fact that I'd be a great dad with her help. But after she died, I started to worry that I was going to fail her and our baby. I was convinced that I didn't have any sort of inborn abilities to raise a child successfully.

And apparently, I wasn't the only one who thought so. While my family and friends seemed confident that I was up to the challenge, encouraging me as if simply telling me I'd do well with Madeline meant that I actually would, others were not so sure. A few days after Liz died, a woman saw my mom crying outside the window of the NICU.

"Is your baby okay?" she asked.

"Oh, that's my granddaughter," said my mom. "She's doing great."

My mom—always one to strike up conversations with strangers—volunteered the entire story. When she finished, the woman, stone-faced, asked, "Is your son going to give the baby up for adoption?"

When I heard the story, I was furious. Give her up for adoption? What the fuck is wrong with people?

This woman's reaction and many others left me with the rankling feeling that I had something to prove. Not just to those close to me, but also to the world, because I knew I would forever be judged as being incapable, if not totally incompetent—unless I was great. I had to be better than great. I was going to be the best fucking father there ever was.

And that was my promise to myself and to Madeline.

I pulled out of the hospital driveway and headed toward the freeway, completely alone with Madeline for the first time. No doctors, no nurses, no friends, no family. I thought about how this moment should have gone. Liz should have been in the back—one hand on the car seat, the other hand making sure Madeline's head wasn't bouncing around—telling me to be gentler as I downshifted. She should have been here, cooing at our daughter and relaying her every reaction to me. But my wife isn't here, I thought, snapping back to reality.

There were several other routes home I could have chosen to take, but I felt compelled to drive past where Liz's funeral had been held—I don't know if I was delusional or just feeling sadistic. As soon as I saw the parking lot, I began crying and shaking uncontrollably. If this wasn't a kick to the nuts, I don't know what would have been. Driving under the influence of irrepressible grief was a lot like what it must feel like to drive drunk. I was dizzy and couldn't see straight. I struggled to regain my composure, gripping the wheel as tight as I could, trying to keep my car headed in a straight line, and doing my best not to get pulled over.

I managed to make it into our neighborhood without incident, and as I drove up the big hill leading to our house, there it was: Liz's car, parked in its usual spot. Just like every time I had pulled up to the house in the last two weeks, I felt the excitement in my chest that came when I realized Liz was home before me. And every time, it took a second for my brain to catch up with my heart, and then the feeling disappeared as quickly as the exhale from her last breath. I backed my car up to park and felt the resistance of an object behind me.

Fuck. I hit Liz's car. I'd parked here hundreds of times, and I'd never hit it before. My heart started racing immediately, and with one quick movement I unbuckled my seat belt and lifted myself out of my seat, arching my back to assess the damage I'd done to my child. She was expressionless and in no obvious pain; relief blanketed my body. I knew I was being ridiculous—the impact was barely noticeable—but I was convinced that the slightest misstep would forever damage Madeline. And I would be the only one to blame if something went wrong.

I pulled the car forward a few inches, finally putting it into park just as my dad and Anya both arrived. I would have been fucking mortified if they had witnessed the collision—I didn't want to put any doubt into the minds of some of my most ardent supporters. I walked around my car to open the back door, and after a few seconds of fumbling for the car seat release, Madeline was out. I felt terrible about hitting Liz's car. She would have been pretty pissed at me if she had witnessed it. Then I felt sad that I'd no longer have her there to be angry with me for doing stupid shit like bumping her car with mine.

I carried Madeline to the front door, and the instant we walked into the house, it felt different—it felt better. It was less lonely now with Madeline. I'd been in and out of my house several times in the past two weeks, and no matter how many people stood in the living room or the office or the kitchen with me, and no matter who the people were, the house seemed empty. I could feel Liz's absence, the gravity of her death weighing heavily on my mind and in my heart, but with Madeline next to me, the house felt alive. And so did I, because now that she was home with me, it was time to start living life with my beautiful baby girl.

Getting her safely home felt like a great accomplishment to me. Despite the smallness of the task, my confidence was boosted by this feat; I was now just a little bit surer that I could handle the job of being a single parent.

At the time of Liz's death, I had worked for Yahoo! for almost six years. The day after she died, I received a call from my department's HR representative. She expressed her sympathy and told me that everyone there was thinking about Madeline and me. "Matt, please don't worry about work. I'll call you in a couple of weeks and we can talk about your plans for the future."

That next conversation never happened, though, because I got a different phone call from the vice president of my department, who offered me an indefinite leave from my job to help me deal with Liz's death and to spend time at home with Madeline. "Matt, we're going to treat this situation as if you are working from home. Our only concerns are you and Madeline, so take as much time as you need and we'll do our best to keep you from having to deal with disability insurance or any of that other stuff."

I was blown away. Without his saying it, I knew that this was a decision he came to without consulting any employee handbook; it was done out of the kindness of his heart, because as a married father, he could actually imagine himself in my shitty situation, and this was the only possible way he could help me. The only other people who knew about the arrangement were the HR representative and the senior director of my department. I was so thankful for their decision, but I wondered how much time I could take off without appearing to take advantage of their generosity. Even if I lived another ninety years and kept Yahoo! hanging on the line that entire time, I would never be over Liz's death. I decided to take it day by day and worry about nothing but Maddy and me. I had no idea when I'd consider working again, but I knew I'd return someday.

My responsibility now was for another human life, and fucking up was not an option. Because Maddy was still so tiny, the NICU doctor had placed her on a strict feeding schedule. Every three hours she got a bottle of formula and a diaper change, day and night. I thought about all the times Liz would yell at me for forgetting to stop and eat while she was out of town, and how it wouldn't go too well for Madeline if I forgot to feed her.

Sensing my fear, or perhaps trying to assuage their own, Tom and Candee, now back in Minnesota, called to tell me that they had worked with a few of Liz's friends to track down some assistance for me. The memorial fund that Sonja and Josh set up had brought in well over sixty thousand dollars since Liz's funeral, and Tom insisted that the best use of the money was to pay for some help.

"You have enough money for round-the-clock aid for at least a month, and that's exactly what this money is for."

He was right, but all I could think about was the future—how we were going to continue to live in our house, and how we were going to make it without Liz's income. But I looked at the memorial fund as an emergency reserve, to be used only in the direst of circumstances. I didn't want to dip into it to pay someone to do a job that I saw as a labor of love. I got on the phone with Tom.

"Matt, good news. We found a postpartum doula who's

willing to donate one night of her services for free," Tom said. "She heard about your story and wants to help."

I had no idea what the hell a doula even was, but I remembered Liz telling me that some of her friends had them before and after their pregnancies.

"Great," I said, as I looked up the definition of the word.

I was hopeful that a doula was some sort of baby sorcerer, ready to impart upon me secret child-rearing knowledge that had been passed down through generations of doulas before.

"Now, if we could find another 365 like her, you and Maddy will be just fine."

"Maybe. Hey, Tom?"

"Yeah?"

"Did you know that the etymology of the word *doula* is from the Greek *doule*, meaning 'female slave'? I'm pretty sure I don't really want a slave, even if she's only gonna be here for one night."

Tom spent the next few minutes convincing me that this woman wasn't really a slave at all, just a kind soul willing to volunteer her time to help someone in need. I really wanted to just start this parenting thing on my own, but after the long day, I didn't have the energy to put up a fight. I agreed to allow a doula into my home to help me with Madeline. Besides, getting a good night's sleep wasn't the worst idea.

When my hoped-for savior arrived at the front door, I instantly concluded that a doula was more like a hippie-nanny hybrid than anything else. We spent most of the night sitting on the couch, talking about the kinds of things strangers discuss. She shared with me her strong opinions about natural birthing methods, natural medicine, and, naturally, raising a child. She picked a parenting book up from the coffee table. "You may as well throw this in the trash," she declared.

Now, I probably would have agreed with her a few weeks earlier—I was a firm believer that most parenting books are useless. Humans have been raising babies for over two hundred thousand years, and during most of that time there were no doctors, doulas, books, or websites to help them figure it out. But at that moment, her pronouncement left me seething: the book she held above her head, the book she suggested was garbage, was the last book Liz ever held in her hands, and she saw it as her parenting bible. I didn't say anything to the doula because I knew she hadn't intentionally tried to piss me off, but I took it as my cue to exit and try to get some sleep.

A little while later, I woke up to silence and walked from my bedroom into the living room to find her still sitting on my couch. I looked around and was surprised to see my house a little cleaner than it had been when I went to sleep. Even more surprising was that I'd only slept for two and a half hours, and I had missed just one of Madeline's diaper change/feeding cycles. If this doula had generations of baby knowledge, she sure didn't share any of it. She didn't suck at what she did, but I'd had such lofty expectations for her that she was never going to live up to them. She did teach me an alternative swaddling technique that was rather impressive, but otherwise I found her services basically useless.

The next night's slave wasn't a slave at all. In fact, she was an extortionist. This second doula was at our house for twelve hours and things went pretty much the same as the night before. In the morning, before she was to leave, she informed me that her services cost sixty dollars per hour. "US dollars?" I asked, only half kidding.

She didn't think I was very funny. As I tried to multiply 12 times 60 in my head, she blurted out "Seven hundred and twenty dollars."

Seven hundred and twenty dollars for supposed help that

paled in comparison to the actual knowledge I had gained from the doctors and nurses at the hospital.

But the doulas *did* do one thing for me: they gave me confidence. Confidence that lack of sleep wasn't as big an issue as everyone told me it would be, and confidence that at sixty dollars per hour, my emergency fund would run out far sooner than we had anticipated. Most important, because the doulas didn't provide any precious advice or information, I was confident that I would be able to take care of my child on my own. I still didn't really have all of the answers—or even know the questions, necessarily—but I now felt sure that I could become the great parent I wanted to be. Besides, Madeline seemed pretty easy, just eating and requiring a diaper change at regular intervals. In the hospital, she had been a fragile doll in an incubator, wires attached to her body, feeding tube in her nose. But after two days at home with her all of that seemed to disappear—she was simply my kid. I knew I was never going to be perfect, but I was going to try my damnedest.

I made a check out to the doula while she used a green Sharpie to write her name, address, and phone number down on the back of a receipt I found lying on my desk. "Give me a call if you'd like me to come back."

I told her I would, but I already knew she'd never hear from me again.

i can't help but
think that
madeline
lost the better of
her two parents.

Chapter 13

I knew that I was going to have to learn to live alone with Madeline, so I figured the best thing to do was to jump right in. As the sun went down on our first evening alone in the house, I sat on the top stair of our front porch. Madeline was cradled in my left arm, and I was staring across the small valley that separated our hilltop house from the next, trying to keep from thinking about what should have been. As hard as I tried to focus on the distant sounds of birds, the thoughts just kept creeping back into my head. Liz should have been sitting here next to me, just under a month to go until her due date. I should have had my left arm around her, my hand gripping her shoulder, while the other, placed firmly on her belly, waited to feel our unborn daughter's next kick. We should have been making fun of the annoying couple in our birthing class and talking about when she planned to start her maternity leave. Madeline shouldn't have been here, not yet, anyway. And sitting there alone with my daughter, I tried my best not to completely lose my shit.

I was emotionally exhausted, and I knew that I should go to sleep because Maddy would wake up in a few hours, ready for her next diaper change and feeding. I walked through the house turning off the lights, careful to leave one on in the living room just so any potential burglars would know that someone was home, which I'd been doing nightly since the incident last January. I went into the bedroom, my bare feet sliding over the silk rug Liz had purchased during our trip to Nepal. I placed my tightly swaddled baby faceup in her bassinet and climbed into my bed still wearing jeans and a T-shirt. No sense in getting undressed, I figured, since I no longer had any idea of whether it was morning or night. I lay there, watching the ceiling fan spin above me and listening to the analog clock on Liz's dresser tick away the seconds. I don't know how long she'd had it, but this was the first time I had ever heard it. Suddenly I felt a pulsing in my head that was beating in time with the clock. I closed my eyes and rubbed my temples, just like they do in those commercials for Tylenol, trying to massage away the pain.

I reached for the television remote on my nightstand, hoping to find a new episode of *Robot Chicken* on the DVR to make me laugh without having to think. There were some shows that Liz had recorded but hadn't had a chance to watch: a few episodes of *The Hills*, three hours' worth of *A Baby Story*, and some other pieces of supreme television shit. I hit the menu button on the remote and moved the cursor to Delete, but then I paused. I had no desire to ever watch any of this trash, but I couldn't get rid of it. By deleting Liz's shows, wouldn't I be deleting part of her? I let out a mixture of laughter and tears as I thought about how stupid that was, and decided to turn off the TV and read a book instead.

I wasn't sure how long I'd been asleep, but the sound that awoke me sent a wave of panic through my body; it was the same noise I'd heard come from Liz the day that she died. I jumped from the bed and found Madeline with vomit coming from her nose and mouth, choking and gasping for air. Independent from my mind and the rest of my body, my arms reached for her and my hands lifted her from the bassinet.

I didn't need to remember what I'd learned in the baby CPR class I had taken in the hospital—I just started doing it. I flipped Madeline over, her stomach on my leg, her head hanging over my knee. I firmly smacked her back, hoping I'd be able to clear her airway. It didn't work. My baby cradled in my arms, I ran to her room and with my free hand, searched through the mountain of unopened baby products piled in the corner. Frantic, I found what I was looking for: the booger sucker, as it had been known in my house while I was growing up. I ripped open the package and placed my thumb on top of the bulbous blue rubber thing, with the stem between my index and middle fingers.

I had never actually used a nasal aspirator before, but I didn't think it could require too much instruction. I thrust the skinny end into her nose and pushed my thumb down hard on the round part. Madeline started coughing and squirming harder. Fuck! I forgot the one and only rule for using the thing: squeeze all of the air out of it first. I removed the aspirator from her nose, scared to death that I had done some permanent damage to my daughter by forcefully blowing the vomit further into her nasal passage, but I knew I had to try it again—no one else was going to, certainly. I reinserted the aspirator, this time correctly. When I took my thumb off, I heard a sucking sound, indicating some form of success. I emptied its contents right onto the wood floor of her bedroom and repeated the steps.

By the third round, it sounded like Madeline was breathing fine, so I stopped trying to clear her airway. Mentally exhausted, I dropped the aspirator, lay down in the middle of the now-dirty floor and cried, holding Madeline to my chest and gently rubbing her back.

I couldn't help but think how different things would have been if Liz had been here to help. I would have been freaking out, and she calmly would have dealt with our choking baby. Or maybe it would have been the other way around. But no matter what, we would have been able to responsibly handle the situation together, instead of it being just me, alone with our child, in pieces. My confidence was shaken a bit, but I was pretty damn impressed how well I handled the crisis in the end.

I spent a great deal of those first few weeks in tears. Often they would come upon me suddenly; I was as overwhelmed by the ordinary as I was by the inconceivable. I couldn't help crying, but I worked very hard to avoid doing so in front of Maddy. It's not that she would have necessarily known that I was sad, but I wanted to ensure that she didn't feel my pain. Happy father equals happy baby, right? So as soon as she was comfortably sleeping, her tiny chest rising and falling, I'd sneak out to the garage to cry over old photos of Liz and me. Or I would shower, not to get clean, but to hide behind the green and white curtain, letting the sound of the water drown out my bawling.

But even in the depths of my grief, when Maddy was just a few weeks old, there had to be laughter and I had to have a sense of humor, because it was fucking awful to keep thinking about Liz dying. It's not that things were necessarily funny—I just made light of certain situations. An avalanche of greeting cards steadily flowed into my mailbox, usually with two cards from each sender: one congratulating me on the birth of my daughter, the other offering condolences on the death of my wife. I found this to be as absurd as it was comical. I was baffled that friends and family didn't have the words in their minds or their hearts to be able to say both things at once. They had to buy two cards at Target and get two fucking stamps. I understood the sentiments were difficult to express, and I did appreciate that they made the effort to let Hallmark say it for them, at least. If I hadn't been able to find the humor in it, though, I would have lost my mind.

As much as I joked about the incongruity of the cards, I know it was this type of support that got me through those first impossible weeks. Being alone with my baby and without my wife, support was what I needed the most, and my personal community stepped up to the challenge with grace—and generosity.

Countless local friends stopped by the house with gifts for Madeline, and on most occasions they'd arrive with food and beverages, too. Liz and I had cooked together all the time, but now that she was dead I just couldn't do it. Friends would try to make me feel better by saying, "It's hard to cook for one," which was valid, but the real difficulty for me was actually entering our kitchen. Every drawer I opened contained some item or another that we had been given for our wedding, and I couldn't take the reminders constantly transporting me back there. Liz had such a great time opening up these gifts and stocking the kitchen with them, and I had an equal amount of fun laughing at some of the stupid shit we'd registered for.

"What the fuck are we going to do with this crack torch? Neither one of us smokes crack, I don't think."

"It's a crème brûlée torch, you ass."

"I hate crème brûlée," I said.

"It's my favorite, so you better learn to make it."

During the day it was easier—a phone call from a friend would distract me long enough to dig through the cupboards to find all of the pieces of Maddy's bottle. But the anxiety was especially bad at night. There were no visitors. No calls. No support. Still no wife. Everyone was asleep or up late dealing with their own crying babies. The quiet darkness brought out my weakness and anguish. Things got so bad, I tried so hard to avoid going near that pain, that I moved a supply of bottled water, powdered formula, and a bottle warmer into the bedroom so I wouldn't have to make up Maddy's bottles in the kitchen.

At first I had been pretty much unable to eat at all—the feeling of perpetual nausea had followed me home from the hospital. I probably dropped twenty-five to thirty pounds in the first few weeks after Liz died. I was a fucking skeleton. The unmistakable look of grief emanated from every part of my body. I was destroyed, and a mess. My eyes looked as if they had been shoved two inches back inside my head; my face was ashen and expressionless, except when I was crying. I'd lost so much weight that I looked like a little kid wearing clothing stolen from my father's closet. I was pathetic and visibly not okay. But I had to hold it together for my daughter.

I was learning as I went and making adjustments as needed. Madeline's very strict schedule for the first few months of her life of course meant that I was on a very strict schedule for the first few months of my new life, keeping me from completely falling apart and withdrawing from the world. Despite multiple warnings, I broke the one rule that every parent shared with me: sleep when your baby sleeps. I found it nearly impossible. I was never much of a sleeper, but when Maddy first came home, I only slept for three or four nonconsecutive hours per day. She kept me regimented, but I also needed ways to keep

myself busy while she slept. Too much alone time led to thinking and overthinking and usually breaking down. I did all the
chores around the house that I had actively avoided while Liz
was alive and asking for my help, simply because they kept my
mind occupied. Wilco's "Hate It Here" repeated over and over
in my head: *I even learned how to use the washing machine, but keeping things clean doesn't change anything.* The lyrics seemed written
specifically for my situation.

I also used Madeline's sleep and feeding times to keep up
with the things I used to do before. I'd sit in my office in front
of my computer, reading record reviews and catching up on
the news while holding her in my arms. After a while, I had a
general sense of how long it would take her to drain a bottle.
She was drinking maybe four ounces at a time over the course
of fifteen minutes. One night I put a bottle in her mouth and
propped it up with a blanket under her chin so it could rest
stably while she drank. That way I'd still have one hand free
to maneuver the mouse and keyboard. I started typing, and it
couldn't have been more than twenty seconds till I heard the
schlshh, schlshh sound of sucking air. I looked down and saw that
the bottle was empty. There was a little bit of milk around her
lips, but I definitely didn't see it all over her or anything else.
What the hell?

Fuck, I realized, the nipple had a giant hole in it. My
daughter had just done a beer bong out of her bottle; she'd
just sucked it down like the drunk wannabe sorority girls with
whom I went to college. Oh shit. I was starting to panic. I
had no idea if I should induce vomiting or call the hospital or
something. I grabbed for my phone to make the call, but as I
watched her, she seemed completely fine. And right then, my
panic turned to self-loathing—Liz would have known exactly
what to do, because it was probably covered in one of those
fucking parenting books that I made fun of her for reading.

In addition to such crises, I was also dealing with a host of new feelings that came with being a parent. I felt love, exhaustion, nervousness, and, perhaps least expectedly, disgust. Parenting an infant requires a whole new relationship with bodily fluids. With Maddy around, I had to let go of a lot of my hard-lived obsessive-compulsive tendencies. I'd always sort of had them, to the point that Liz once accused me of being bulimic because I rushed to the restroom after every meal. I had to work hard to convince her that I was simply going to wash my hands because I couldn't stand to have them smell like food. Since most of my clothes are recycled from the thrift store and I insist on keeping a grimy-looking beard, this may be difficult to believe, but it's true: I am a clean freak. But kids are not clean. They're dirty, filthy little creatures, and I had to come to terms with the fact that Maddy was going to get me sticky and sneeze on me and wipe her boogers all over me.

Madeline was in my arms one morning, and for no reason at all she vomited. All over me. My adorable little girl opened up her mouth and released a stream of pureed peas, *Exorcist*-style, all down the front of my Hold Steady T-shirt. There I was, cradling this child, and my first thought was not to put her down and clean myself up—which it absolutely would have been before she was born. Immediately, I made certain that nothing was obstructing my daughter's breathing. I was covered in green vomit, and I didn't even care. I wished that Liz had been there to see the vile mess—she would have laughed her ass off.

Without Liz, I now had to deal with our finances, bills, and the rest of the real-life, grown-up responsibilities that came along with them. One of my biggest and most immediate concerns was how we were going to survive financially. As a part of the survivor benefits extended to me through Disney, Liz's em-

ployer, I met with a financial adviser who walked me through
the process of creating a budget. Looking at our expenses, I
wondered how the hell Madeline and I were going to make
it without Liz's salary—more than half of our income. Ten
months before she died, we bought a house at what turned out
to be the peak of the real estate market. I now saw it as my
duty to ensure that we didn't lose the house of our dreams, the
one Liz fell in love with the moment she saw it. The one she
spent countless hours decorating to make perfect. The one we
wanted to start our family in.

"With the money you have, if you live conservatively, you'll
be able to stay here for about three years," said the adviser.

Three years sounded like a long time to me, but then what?
Would I have to get a second job? Would I have to short-sell my
house, or, even worse, walk away from my mortgage, take the
hit to my credit, and move in with family members? According to the financial adviser, I was eligible to collect some form of
Social Security benefits on behalf of Madeline, and as Liz's surviving spouse I'd get a small onetime payout. I wasn't exactly
eager to deal with any sort of government bureaucracy so soon,
but I knew that it would ease some of the financial stress and
anxiety I was already feeling, so I made an appointment.

I arrived at the Social Security office in Glendale and took
a seat near a couple of old women, both probably in their sev-
enties. I figured that they were there for the same reason I
was: their spouses had died, and they were hoping to find some
financial assistance in this dismal office. But I couldn't help
think how lucky they were to have had forty or fifty good years
with their husbands. It was all conjecture—I really had no idea
why these women were there, and frankly, I didn't give a shit.
All I could think was that I'd had twelve great years with my
wife, and now I would have maybe forty or fifty without her. I
couldn't believe how much my life sucked.

I lifted Madeline out of her car seat and held her in my arms, talking to her about where we were. I'd been doing that since I'd brought her home, talking to her like she was an adult who couldn't see or hear what was going on around her. I probably sounded like a complete lunatic to those around me as I laid out the scene for my newborn. The old women moved closer to us.

"You have such a beautiful baby. Is it a boy or a girl?"

I thought that to be an odd question, considering Madeline was covered in pink from the neck down.

"It's a girl, and its name is Madeline," I said snidely, already pissed off at them based on the story I'd made up in my head. I could tell they completely missed the fact that I was patronizing them—old people often didn't understand my sense of humor.

The women took turns touching her cheeks and cooing at her with the kind of baby talk I'd sworn I'd never use with my child. Thankfully, before Madeline's brain was fully turned to mush by their inane chatter, my name was called. Someone led us through a doorway and directed me to sit down at a desk across from a young woman who shook my hand, introducing herself with a name I forgot immediately. Without making eye contact or acknowledging the baby I held, she began to read from a sheet of paper in front of her. Just as the financial adviser had promised, she informed me that I was eligible for a onetime payout.

"The Social Security Administration will directly deposit two hundred fifty-five dollars into your bank account..."

Two hundred fifty-five dollars? That's it?? Two hundred fifty-five dollars??? Are you fucking kidding me? I tried to find a proper response to the woman's words. No amount would have taken away the pain of Liz's death—but seriously, couldn't they have at least given me enough to buy a couple of months' worth of diapers?

During my internal rant, I missed the end of her script. I zoned back in when she finally asked if I had all of the necessary paperwork to get my benefits claim started.

"I hope so," I said, trying to lighten up the mood. I reached into Madeline's diaper bag to grab the manila folder full of documents that had come to rule the last few weeks of my life. I handed her Madeline's birth certificate and Social Security card, but hesitated before pulling out Liz's death certificate—the grim reminder that the two most important dates in my life will forever be connected.

I didn't want to give her the death certificate; I didn't want to show it to anyone. It was a private thing, and it took an emotional toll on me every time I had to watch another bureaucrat scan it for information. I hated that the death certificate would now be the defining document of Liz's life. And really, I didn't need to be reminded that my wife was dead; the emptiness in my heart was reminder enough.

I wondered if I could get away with not handing it over—after all, I was able to describe its every last line by heart. I knew every square inch of it like it was the ceiling in my childhood bedroom, and I knew every word like it was my favorite poem. I could tell this woman that the seal of the state of California was in the lower left corner of the document, and that the city of Pasadena was incorporated in June 1886, according to the city seal found in the lower right corner. I could tell her that Evonne D. Reed was the coroner who signed it, and that Takashi M. Wada, M.D., was listed as the health officer at the bottom. I could describe in great detail the way the colors faded from pink to blue from both the left and the right sides, and the ornate patterns created by the blue and white lines bordering the entire paper. I could tell her that in Box 8 was the number 1511, noting Liz's time of death at 3:11 p.m., and that Box 41 listed the letters CR/RES, indicating that she had been cremated and that her remains had been removed from the state. I could tell her that Box 107 listed two causes of death, and that the document had been issued on April 1, 2008, one week to the day after Liz died.

But I knew that for the Social Security Administration, this recitation would not be proof enough that my wife was dead. I reluctantly slid the document across the desk and sunk deeper into my chair.

"Did the marriage end in death?" she asked, still reading from her script, still not looking at me.

What kind of question is that? *What the fuck do you think?* I wanted to scream, but what came out of my mouth was far less eloquent: "Technically, yes, but I'm still wearing our rings, so no. Well, yes. Um, never mind." Jesus.

Even though Liz was dead, I really did still consider myself married, but to this woman, there was no room on the paperwork for any explanation. All she wanted was a simple yes or no so she could check the correct box on the form in front of her. She finally glanced up, making eye contact for the first time since I had sat down.

But all she did was look at me. I felt like I was back in elementary school, taking part in a playground staring contest. I lost.

"Yes. The marriage ended with her death."

I overthought and had a hard time with the rest of her questions, but ultimately answered in the way she wanted. When the interview ended, she informed me that we'd be getting just under $1,800 per month to be used to provide for Madeline. After the paltry $255 death benefit, this amount made me feel as though we'd just won the lottery. Mostly, I was thrilled that Madeline wouldn't have to join the workforce just yet, and that we might be able to stay in our house longer than I'd anticipated.

With the formal interview over, the woman became almost human and began making small talk with me. I would have obliged her, but at that moment, I smelled something awful. While she was still talking, I grabbed Madeline's car seat and stood up.

"I have to get going. My daughter just shit herself."

The woman looked flustered, obviously unprepared for my crassness. If only she could have read my mind during her interview, she would have known just how unrefined I really was. Pointing to her right, she said, "Uh, you can use that conference room to change her."

"Thanks."

I walked into the conference room, closed the door behind me, and pulled out the changing pad that matched the diaper bag now permanently attached to my shoulder. For the first time since bringing her home from the hospital, I changed Madeline's diaper in public, right there on the middle of the table. As I dropped the diaper in the trash can and walked out, I smiled at the thought of someone else entering this room and wondering where the shit smell was coming from. Hilarious—especially after the interview I had just endured.

sometimes it feels like
yesterday.
other times it feels
like a lifetime ago.
i'm having a hard time
remembering her voice,
but i find myself
saying things that
liz
would have said if
she
were standing next to me,
looking at our child.
like cute.
and pretty.

Chapter 14

The people I encountered in public had no clue what I was going through. It's not that I expected them to—obviously strangers don't generally know what's going on in another stranger's world—but my entire life had fallen apart, and it felt crazy to see everyone around me continuing on as if nothing at all had happened. Drivers honked and gave me the finger when I hesitated at a green light because I was thinking about the last time I'd driven down Fairfax Avenue with Liz. Baristas turned up the snark when I took too long deciding between Earl Grey and Darjeeling because I was lost in a memory of drinking tea while we watched the sun rise over the Himalayas.

Sometimes, though, strangers could be the greatest source

of comfort. I went to my bank to make a deposit, and as I approached the bulletproof glass that cascaded from the ceiling to the counter, I couldn't help but think about all the times I had visited Liz at her college summer job as a teller in Minneapolis. I did my best to hold back the tears, but when I was about to speak to the young woman at the counter, I completely broke down. "Are you okay?" she asked. I looked up and made some sort of unintelligible sound that clearly indicated I wasn't. I'm not sure if it was the noise I made or the sadness plastered across my face, but the teller immediately started crying and looked at me with an expression I would never have expected from someone I didn't know. It wasn't pity—she didn't even know my story, so it wasn't shock, either. It was the purest and most sincere form of sympathy a human could relay. When I pulled myself together, I told her all about Madeline's birth and Liz's death. I told her about the uncertainty I felt and the fear I had about my financial situation. I must have sounded like a total fucking lunatic. But if I did, she never let on.

On another occasion, I was picking up some supplies at Home Depot and the person who was helping me, a tough-looking Hispanic guy wearing an orange smock over a white muscle shirt, his arms and neck covered in tattoos, took one look at me and knew there was something wrong.

"You okay?"

"No. Not really," I replied.

"What's up?" he asked.

"My wife died a few weeks ago and I'm a fucking wreck."

"I'm sorry. I lost my son in a shooting last year. It's not the same, but I know pain."

Just feeling that hurt was something that a lot of people couldn't relate to or even fathom, but by simply asking me if I was okay I knew that this man *got it*. He knew that no matter how tough or together you tried to look, there were moments when nothing but a good cry would do the trick. And that helped.

When I walked down the street with Madeline in my arms, it seemed like everyone was looking at me as if I'd stolen her. When I walked into a kids' clothing store, I felt like everyone thought I was using her as a prop in order to kidnap their children and use their skin to make lampshades or something. The people I encountered on a daily basis could jump to any number of conclusions: to some I might be a deadbeat dad, babysitting my child on weekends; to others, maybe I was a child predator. But, as is the case in all encounters with strangers, the only way to really know what was going on in my life was to ask questions. And it was always the same one: "Where's her mother?" No one ever asked where my wife was.

Seriously? A father alone with a baby is not such a rare occurrence in modern society, but it seemed that some people's attitudes needed adjusting. When was the last time a mother was out with her child and a stranger wanted to know where the father was? The very idea of asking such a question would not only be rude, but it would also be a complete invasion of privacy. Yet I got that question almost every time I went out alone with Madeline.

I always answered the question as honestly and directly as I could, which often made me feel like I had somehow been tasked with pissing in everyone's lemonade. It's not fun to ruin people's days by answering a simple, terribly inconsiderate question, but I couldn't avoid the truth of my own situation, and I certainly wasn't about to soften things for someone I didn't even know.

But it wasn't just the sad look on my face or the baby in my arms. I know I brought some of this attention on myself by continuing to wear Liz's rings, but I just couldn't take them off. They had been on my left pinkie ever since I put them on in

the hospital, and I was too afraid to leave them unattended in
the house. I would have been seriously pissed off if something
had happened to them. Besides, with my unexpected weight
loss, they fit perfectly. What dude doesn't need a few diamonds
on his finger? And still, I needed that physical reminder of our
closeness; I wanted Liz's most prized possessions to become a
part of me, just as they were a part of her.

When Anya and I took Maddy to the pediatrician, the assumption in the waiting room must have been that we were a
very happy family—mother, father, and daughter. But I could
feel the other parents' puzzled looks: Why was he doing all the
caregiving? Why was he holding their baby up and pointing
at the fish in the tank? Why was he carrying the diaper bag? I
mean, the sign-in sheet at the desk had the word *mother* written
on every line from top to bottom, with my lone *father* scribbled
in the bottom row.

A woman sitting next to us noticed the rings on my finger.
She was there with her two children, an infant and a girl
about eight years old. "Those are lovely," she said, then cast her
gaze in Anya's direction. "Why isn't your wife wearing them?"
When I gave her the truthful answer, she couldn't deal with it;
overwhelmed, she left her daughter in charge of the baby and
fled the waiting room in tears.

The varied reactions I got from total strangers were something of a surprise, but I suppose my answers to their questions
were equally surprising. No matter what the situation that
brought forth my story, I found that mothers always had the
most extreme response, maybe because they could see their
partners in my situation, and that scared the shit out of them.

I met one mother in a coffee shop. Maddy and I were there
hanging out with Deb when Windy approached us. Looking at
Deb, she asked, "How old is your baby?"

"Three months," Deb responded.

"She looks so small."

"Well, she was born seven weeks early."

"Was it a tough pregnancy?"

"Yes, five weeks of bed rest."

"Wow. Good luck to you," Windy said to Deb, as she headed toward the exit.

I was a bit dumbfounded. Dealing with strangers who assumed that I was not Maddy's primary caregiver was one thing; leaving them with the impression that Deb was her mother was quite another. It was obvious that Deb didn't want to discuss the circumstances that led her to be *the* woman in Madeline's life, but hearing her speak as if she was the one who had given birth to Madeline really hit a nerve. I couldn't believe she didn't at least hint at what had actually happened.

When I thought about it, though, I understood why Deb had responded that way. My wife was dead, the person who had been my compass for the past twelve years, and I had my own feelings about that. But Deb had lost her sister, whom she had loved and been so close with for her entire life. I addressed the grief in my way, and Deb in hers. There was no right or wrong way to mourn—this much I knew. But in that moment, Deb's handling of the questions had been unbearable for me.

I felt very upset and more than a little angry, but I wasn't about to lecture Deb on how to deal with her sister's death. I got up from my chair, grabbed Madeline from her car seat and said, "I'm going for a walk. I'll be right back."

I went out the door and took a left, heading for nothing in particular, just hoping to clear my head. About a quarter of a block down the street, I noticed a kids' clothing store and went inside. I hadn't intended on doing any shopping until I saw the place, but I figured I might as well pick up a few things for Madeline while I was trying to distract myself. I spent a few minutes browsing a rack near the front of the store, choosing a pink onesie with a green cartoon character on the front. As I made my way toward the register, I bumped into Windy and her daughter.

"Hi," I said.

"Oh. Hello."

"Just so you know, you didn't get the full story in the coffee shop," I abruptly told her. For the first time I *wanted* to tell a complete stranger everything, up front and without prompting. This felt different.

For the next fifteen minutes, Windy held her daughter tight as I shared with her that my seemingly picture-perfect family was not what she had been led to believe. When I finished, she wiped the tears from her eyes and reached into her purse for a pen and paper. She wrote down all of my information and promised to get in touch so we could catch up again soon.

Within a few days I heard from her, and she told me that she belonged to an online parenting group. It had started out as a resource for moms who were breast-feeding, but it had evolved into much more, with discussions about everything from what kind of stroller to buy to where to go on a play date. She said it had a huge membership and that it would be really helpful for me to join them. Help sounded great. Windy told me that she was trying to get me into the group, but she warned me that even though there would be a lot of practical information I could use, there would also be a lot of talk about vaginas and menstrual cycles and breast-feeding.

"No problem," I told her. "I lived with a woman for a very long time. I can take it."

But the next time I heard from her, she told me that although the overwhelming majority of the women in the group wanted me in, the leaders would not allow it. They had decided it wasn't a good idea to have a man in their midst because there was so much personal talk among them, and they didn't want other women to feel inhibited. Bullshit. My wife was dead and I didn't give a shit about women's body parts or bodily fluids or any other personal talk. All I wanted was access to their valuable information about parenting in Los Angeles, setting up play dates, and finding good day care.

"Matt, I'm just floored by this," Windy said. "I know two gay men who adopted, and they won't let them in, either. So you know what? Fuck 'em. We're going to start our own group."

If Liz had been there, we probably would not have been seeking out such help, but without her I not only wanted this support system, I needed it. I knew it would be invaluable as I tried to raise Madeline on my own.

And so Windy and I began to meet for coffee to talk about how the group would take shape. It started small but continued to grow, mostly thanks to Windy's efforts and organization. The more she and I planned, the closer we got, and eventually Windy shared with me that she was a lesbian. Strange as it may sound, that gave us a lot of common ground to walk on, as neither of us was necessarily what people thought us to be when we passed them on the street with a kid. The potential assumptions about me as the father of a baby girl were obvious: he's lazy; his wife must be at work; he doesn't do shit. As for Windy, most would figure that she was a stay-at-home mom, that her husband was the breadwinner, and that she and her partner were just friends.

One day while we sat at the coffee shop talking, Windy's daughter, almost two at the time, was in the playroom with some other children. A guy walked in and saw her picking up toys. "Your daddy must be so proud of you!" he exclaimed.

We looked at one another and just burst out into raucous

laughter. I felt I had more in common with a gay parent than I did with anybody else, and Windy became part of my chosen family. It was a fantastic feeling—no matter how different we might have seemed, we had a bond. Without Liz, I was now the one responsible for creating a community for Madeline and me. Without her, I was learning, I had to be the friendly one.

When I started to blog again, my community expanded even further, and my encounters were no longer limited to people in my geographic location. I hadn't thought that blogging was something I would continue after Liz died. On March 28, A.J. posted the obituary that his wife had written about Liz, the one that I still have trouble getting through. I believed at the time that it might be the blog's final post, but a few weeks later I found myself turning back to it in hopes of some kind of emotional release. In the days after Liz's death, writing my thoughts down—like the thoughts that had turned into the words written on her funeral program—had been really effective in helping me deal. As time passed and I continued to write, the blog just seemed like a natural place to put them.

It felt great. At first I thought there would be nothing much to say, but with Maddy home, something in me wanted, or maybe needed, to record everything. Were my posts revelatory? Not exactly. But having an outlet where I could say whatever I wanted and work through my constantly shifting emotional state was invaluable. I knew it when I wrote that first post after Liz's death; I knew it again the next day, when I wrote a post about how the better of Madeline's parents had died; and I knew it every day thereafter, as I rambled about life with my daughter.

Years earlier, the blog had originally been for photos of my travels, and then, when Liz went into the hospital, it was a convenient way to keep all of our friends and family updated on her status. But now, it was different. As I wrote, I realized that the blog was becoming Madeline's baby book. No, it wouldn't contain locks of hair or tiny impressions of her handprints and footprints, like my mom has of me. Instead, it would be a chronicle of our day-to-day lives. And this way, I wouldn't have to rely on my memory for everything. I could record what her first word was, how much she weighed at her three-month doctor appointment, how tall she was, and the circumference of her head. Those are things you think you'll remember forever, but if you don't write them down, they disappear.

At first all I wanted was to give Maddy something tangible to refer back to someday. It was 80 percent for her and 20 percent for my friends and family—well, mostly for my family, because my friends don't read that kind of shit. In the weeks and months immediately following Liz's death, it was important for me to let everyone close to me know that I was surviving, and that our baby was doing well. I was writing down the things we did to prove to them, and eventually to Maddy, too, that after Liz died I didn't just curl up into a ball while my kid jammed forks into the light socket in the living room. It felt especially important for Liz's parents. I wanted them to know more about their granddaughter than they otherwise would have—even more than they would have if Liz were alive. I wanted to reassure them that they would always be a part of our lives.

Every new parent gets advice—from their own parents, from friends who have recently had children, from random people in the grocery store who tell you that children should have socks on even though it's ninety degrees outside (yes, that actually happened). And while some of it bordered on the ludicrous (because children like to play with their toes, by the way), I needed all the advice I could get. Writing my own blog made me look at other blogs out there, and I soon discovered that my hometown newspaper, the *Minneapolis Star Tribune*, had a website with an excellent parenting blog. It was run by two women, but they didn't just write about mothers. They also wrote about fathers and their relationships to their children. I e-mailed them:

> Hello...
> I just came across your blog...
> I'm a proud new father (originally from MPLS, now in Los Angeles) who is definitely in the process of managing changing priorities. I'm doing it on my own (my wife passed away the day after our baby was born).
> I'll be reading your blog often (while baby sleeps). I'm finding much of the content very helpful.
> I'm writing a bit about my experiences. Some of the language is a little blue, but I can't help it.
> It's been tough.
> Matt

The next morning they wrote back asking if they could put my story on their website. It ended up both there and on the front page of the paper. The reaction was amazing: that same day, my blog picked up tons of new readers, and after that it just continued to grow.

I was grateful. Now, I'd made a connection to a whole community of caring people online. To write up a quick post and receive a bunch of responses with advice and reassurance really validated the work I was doing as a father. So I solicited more. I used the blog to ask questions, often beginning "What do I do...?" I always filed every answer away, just in case I might need to refer back to something later. Eventually, I could get sound advice within minutes from people who were reading my blog, even if it was three in the morning in Los Angeles. It was awesome.

This outpouring of advice and kindness was yet another demonstration of the power of community, and of community as extended family. I was lucky to have a great group of friends nearby who did their best to make our lives easier, but most of our family was in Minnesota, and it was impossible for them to help us on a daily basis. And because I didn't belong to a church or any neighborhood groups, there was no organized effort to assist us. Nevertheless, I'd stumbled onto these sympathetic individuals online and expanded my circle far beyond what would have been possible before the Internet age. I received e-mails from Indonesia, Thailand, Europe, South America—from all over the world. What began as something I wanted for my daughter, my parents, my in-laws, and my friends became a forum of communication for and with parents everywhere. I had built my own virtual support system.

Many of these people also wanted to help in a material way. Just after Liz died, A.J. had set up a PayPal donation link on my blog with the money going directly into a memorial fund in her name, and people had also been sending money separately to help me raise my daughter. There was an address listed for the bank through which the fund was set up, and soon people were also sending actual stuff there.

Tons of it.

They also began to ask for my home address so they could send us stuff directly. Initially I said no. I didn't want there to be any possible insinuation that I was profiting from my wife's death, even if those profits were coming in the form of diapers, formula, and clothing for our daughter. That was something I could never, ever do. And to be honest, I was a bit leery about giving my address out to total strangers. It wasn't that I distrusted them, or that I was worried that they'd show up at my house and attempt to steal my baby. But making friends with strangers had been Liz's job.

Tom set me straight. "Matt," he said, "you have to let people help. If they're asking for your address, you give it to them."

"I don't know. I just feel a little weird just handing my address out to random Internet people."

"Matt, this isn't just about you and Madeline right now. This is about them, and their desire to help a human being who is in pain. Let them help you."

He was right. Our conversation allowed me to realize that there was absolutely nothing wrong with accepting help. So I threw off the shackles of the possible negative perceptions of others, and opened myself up to the kindness and support of total strangers.

And help they did. Every time I walked up to the porch, I found boxes sitting there. Stuff came in constantly, so often that I couldn't keep up with opening all of it. Several people mailed me perishable items that I unfortunately didn't always get to in a timely manner. A woman from Duluth, Minnesota, sent me all the fixings for chicken noodle soup after I had written that I was sick. I didn't open the care package until months later, unfortunately to find rotting garlic and a leaking container of chicken stock.

Some gifts were incredibly thoughtful but simply too difficult for me to deal with. One of Liz's best friends from high school put together a book written from Liz's point of view with photos captioned "I love you," "I'm sorry I'm not here," stuff like that. It was very kind and very touching, but for many months it was much too painful—I wasn't yet strong enough to confront what was in it. More than one person sent me a pillow with an image of Liz on it. I know they meant well, but for me that was just a bit creepy. But at the heart of this outpouring of generosity was something very basic and very human: the fundamental goodwill of each sender. People wanted to help, and so I let them—Tom helped me understand that they felt good by reaching out to Madeline and me.

It quickly became impossible for me to look at these expressions of sympathy and generosity without thinking about how I could help other people. Something about all this support made me feel ready to focus on others in need. How could I acknowledge these many acts of kindness? I didn't have the money to assist anyone financially, but I had all of this stuff—more than Maddy and I could ever possibly use.

The answer was to give back. Through the blog I had become friends with a woman in New York City whose boyfriend got her pregnant and then took off. When she decided to leave the city for Oregon because she couldn't afford to stay in her apartment, I shipped her seven or eight giant boxes of clothes. I sent many more to a battered women's shelter nearby because someone explained to me that the women there had often abruptly fled their abusive partners with their children. They arrived at the shelter with literally nothing but the clothes on their backs.

Just like people wanted to help me and Maddy, I wanted to help the people around us, and so I passed on what I received to those who needed it more. It became a really important part of what the blog brought to my life, and an important part of my beginning to heal after Liz's death. Concentrating my attention on others allowed me to remove some of the focus from my own situation, and finally I felt less like a victim of my horrible circumstances.

she's got so
much of her mom
in her.
as a kid,
sitting on a swing
(more than capable of propelling herself)
liz
would say, "somebody push me!"
she wanted attention
and loved having
people around.
madeline is obviously no
different.
her cries said,
"somebody hold me!"
so i did.
almost all day.

Chapter 15

Though I had many sources of advice, there were some things I was beginning to realize I could figure out for myself. While some parents claimed allegiance to Dr. Spock, I was more from the MacGyver school of parenting, which was less about having an arsenal of baby equipment and more about troubleshooting with whatever was available. Early on, I took Maddy to a Dodgers game. This was something that Liz and I had imagined doing with our future child from the moment we put the down payment on our first year of season tickets—way before Liz was even pregnant. And just like in our dream, Maddy was dressed in a pink and white pinstriped Dodgers onesie and wrapped in a free blanket we had been given on one of the team's many promotional nights. Of course, the dream included the two of us here with our baby, but in reality Liz was dead and I was at the stadium with her friend, Diane. Madeline was still so small that she was only drinking formula. I had remembered the diapers, I had remembered the wipes, I had remembered the formula, but I had forgotten the bottle.

What the fuck does a guy do for a kid who doesn't have a bottle to drink from? I felt like an asshole. She needed to eat, but I didn't want to leave the game, defeated by my forgetfulness and ruining my daughter's first Dodgers experience. I sat there for a couple of minutes thinking that there had to be a solution.

I bought a bottle of water from the concession stand, which I needed for the formula anyway, and I asked for one of the lapel pins behind the glass case—the kind they sell with the Dodgers logo. I removed the pin from the packaging and sterilized it with a lighter borrowed from a man behind me in line, and then jammed it through the water bottle cap. I mixed the water with the formula and squirted it into Maddy's mouth, just a little bit at a time. I felt as victorious as I used to when I beat Liz in a game of Scattergories—I had to think on the spot. It worked for us, but that's not something you're going to see in any parenting book.

And once during our travels, I didn't realize until we were already on the plane that the pants I had put Madeline in were way too big for her tiny waist. With her other clothes in our checked luggage, I had to come up with some way to keep her pants from continuously falling down. After considering—and ultimately deciding against—tying my BlackBerry USB charger around her waist, I decided the simplest and most effective way to deal with the problem was simply to button her onesie over her pants. After I posted a photo of it on the blog, some of my readers questioned whether or not I had any idea how to dress a baby girl, but others defended my function-driven sensibilities and left comments telling me that they were now dressing their babies the same way. Well, with that slick move, Madeline and I had accidentally started a mini fashion trend. I used to make fun of Liz when she wore heels in the rain or didn't wear a hat in winter because she was concerned her hair would get messed up, taunting her with the words "fashion over function." Liz would have been proud of me for figuring out such a practical solution, and she certainly would have found my effort adorable, but she most definitely would have questioned my style sense.

With each experience Madeline and I had together, my confidence level increased. After a while, I kind of felt like I could handle any parenting challenge thrown my way—what a big difference a few months had made. Though I initially had been preoccupied with the possibility of ruining or breaking my daughter, through everything she was thriving. Each successive trip to the doctor brought more words of encouragement, and with that encouragement came more confidence, too.

Despite being born seven weeks early, Madeline's measurements were in the average range on the growth charts at her three-month appointment, though the NICU doctors had warned me that might not happen until she was two years old. Madeline's pediatrician, Dr. Jennifer Hartstein, would ask me all sorts of questions to get a clear understanding of Madeline's physical and mental development, and when the appointment was finished, she would offer a simple but effective "Matt, you're doing a great job." Considering how out of control my life seemed after Liz's death, it was incredible for me to know that I was succeeding at the most important job in the world—a job I didn't know I had been so well prepared for—or prepared for at all.

These day-to-day experiences, early successes with Madeline, and praise from real experts led to an interesting transition in my blog. There were people who'd been reading my blog since Madeline's birth, many of whom had found it because they were pregnant. By now, some of their babies had been born, and with infants of their own at home, they didn't have a clue what they were doing. So they turned to me, a guy they knew had been through it.

Everyone assumes—and society encourages—that all women are experts at being mothers. What I found, however, was that women are just as fucking clueless as men are; they're just more willing to ask for and accept help. Here was a man—me—who just months earlier had no goddamned clue what he was doing, and now I was giving advice to many of the same women who had given it to me.

Not that what I was offering was really "advice." I would never tell anyone how they should do things. All I could offer was my own perspective: "Here is how I did it. It may not work for you, but this was my experience." For the first time since I had begun talking to other moms and dads, I felt that I could hold my own in any parenting conversation that arose. In fact, I not only felt as if I was equal to the rest of them, but I also felt a little bit like being a single father somehow gave me a leg up. I was, after all, doing at least twice as much work as I would have been if Liz were alive, and I was doing it as a stay-at-home dad. If that didn't make me an expert, I don't know what would.

Many questions also came my way regarding the death of a spouse. After all, fathering a newborn was only half my story. People wrote to find out how they could help in the immediate aftermath of a death in the family. Asking the bereaved what they need may be kind and well-intentioned, but ultimately it didn't help me at all. When Liz died, all I knew was that I wanted my wife back, and that that was not possible. I didn't know that I needed to have the floor swept. I couldn't recognize that there was no food in the refrigerator. I had no idea that my mail was piling up and I was probably not paying my electricity bill. My most common advice for these people was anti-advice—what not to do. "Don't touch anything in the house. Don't throw anything away because who knows what she may be attached to. Don't wash the sheets, because maybe she wants to be able to smell her husband's cologne awhile longer." I told people to find what little tasks and chores needed doing and to do them without having to ask the surviving partner any questions.

I also, and without intention, became the voice for a small community of young widows and widowers. They heard about my blog and began writing to me almost daily, and I became great friends with most of them as we shared our experiences via e-mail and phone. It was a bit like the parenting community that I'd found myself a part of, but this group was much smaller and more intimate. It was one thing to bond over the birth and raising of a child, but it was another to find an incredible group of widowed people under eighty years old, all of us united by the worst moments of our lives.

Liz's death had turned me into an uncertified expert in death and dealing with it, which was both a blessing and a curse. The blessing was that I could offer a truly informed opinion based on personal experience, rather than the kind of bullshit advice that spews forth from the countless grief books that line the shelves of every store. The curse? Well, to be confronted with so much death and sadness on such a regular basis really took a toll on me emotionally. Every time I heard another heartrending story about a husband dying, I was transported back to those seconds just after I realized Liz had died, and the hideous feeling that came over me every time was as real as it had been on that day.

Hearing these stories was awful, but I had to think that I

was helping these women in some small way. And the truth was, they were helping me, too. Realizing that I wasn't alone in my sadness was a valuable tool for fighting through it, because in talking to this group I understood that there was no such thing as moving on after what we experienced. With each other's help, though, we could continue to move through. Without their companionship, wicked jokes, and sarcasm, I wouldn't have laughed nearly as much.

Just a little while after I brought Madeline home, three of my best guy friends from Minnesota offered to come out to Los Angeles to stay with Madeline and me. They coordinated their trips so as not to overlap, ensuring that I would have maximum time for help and company. A.J. came first. When I picked him up from the airport, I kind of got the feeling something was different, and it became obvious what it was within the first few hours of his arrival. He hadn't told me, but I was positive. My suspicions wouldn't be confirmed for another few months, but the questions he asked and the way he interacted with Madeline had me convinced that Sonja was definitely pregnant. A.J. immediately took a very active role in feeding, burping, and changing Maddy—things I didn't think a childless man would want to do, let alone *could* do.

This was not the type of help I had expected. I thought these guys were coming out to Los Angeles to make me laugh, to shoot the shit—mostly to keep my mind off Liz. They'd probably cook and do some other stuff around the house, and only help me with Madeline if I asked them to. I was sure they'd never even touch a diaper, but it became apparent very quickly that I had assumed incorrectly.

When Steve arrived a week later, he immediately told me that his wife, Emily, was due to give birth within the next few months. My theory was spot-on. Here were guys with whom

I used to speak only about booze, sports, and music, and now they wanted to discuss the best methods for preventing diaper rash.

While he and I were out one day, we sat on a bench watching the world go by. Two women walked by, each of them pushing a baby stroller. We looked at one another and Steve blurted out, "See that stroller on the left?"

"Yeah."

"That's the stroller Emily and I registered for."

"Yeah. I know Liz looked at that stroller as well—" I interrupted myself midsentence. "Jesus. Do you realize how fucking old we are?"

"What do you mean?" Steve asked me.

"Well, did you see the two women pushing those strollers?"

"Yeah. They were totally hot."

"I know. And all we could talk about was the strollers they were pushing."

I rolled my eyes and shook my head with mock disapproval of just how adult we'd become since our college years. Steve let out a laugh, then I made a joke about the frozen chocolate-covered banana he was about to insert into his mouth.

John was the last to visit. On the way to my house from the airport, I asked up front, "Is Andrea pregnant?"

"I hope not," he replied, laughing. "Why?"

"Just testing a theory," I explained, then turned the conversation to his upcoming wedding.

I taught three grown men how to hold, feed, and burp a premature baby—skills that they then demonstrated via video-conference to their impressed (and relieved) women. It was about to become a reality for two of them, and it was kind of awesome to be showing them the way. To be the one who'd already been there.

They knew they could rely on my experience and probe

my ever-growing knowledge base for future use with their own children, and they were determined to learn as much as possible from me before they flew back to Minnesota. And I felt confident that the guidance and practical experience I could give them was the real deal. I wasn't pretending to be a father; I was a certifiable success. I got to be their friend with the baby instead of their friend whose wife had died. It was a relief.

No matter how eagerly they tried to provide diversions and distractions, though, there were always reminders of Liz. Some of them, like her perfume bottles on the dressers or her shoes in the corner, were constant and to be expected. But others, like the calls my friends made to their ladies before going to bed, made me sick to my stomach; I no longer had Liz to say good night to. But I did have my baby to tuck in every night, and holy shit, was I thankful for that.

One morning when Steve was still in town, I got out of the shower and heard him call my name from the living room.

"Is everything okay?" I asked.

"Yeah. Maddy's fine," he replied. "Your phone rang, but I didn't know if I should answer. I let it go to your answering machine."

"Shit. You didn't happen to hear who it was, did you?"

"United Airlines? Something about your trip to Hawaii?"

"Are you sure? I'm not going to Hawaii."

"I'm pretty sure I heard the automated message say something about an itinerary change for your trip to Oahu."

"Fuck. I'm gonna call them."

"Do you want to listen to the message?"

"No, I can't."

What I couldn't tell Steve was that I was hiding from the answering machine. There was a message somewhere on there from the Los Angeles County Coroner's office, and I didn't want to hear it. There was also another message that I'd been avoiding—it was from Liz. She'd left it from the hospital when she was on bed rest. I'd never listened to it, but I knew it was there. I hadn't heard her voice since the day she died, and as much as I thought I wanted to, I was afraid that if I did, everything would start to seem unreal, as if she were on an extended business trip or something. So I had been avoiding the answering machine altogether.

I called the airline later that day. "I received a message about an itinerary change. Do you have the details of that?"

"Yes, Mr. Logelin. It looks like your flight to Oahu on May tenth has been moved up by two hours."

"Okay. This may sound strange, but I had no idea that I was going to Oahu. Can you give me any more information about the trip?"

The agent laughed. "It looks like the flight was booked by Elizabeth Logelin, and was originally scheduled for one year earlier. Elizabeth rescheduled the flight for May tenth, 2008."

It all suddenly came back to me. I hung up the phone without saying thank you or good-bye, and instantly fucking lost it. All six feet seven inches of Steve got up off the couch and hugged me, making me feel like I was a child again, back in the arms of my father.

I sobbed, now remembering everything about this trip. We had booked tickets to Hawaii the year before for a wedding, but we both ended up having to travel for work. Liz rescheduled the trip as a vacation for us, choosing the furthest possible date from the original reservation. This had all happened a few months before we found out Liz was pregnant, and like me, she must have forgotten about it. Madeline's original due date was May 12, and there was no way we would have been able to travel, even if everything had gone as planned.

All it took was this one phone call to knock me back down and crush my confidence. All of the positivity I had been building instantly evaporated, and I wondered if I had made any progress at all. My face remained buried in Steve's chest for what seemed like hours. When I finally pulled myself together, I called Liz's dad. Before he even had a chance to say hello, I launched into my proposition.

"Tom, I just got off the phone with United Airlines. Liz and I were supposed to go to Hawaii in May, and I just can't do it alone. Can we take a trip together? You know, you, Candee, Deb, Maddy, and me? Maybe we can go in a few months for our wedding anniversary or something? I don't want to be alone, and I can't be in Minnesota, Los Angeles, or Greece on August thirteenth." I didn't take a breath until I'd said it all—it must have been a lot for Tom to take in without warning.

"Yes," he responded calmly. "We can do whatever you want, Matt. Let's talk about this tonight with Candee and we can plan something."

That was all I really needed to hear. Later on, we agreed that we would take a trip together on what would have been my third wedding anniversary. I informed Tom and Candee of my self-imposed travel parameters: somewhere outside of the United States, and somewhere none of us had ever visited before. By the next night, we had a flight and a condo booked for a week in Banff. I felt sure that Liz would have been thrilled to know that I planned to spend time with her family. I was just relieved to know that I wouldn't have to be alone on our anniversary come August.

she's a little
too little
to fly.
but,
she won't be
alone in her
bassinet with one of
those hamster feeders.

Chapter 16

Many of our friends and family had been unable to attend Liz's funeral in Pasadena and so had been unable to get any sort of closure about her death. What's more, my decision to have Liz cremated and her remains stored until I decided what to do with them also left people without a permanent place to go to mourn her. Everyone I was now spending time with in Los Angeles—all of Liz's college and work friends whom I'd rarely spent time with previously—was still devastated. Everyone was still buried in grief. Tom, Candee, and I decided that we should have a second funeral for Liz.

We would have the service in our home state of Minnesota so that those who hadn't been able to travel previously would have a chance to say good-bye. The funeral home in Pasadena had sent Liz's ashes to a funeral home in Milaca, Minnesota, a town that held my family's roots. It was where my mom was born, and where my grandfather's hardware store had been.

Initially, I thought having a second funeral was insane. I understood providing an opportunity for more people to mourn, but I wasn't ready to stand up and give another fucking eulogy for my wife. The first time I had done it was pure hell, and it would never get easier, even if I did it a thousand times. Besides, who the hell has two funerals? Then my thoughts went to Madeline. Though nothing would bring about closure in her situation—and even if it could, she wouldn't have any clue what was going on—I couldn't help thinking that she needed to be at her mother's funeral.

I called Dr. Hartstein.

"I'm flying to Minnesota so we can have another funeral for my wife. I want to bring Madeline with me."

"Matt. It's not a good idea."

I knew that was going to be her answer. Maddy wasn't even supposed to be out of the womb yet, so the notion of taking her on an airplane was kind of absurd. But I kept wondering how I'd someday explain to my daughter that she missed not one but two funerals for her mother. Of everyone whose life Liz had ever touched, the one who would endure her death the longest and hardest would be the child she never held.

I was also scared shitless about heading to Minnesota without Madeline. It would be my first trip back since last Christmas with Liz, and I knew I'd be confronting a lifetime of memories by returning to our childhood homes. What I needed most was not friends, family, music, or booze. I needed my security blanket. I needed my baby. But faced with the very real prospect of jeopardizing the well-being of my otherwise healthy preemie, I had to heed the doctor's advice and leave her in Los Angeles. I asked my friends Ben and Dana if Madeline could stay at their house while I was gone. Their first baby had been premature, too, so they would best know how to attend to Madeline's needs.

When it was time to send Maddy home with Dana for the three days I would be in Minnesota, I did my best to keep from crying. I wasn't ashamed to let my tears flow in front of anyone anymore, especially a friend, but I'd recently started to notice how my crying affected those around me, and so I began attempting to hold it in. My success rate wasn't 100 percent yet, but I had become rather good at it. I took it as a challenge, and better still, a way to get my mind off of the reason I felt like crying in the first place.

And oddly enough, I had even started to enjoy it. There was a strange sensation that came along with holding in tears, and it became more and more intense the longer I held them in. As they welled up in my eyes, the bridge of my nose started to tingle, the feeling slowly traveling down to its tip and finally sending pulses of numbness through the rest of my head. I became obsessed with trying to hold on to the feeling as long as possible; at one point I thought about carrying a stopwatch around so I could time myself and see if I could set a record each and every time I was about to cry. That seemed a little crazy, though, so I decided against it.

Dana's voice brought me out of my game.

"Don't worry, Matt. We'll take good care of her."

"I know you will. In fact, I'm pretty sure you guys will take better care of her than I do." I'm just really going to miss her, I thought.

I buckled Maddy into her car seat (now in Dana's car), gave her two kisses, and whispered, "I love you." With my palm on the car window, I pushed the door closed. I left my hand there as the car started, still reaching out for my daughter. Even after they disappeared over the hill, I still held my hand out, frozen in place, my feet firmly planted in the grass below. Driving away from me was the only person left in the world who I actually cared about, and I couldn't believe I was going to be without her for the next three days.

The tears were welling up again, but this time I didn't want to play the game. I just let them flow; I knew it would be impossible to stop them. I felt myself sinking into the wet ground outside my house, the moisture and mud soaking through my socks. Shit, I thought. Where the fuck are my shoes? I looked around, hoping that my neighbors weren't watching. The last thing I needed was for them to know I'd lost my mind.

I walked up the stairs to my house, leaving wet footprints, and thought about how pissed Liz would have been that I had just ruined a pair of perfectly fine socks. I stood in the doorway removing the soggy things, thinking I shouldn't make matters worse by tracking wet footprints into the house. I pulled them off and pushed the front door closed, slowly realizing that this was the first time I'd been completely alone in our house since Liz died. Though fewer than 1,200 square feet, it then possessed the kind of cavernous emptiness I imagined could only be felt in palatial structures. I melted into the couch and listened to the music I had left streaming into my living room. The words from "Last Tide" by Sun Kil Moon reached my ears and the torrent of tears continued to flow.

Every bird fall weak on lifeless ground
Every eye swelled from tears ever clear
Every seed broken in spring lived till fall
All your babies be around to see them growing up.

Will you be here with me, my love
When the warm sun turns to ash

And the last tide disappear
All darkness near.

I kept quiet so you'd think my heart was tough
I never showed you if I loved you enough
The dreams I had, yeah, I kept but I wouldn't dare
Share with you for fear of things still living in me.

Will you be next to me, my love
When the cold moon vanishes
And the last cries no yells
For it to hear?

It was one of Liz's favorite songs, and it would be echoing through the chapel at Lakewood Cemetery in Minneapolis in fewer than twenty-four hours.

"What the fuck is up with this weather?" I said with exasperation.

"It's Minnesota," A.J. replied. "Have you forgotten?"

He was right. Spring snow at the end of April was not unprecedented, but it seemed unreasonable and more than a little cruel. I guess after six years of living in Los Angeles, I'd officially become a weather snob—I couldn't stand any temperature below seventy degrees. I tentatively shuffled my feet through the icy snow, hoping to avoid falling on my ass in front of the large group of people already lined up outside of the chapel.

I gave depressed looks of acknowledgment to the couples clutching each other as they walked in, and I was sure that after seeing me they'd look into each other's eyes and squeeze each other a little tighter. I knew what they were thinking: *I'm glad this isn't us.* No person with even one ounce of compassion would say those words in front of a grieving widower, but the way they gripped each other's arms, the looks—that said it all.

I wished so badly that I were in this line with Liz, waiting to walk into someone else's funeral. I wished that she were holding tight to my side, her teary blue eyes looking up at me, saying, "Those poor motherfuckers. I love you." I wished that it wasn't us.

More than anything, that's what I wished.

But it was.

An hour later I was standing at a podium, microphone just below my mouth, staring out at a sea of people. This was an exceedingly shitty feeling, waiting to give my wife's eulogy again. Before I'd walked in here, I thought it might be easier to do this a second time, but as I strained to hear Liz's funeral soundtrack, the same one we'd played in Pasadena, I realized just how wrong I was. I wanted so badly to hear a familiar song, no matter what it was, something other than the depressing-ass one in my head at that moment. "If I Needed You" by Townes Van Zandt was playing over and over again, and the line "If I needed you, would you come to me?" was making me think about how impossible it was for her to come to me now, when I needed her most. But the sounds of people shuffling in drowned out the music we had playing, leaving me stuck with that one. When all the pews were taken, people filed into the side aisles, and when those spaces filled up, too, they sat on the floor behind me and in the aisle running up the middle of the chapel. The place was packed like the Animal Collective concert I had seen at the El Rey.

I could just picture the look Liz would have given me if I had sat down on that floor, ruining my only suit. A mess of melting snow, dirt, and salt had been tracked into the chapel and was now being ground into the funeral clothes of everyone who had come out for Liz. I looked down at my suit and tie,

and thought, I really need to retire these things. After wearing the ensemble to my wife's funeral—twice—I knew I could
never put it on again.

Standing there, I thought about the conversation I'd had
with the funeral director in Pasadena. With the emotionless
tone expected of an undertaker, he'd said to me, "You know,
you're the first person to use the word *fuck* in my chapel." I
don't think he was admonishing me as much as he was trying
to tell me he was proud...but then again, I might have been
projecting. "Well," I'd replied, "it was the most accurate way
to describe my feelings."

The shuffling stopped before I could replay any more of the
conversation, and I knew it was time for me to speak. I felt the
same way I had the first time around, so I began with the same
words: "This fucking sucks." And for the next hour, we all remembered Liz.

Once the service concluded, people made their way to Tom
and Candee's house. I caught a ride with A.J.—I needed to be
with my best friend at that moment. We drove out the gates
of the cemetery in the direction of Liz's parents' house, and after sitting in silence for a couple of blocks, I suddenly yelled,
"Take a right!" just as we approached Lake Street. A.J. took the
turn without question or hesitation, even though we were now
heading in the wrong direction.

"I need to stop at the record store. Those Replacements re-
issues came out on Tuesday and I need to get them."

He laughed. "Do you think that's a good idea right now?" I
knew what he meant. The few hundred people on their way to
Tom and Candee's would likely want to talk to me, or would at
least expect me to be there.

"Liz wouldn't have it any other way," I replied.

Actually, Liz probably would have been pretty pissed about
me stopping for records after a funeral, but in this case, I felt

like she'd understand. Yeah, I was being a little selfish, but she knew that one of the great joys in my life was buying records, especially when I was having a bad day. This was a bad day of epic proportions. She'd grant me this stop, and she'd be glad to know that I was keeping my shit together, even if doing so meant that I kept some friends and family waiting.

"I know exactly what I need; we'll be in and out," I promised.

Five minutes later we were back in the car and heading over to the house. A.J. followed the road on the north side of the lake, and my stomach sank when the stoplight turned green. Just ahead was the Calhoun Beach Club—the place where Liz and I had gone to dinner before our prom, and the place where we had been married not even three years earlier. As A.J. and I approached the building I did my best to avoid looking at it, but the harder I tried, the faster it came at me, and I started sniffling before we had even reached it. It was like the drive home from the hospital past the funeral home all over again.

A.J. looked over at me, tears welling up in his eyes, too. "Matt, I'm so sorry. I didn't even think about it."

I managed to say, "It's okay." But I wasn't okay, not yet. I would be, though—or at least I tried to think so, until we got to Tom and Candee's house.

This miserably failed attempt to ignore the unavoidable forced me to realize that after more than twelve years together, it would be impossible to steer clear of all the places that held memories of my life with Liz. It would be to my advantage to go to these places, to embrace them, and to remember the moments that shaped our relationship, no matter how painful confronting them was. As A.J. and I continued driving, I thought about all the significant places we had passed that day just going to and coming back from Liz's funeral. The gas station where we had met, the restaurant where we had our first date, the spot where we had our rehearsal dinner, and the countless stores, streets, and restaurants that had been a stage to so much of our lives. And it wasn't just Minnesota—I had felt this way in Los Angeles as well. I wasn't going to the farmer's market at the Grove or the Oinkster or Whole Foods anymore.

Just thinking about stepping foot in a produce aisle brought me back to a memory of the last New Year's Eve Liz and I had together. That night, Liz, her pregnant belly not showing quite yet, spotted one of her many celebrity crushes, Joel McHale, at the Glendale Whole Foods. The well-trained LA girl that she was, Liz never said a word to him; she just trailed him like a puppy. While we waited to check out only one line over from the subject of her stalking, I said, "Liz, it's pretty fucking creepy that you followed him around the entire store."

"He's so hot. And a lot taller than I expected."

"Jesus."

"I wished you dressed more like him."

"That is *my* child in your womb, right?"

"I think so."

I smiled thinking about that moment, realizing how much I missed her sarcastic sense of humor. I wanted so badly just to talk to her.

But if I went to these places, embraced them instead of avoided them, maybe I could recall other long-forgotten, tiny moments that illuminated just how amazing both my wife and our time together were. I could share these memories with our daughter and hopefully create some damn good new ones, too—in Minnesota, Los Angeles, and around the entire world.

starting to feel like a
divorced parent,
sharing custody,
arranging pickup/drop-off times,
carting baby supplies
from house to house.
this is weird.
and not how i
pictured fatherhood.
damn it.

Chapter 17

After the difficulty of leaving Maddy behind for Liz's second funeral in Minnesota, I was thrilled to finally bring her with me when I went back for my cousin Josh's wedding in June. It would be her first trip anywhere outside of Los Angeles. Attending the event was going to be incredibly difficult, but Josh had asked me to be in his wedding party, and in going I would be keeping a promise I had made to Liz—or rather, a promise Liz had made for me.

Madeline's original due date fell just before Josh's wedding, but Liz definitively told me, "You're going to his wedding." She was adamant because she knew how important the event was for Josh. We thought Madeline would be barely a month old, so the plan was for my girls to stay behind in Los

Angeles while I headed to the wedding in Minnesota. So now, even though it would be painful to face all of the reminders of the life I no longer had, I was determined to be there for my cousin. I didn't want my bad days to cast a shadow over anyone else's good days, and I certainly didn't want to disobey Liz's orders.

A family friend took it upon herself to call the airline and tell them it was Madeline's first flight. When we boarded the plane, the flight attendants presented us with a First Flight certificate and a book in which we could record all her travels. I knew already that this would be the first of many trips together. Of course we'd be regularly visiting family and friends in the Midwest, but a list was already forming in my mind of everywhere else I wanted to take my daughter. The world was full of places where Liz and I lived together and loved each other, and I pledged then that I would take Madeline to see all of them.

Thanks to the advice of my blog readers I was well prepared for the flight, but I might have overdone it a bit. A few people had suggested I bring an extra outfit for Madeline, in case of the dreaded diaper blowout—I brought five. They told me to bring a few extra diapers—so I brought eleven...for a four-hour flight. Though I was physically overprepared for the trip, I was seriously underprepared mentally. I hadn't even considered how difficult it would be to face the stares and whispers of the other passengers who were expecting my baby to be the crying, whiny horror story they could tell once they landed in Minneapolis. I tried my best to ignore them and focus my attention on Madeline.

Thankfully, she slept almost the entire way to Minneapolis. I didn't need any of the extra outfits, and I didn't have to try to change her diaper on the plane. But I was the mess, spending the entire flight awaiting the expected meltdown or the

promised diaper explosion, so I really didn't get a chance to enjoy Madeline's perfect behavior.

One of the first events of the weekend was a round of golf as
part of Josh's bachelor party festivities. When I arrived at the
course to the company of twenty or so guys, many of whom
I'd known since fourth or fifth grade, few of them said a word
to me. Most gave a polite wave and avoided eye contact, not
knowing how to talk to the guy whose wife had died. I felt
as though I was a ghost they couldn't see. It was just fucking
weird for some of my oldest childhood friends to treat me like
an outcast: I expected this kind of reaction from the strangers I
encountered, but not from them. Thankfully, A.J. and my good
friend Nate were on the golf course, and they were perfectly
willing to talk to me. I just wanted people to be normal, but
nobody could be—nobody knew how to be. It may have had
something to do with the amount of booze in their systems,
or the fact that I was acting completely normal (apparently to
their surprise), but by the end of the night all the weirdness
disappeared, and I was once again just one of the guys. I had
found that people often followed my lead. If I cried, they cried,
and if I laughed, they laughed. That night, there was a lot of
laughter.

But the wedding itself was more difficult for me. I struggled to keep my composure, trying to be strong for my cousin
and wanting not to cry openly on his wedding day. I felt like
I occupied an awkward position in the celebration: I wanted
to be social and catch up with as many people as possible, but
without taking the focus off the bride and groom. I tried to
blend in, but it seemed like wherever I was, people were giving me too much attention. Sure, I might have been imagining
it, but it really felt that way: like I had some spotlight following me everywhere I went, illuminating the fact that I was the

guy who had already experienced the "until death do us part" line of the vows. I was even more worried that Madeline would deflect attention away from Josh and his wife, but I was happy that my family got to see her.

The evening ended up going way better than I expected. Madeline did draw a lot of attention, but she went home with Tom and Candee before the reception really kicked into high gear, and the rest of the night was exactly the kind of party that Josh had planned. Liz would have loved the wedding, and knowing that I had successfully survived the day, she would have been proud.

In addition to getting to know more distant relatives, this trip was a great opportunity for us to start spending more time with the grandparents—even more than I might have if Liz had been with me. When she and I came home, family hadn't always been our first priority. We both had a lot of friends still in town, and would often head straight from the airport to someone's house for a dinner party that had been arranged just because we were visiting. But this trip was different. With Madeline in tow, I had to pay more attention to our families because they wanted (and perhaps needed) to spend time with her as much as I did. So during this trip we began a new tradition: my two sets of parents would meet us at Tom and Candee's house on the night of our arrival for dinner and some shared time with Maddy. Thankfully, everyone had always gotten along well, but after Liz's death they became even more willing to spend time together.

During that first trip back, everyone sort of swapped her around, eager to have her in their houses—I like to think that Madeline's presence brought their homes to life in a way that Liz had. But it wasn't just the grandparents who wanted to hang out with Maddy; each set also made sure that their friends and extended families were able to spend time with her as well.

Though I was happy to lend out my best girl, it felt fucking strange that she was having new experiences with new people, and I wasn't there to witness it all.

But while everyone else was getting their fix of Madeline, I got to take a short fishing trip with three of my five brothers. It was something I wanted to do to recapture a camaraderie that had disappeared long ago, so we went up to the family cabin, where I hadn't been since the late '90s. We headed out to the middle of the lake in a boat, drinking beers, joking around, and doing some fishing. For a second, it felt like it used to feel when we all lived in the same state and could get together more easily. It was great to be back with my brothers—there was no pretense. We didn't have to worry about awkward silences, and no one had to fear saying the wrong thing.

Going back home again, this time with my daughter, was exactly what I needed to refocus and remind me that my life would continue to move forward, even if I thought it never again would. The trip to Minnesota had been a refreshing and much-needed escape, giving me a chance to spend time with family and friends who kept my mind off of Liz's death. It was these people who'd be there for me to make sure I'd someday be happy again. And with their help, I'd been able to start making new memories with Madeline in this old place.

When we arrived back in Los Angeles, I was jarred into the present. One of Liz's friends had arranged for a housekeeper to come in and give our house a thorough cleaning while we were gone in Minnesota, which it had not had since Liz died. When I set our luggage down in the living room, I was surprised to see a path carved through the piles of unopened packages that had been arriving from blog readers. The outpouring of kindness had been unreal—and now the boxes were stacked neatly, which was a massive improvement.

With Madeline in my arms, I walked through the house as if for the first time. The kitchen was immaculate: the sink free of dishes, bottles behind the cabinet doors, counters clear and devoid of anything but small appliances. I walked into the hallway. The kitchen door closed behind me and I stopped in my tracks; one of Liz's black elastic ponytail holders on the doorknob had caught my eye. She had left one on every door-knob in the house so that anytime she needed to throw her hair back she could do it without having to dig one out of a drawer in the bathroom. They'd always been there, but see-ing the little bungee cord now—without being distracted by messiness—was like being stabbed in the heart all over again. Like when I saw her car parked out front, for a brief second it felt like Liz was still here. Like she was just in another room and would be coming back shortly to put her hair up in a pony-tail. I missed her so fucking much, and those little black things were a big enough reminder to set my heart racing.

I wanted to run away, but with a sleeping baby in my arms, where the hell could I go? Exhausted, I opened the door to my bedroom. When I walked inside I was completely awestruck. It looked like *our* bedroom again. Since Liz had died, only the color of the walls had changed. They had been covered in a sponged-on yellow when we bought the house, giving them the appearance of having been pissed on. It really was like urine—that was Liz's interpretation of the color. I vowed that when industriousness got the better of me I would paint the bedroom, because that was what Liz had wanted, and I may have been the first man to arrive at Home Depot with a pillow-case to match to a bucket of paint. But regardless of the color on the walls, the housekeeper had made the room look exactly like it had the day Liz went into the hospital. The books on the nightstand were perfectly lined up. The clock that used to blink *12:00* was plugged in and reset. The piles of clean clothes stacked against the dresser and the shirts hanging from the doorknobs were no longer visible. I'm not sure where there had been room to stash everything, but I was pretty sure I didn't want to open any closet doors to find out.

But more than any of these small details, seeing the made bed really put me over the edge. Since Liz died, I hadn't made the bed at all. Yeah, I'd washed the sheets and done a half-assed job of putting them back on and throwing a comforter over them, but never the right way—never the way Liz would have done it. Now on the bed were the three big square pillows that matched the comforter, the ones she never let me use because, as she explained, they were for decoration only. They had been on the floor since Madeline had come home from the hospital. There, on Liz's dresser, was the silver tray with peacocks on the handles that held seven bottles of perfume. Next to it was the black velvet jewelry stand that she had purchased in downtown Los Angeles, displaying her newest bracelets and necklaces. I stared at all these things until my eyes started to burn, then closed them tight and tried to remember what Liz smelled like and when she had last worn each piece of jewelry. I strained my mind, and it returned nothing.

All of a sudden, the room that had been a place of comfort became completely suffocating. Seeing everything set up and arranged how Liz had kept it sent me out in tears. I couldn't be in there, and I absolutely couldn't sleep in there that night. I put Madeline in her bassinet and lay down to sleep an arm's length away on the couch. This would be our arrangement for the next several months.

i can't remember what
we did for our
anniversary last year.
the only other person
who would know
is no longer here
to jog my memory.
so how the fuck
do i figure this out?

Chapter 18

The middle of August came, and with it my trip to Canada with Liz's family. Our actual anniversary fell a few days in. That morning, we took Madeline to Sulphur Mountain, where she experienced her first gondola ride. The apprehensive look on her face made me think that she had inherited my fear of heights and thus enjoyed the experience about as much as I did (not at all). Before Liz's death, I never would have voluntarily gotten into a box suspended high above the ground by a couple of wires, but when I looked up at the mountain that day, I heard Liz's voice saying, *Don't be such a pussy.* Roughly, that translated to: *I'm not around anymore; you have to do the things with Madeline that I would have done.*

So I scaled the mountain with my baby, and I actually felt

pretty proud when we made it to the top—until I realized how frigid it was at those heights. Thanks to me, Madeline was completely underdressed: I had a hat to cover her ears and socks to cover her feet, but I hadn't brought along any mittens—we didn't even own any. Just as I started to worry that my daughter's tiny fingers would get too cold and that the well-prepared parents nearby would judge us, I found a pair of socks in the diaper bag and placed them on her hands. Maddy started waving around happily, and I instantly felt better. It might not have been a pretty solution, but at least my kid was warm. And I had conquered one of my biggest fears thanks to her and to the memory of her mother's urging, too.

Later that night I found myself at a dinner table in Banff, surrounded by Tom, Candee, and Deb, unable to say a word. I just sat there, Madeline in my arms, thinking about how Liz and I would have celebrated this occasion if she were still alive, and trying not to think about our wedding. It was at that moment that I realized I had no idea what the fuck we had done for our second anniversary. Our last anniversary together. I searched the deepest part of my brain, trying to find some hint of a memory that could help me recall what it was we had done the year before. Were we at the beach? Did we go out to dinner? Had we been on a trip? I couldn't remember anything.

I stayed focused on keeping Madeline from pulling everything off of the table, and I didn't manage more than a few bites of my steak. I was silent, staring down at the tablecloth while conversation flowed steadily around me. We toasted Deb for her law school accomplishments, but no one had mentioned Liz at all, or the fact that it was our anniversary. In our few days together in Banff, I was the only one who had so much as uttered Liz's name, and each time the word floated off unacknowledged.

One way of dealing with death is to avoid discussing it altogether—it's not uncommon. But seeing this reaction from Liz's family surprised me, and it made me feel even more lonely and isolated. Worse was that I'd known these people for almost half my life—Tom and Candee were as much my parents as my own mom and dad. They didn't have to change my diapers or pay for my education, but they had been there through so many of my challenges and successes. I wasn't angry or even mildly upset about their silence; it just showed again how different the grieving process is for everyone, and I could recognize that much. But that doesn't mean it didn't make me sad. One of my great comforts since Liz's death had been talking about her—I was afraid that if her name went unmentioned or the stories went untold, our memories of her would forever disappear, and so would she. And I felt like this possibility was already manifesting itself as I struggled to remember what we did for our second anniversary.

By the end of the main course, I really just wanted to be alone with my baby. I loved Liz's family dearly and I knew that they loved me, but we hadn't yet figured out how to mourn together, and I needed that to heal. Especially today. When dessert was served, I grabbed Madeline, presumably for a diaper change, and left for a walk around the hotel where the restaurant was. I sat down in a big leather chair in the middle of the lobby and gave up keeping my shit together. What a scene: a bearded man alone with a baby, crying like a little bitch in the lobby of one of the nicest hotels in Canada. I let myself sit there for ten minutes, and then returned to the table without a word.

After dinner, we all drove together back toward our condo. I was still feeling restless. While we waited for a traffic light in the center of town to turn green, I said quickly to no one in particular, "Would you mind taking care of Madeline for a bit?"

They were kind of caught off guard, and without any fanfare or hesitation, I thanked them and hopped out of the car, striding alone toward the bars I had been thinking about all evening.

The place I walked into had horrible live music, but I needed booze to dull my senses more than I needed to be a music snob. I sat down at a table near a window, far away from the few people who were inside. Minutes later a waitress stood over me, listing off a bunch of Canadian beers from memory. The last one she mentioned caught my attention: Kokanee. Liz and I drank that crap on a retreat we took to Whistler with the first company she worked for. I ordered it along with a shot of whiskey.

The waitress returned with my drinks and placed them in front of me silently. I threw back the shot and quickly downed the beer. I put my hand up like I was in third grade, eager to call out the answer to the math problem on the blackboard. She came back and I said, "Same thing, please." Soon I had a glass in both hands, and soon both were empty again. Up went my hand; over came the drinks. This continued for four more rounds.

As I drank, I sat passing judgment on the guitar player with the awful voice and the asshole businessmen trying so hard to pick up women at the bar. Everyone there seemed so happy and carefree. Fuck them, I thought. I'm in pain, real pain. The kind of pain no one would wish upon anyone else. That night, sitting alone at that table and getting more and more drunk, I wanted every single person in the bar to know my heartache.

A while later, the waitress approached me to see if I needed anything. My slurring made her persist when I tried to brush her off. "Are you alone?" she asked.

Well, that's a complicated question, I thought. "I'm in town with my in-laws and my baby," I said.

"And what about your wife?"

"My wife died," I said.

After months of being asked that very question, I had discovered that people reacted differently depending on how I worded my answer. When I said *she passed away,* I got a very sympathetic reaction and the person I was talking to generally asked more questions about my life. When I said *she died,* well, that was a conversation ender, every single time. The waitress didn't bother me again. I sat there with my thoughts, taking in the shitty music and observing the scene until the bar closed.

When I finally left, I walked for what seemed like hours, eventually arriving at our condo. I went inside and headed straight to my room, where I found Candee curled up in my bed with a sleeping Madeline in her pink pajamas with the white polka dots. Without a word, Candee gave me a hug and went upstairs. I sat down at the edge of the bed and looked back toward my best girl. This was not how our life was supposed to be, but this was not how I should be dealing with it, either.

I hadn't had this much to drink since my last trip to Vegas for a friend's bachelor party, and I knew it could never and would never happen again. I crawled into bed, kissing Madeline twice on one cheek: once for what is, and once for what could have been.

Already jet-setters, a few days after we got back to LA, Maddy and I flew to New York City to visit a friend of mine.

We had a room booked at the Waldorf Astoria, the same hotel where Liz and I had stayed on our way to Greece to celebrate the beginning of our marriage. It was just another stop on the list of places that I wanted to visit—to revisit—with Madeline. The doors were still ornate and the entryway was still grand, but just three years later, she was gone, and I was here with our daughter, just the two of us. Madeline was nestled against my chest in a Baby Bjorn, and I held her hand as the bellhop opened the door and led us up the staircase.

The memories flooded back with such force that without Maddy's little fingers in mine, I might have drowned. I had held her mother's hand when we walked up the very same staircase on the first night of our honeymoon. We weren't giddy, though—we were stressed. We were to stay in New York for fewer than twelve hours before our next flight, and the airline had lost our luggage. Since Liz was such a frequent business traveler, we were spending a night in one of the world's fanciest hotels for free, but because our bags were missing we didn't get to enjoy the massively excessive three-room suite. Liz was teary, worried about arriving in Greece without all of the clothes she had purchased specifically for our honeymoon. I spent the night alternating between consoling my new bride and calmly arguing with customer service agents in the hopes of finding some sort of resolution.

After more than a few hours of this, Liz went to sleep, but I continued working the phones until I found a sympathetic ear on the other end. Instead of granting us the usual policy-mandated few hundred bucks for lost luggage, the agent told us to go out the next morning and have a shopping spree, courtesy of the airline. We could each spend one thousand dollars, and as long as we sent him the receipts, he would personally see to it that we were reimbursed.

And so we did just that. We had less than an hour to complete our shopping spree before we were supposed to head back to the airport to catch our flight to Athens, so we went to Macy's, where we each bought a new suitcase and hurriedly filled them with as many items as we could.

Before we checked in for our next flight at JFK, we stopped by to check the lost luggage area just in case ours had surfaced.

Sure enough, sitting in a corner were our two suitcases. While we waited for our flight to board, I called my contact at the airline to tell him that we had found our luggage.

"That's great news!"

"We'll return all of the stuff we just bought when we get back from Greece."

"No, keep it. You deserve it after everything you've been through. Consider it a wedding gift from the airline."

When I relayed the story to Liz, she smiled.

"Not a bad way to start our honeymoon, eh?" I said, smiling back at her.

"It's as perfect as I could have imagined it."

But this time at the Waldorf, things were a lot less perfect. After we got everything into our room, I transferred Madeline to her stroller and headed down to the restaurant on the ground floor for a little late dinner after our long flight. All eyes in the bar fixed upon me as I wheeled in my sleeping child and parked her stroller against the wall. I sat in a chair next to her and pulled out a book to keep me company.

The waitress came over to me a few minutes later. "What can I get for you?" she asked, a gray-haired woman probably in her late fifties. As I pondered the menu, she said, "Cute kid. Where's her mother?"

Come on. It was the fifth time that day that someone asked where her mother was. Was it that unnatural for a man to be out in the world, alone with a four-and-a-half-month-old baby? Maybe. I tried to think about the last time I noticed a father traveling alone with a child as young as Madeline, and couldn't remember ever seeing it. And then I put myself in the shoes of the waitress, and realized the scene was probably pretty odd—a scruffy-looking dad and his baby girl, hanging out in a hotel bar in New York City well after midnight on a Friday. But still, I couldn't bring myself to be polite.

"She died the day after our baby was born."

"Jesus. I'm sorry. What are you drinking? It's on the house."

"I'll take a glass of water."

The waitress returned a few minutes later with a water and a scotch, even though I hadn't asked for it. I drank the water and ordered some French fries.

Madeline was still asleep as I pushed her stroller through the lobby and into the elevator. When we got back to the room, I picked her up and gently placed her in the crib the hotel had provided. She stirred a bit, but then settled in. I picked up my book and continued reading, but I only made it through a couple of pages before Madeline interrupted me. She was awake, and she wouldn't go back to sleep unless she knew I was nearby. I took her out of the crib, and brought her to the king-sized bed in the middle of the room. I laid her there on her back and sat down next to her, rubbing her stomach until she fell asleep.

A while later, settled back in my chair, I heard her make a noise and I looked up from my book. Madeline was on her stomach, her face buried in the comforter. I immediately jumped from the chair and rolled her onto her back. I was tired, but I was sure that I hadn't put her on her stomach. I was equally sure that she couldn't have just rolled over on her own.

There's no way, I thought. I sat back down in the chair, my eyes now fixed on my daughter. In less than a minute, she was on her stomach again, letting out the same muffled cry. It was confirmed: my child had rolled over.

I crawled onto the bed and rolled her onto her back once again. I sat there next to her, smiling through the tears gathering in my eyes. This was major. But my heart broke to think that Liz had missed it. She would never see her daughter walk, her first day of school, or her prom. But at the same time, I had to rejoice: our baby had made her first move toward growing up. She gained some freedom—and I lost a lot of mine. No longer could Maddy be left unattended on the couch while I ran into the kitchen to make her a bottle; no longer could I leave her on her changing table while I ran to the bathroom to wash her crap from my hands.

Soon enough our child would be crawling, walking, running, dating, and having children of her own. It was beautiful. I was devastated that Liz wasn't there to see it, but I was so fucking proud of how far the two of us had come together. Against all odds, Madeline was thriving, and I, well, I was getting there. And I finally believed myself when I said we were going to be okay.

Part III

i couldn't help but think
that i'm happy to have
what we have,
but
we're totally and completely
incomplete without
liz.
i wish this weren't happening.

Chapter 19

I t was the first day without her, the first week without her, the
first month without her, the first anniversary without her.
When these dates approached, I found myself tiptoeing toward
them, terrified that when I opened my eyes on the dreaded day,
I might completely disintegrate.

Now it was Liz's birthday. The first one without her.

I wished I could say it was the first time I was not going
to celebrate her birthday with her, but that would have been
a lie. On her last birthday on this earth, I was in India
on a business trip instead of at home with my pregnant
wife. When I found out that the trip was necessary, integral,
urgent, all of those words that make us drop everything Personal for those marked Business, I told Liz immediately. I was

apologetic, and she was disappointed. But she was supportive, as always.

"Don't worry," she said, "we'll have plenty more of these."

At the time I of course believed that she was right, and that I was right to go. But we were both wrong. Last year, while I was in India, Liz spent her birthday with Anya. This year, I would be with Anya, and Liz was dead.

I woke up on September 17 and the world did not end, and I did not fall apart. I just picked up my daughter and fed her and played with her, thinking about her mother a little more than usual. Time passed slowly, and when evening arrived, we went to meet Anya for dinner at the restaurant I had suggested. Perhaps because she had been the last person to spend a birthday with my wife, I wanted Anya to be the one who was there with us that evening.

The restaurant I chose was one of Liz's favorites, a Japanese barbecue place right near the Wish Trees, a temporary art installation in Pasadena. It seemed as good a day as any to make a wish, even though I believed that wishes didn't come true and that they certainly were not retroactive. The courtyard was full of these trees, each with hundreds of white tags hanging from the branches—individual wishes. We sat down and I wrote out one wish for Madeline and one for me, and then tied them carefully on a branch. As I watched our wishes dance and spin in the breeze, I looked across the courtyard to the jewelry store where I had purchased Liz's wedding gift—a beautiful blue sapphire necklace, the stone surrounded by diamonds. When I had first seen that necklace, all I could think of were Liz's shining blue eyes, and I knew it had to be hers.

Now I was thinking about how thankful I was that she had been wearing it the night our house was burglarized. I decided right then to make good on my promise to replace Liz's stolen jewelry. We went across the street to Tiffany's and bought a necklace for Madeline. It was a silver necklace with a bean-shaped pendant—it had been Liz's favorite piece of jewelry—and with the blue bag hanging from my wrist and my daughter strapped to my chest, we walked to the restaurant and settled in at a table.

We shot the shit while we waited for our food, catching up on what we'd missed since we had last seen each other. Then something occurred to me. "Anya," I said, "where were you guys last year? What did you do?" Like with our last anniversary, I could not remember what she and Liz had done to celebrate while I was away in India. My mind was a big, swirling blank, and I felt a feverish need to recapture the lost details.

She looked at me. "Here," she said. "We were here."

The food came, plates piled high with food covered in miso sauce, and I stared at the strips of thinly sliced beef, at the walls, down at my baby—anywhere but at Anya. I was breathing heavily, doing everything I could to slow my heart rate down. I felt like I was going to vomit and I swallowed hard to keep it from coming up. How in holy hell did I end up at the very place Liz spent her last birthday? It was a good thing I didn't believe in signs, because if I did, I'd have been scared shitless.

"Are you okay?" she asked.

"I think so," I said. "I should feed Maddy."

Our dinners sat untouched as we focused our attention on Madeline. Anya passed me her bottle, and I settled Madeline in the crook of my arm, holding it for her to drink.

I looked at Anya. "Eat," I said. "It's getting cold."

She picked up her fork. "You eat," she said.

"When she's done."

A few minutes later, Maddy picked up her little hands and grasped the bottle. I let go, lightly, waiting to see what would happen. She had been attempting this trick for weeks, but now the bottle stayed aloft. My daughter was feeding herself. I suddenly imagined the freedom I would have, all of the exciting things I would get to do while she fed herself her lunch, like brush my teeth. Or do the dishes. Or fold some laundry.

"Wow," said Anya. "Liz would have loved this."

I nodded. We held up our drinks.

"Happy birthday, Liz," I said.

"Happy birthday, Liz."

A few days after Liz's actual birthday, there was to be a 5K walk/run in Minnesota. Actually, it would be all over the world. I wanted to honor her in a larger way, so through the blog, we'd asked people to start walking or running at 1:00 p.m. in their respective time zones on September 20. The idea was that we'd collectively be running for twenty-four hours straight.

The event had been organized in conjunction with the Creeps, a group of women who had been following my blog from the beginning—my original supporters. They would leave helpful comments, and some of them reached out in more personal ways, too. These women cared about me and they felt protective of me; whenever a "stranger" said something that they deemed offensive, they would descend upon the interloper with a vengeance that was swift and merciless. When one of those interlopers called their interest in me "creepy," it was all they needed to form a cohesive and loyal group, however different—moms, single women, divorcées, people with children, people without.

When I had visited Minnesota in June, I spent some time with Rachel, a reader who had become a dear friend; after that, she and the other Creeps decided they wanted to raise money for Maddy and me to give us a financial cushion. They asked everyone to donate seven dollars for the 5K, because that was Liz's favorite number.

This trip back would be my sixth flight with Maddy, and I was getting better at it. I'll admit that I had a lot of help—there is something about traveling as a single dad that gets you the immediate sympathy vote. A woman can be standing there with two toddlers, four suitcases, an infant, and a cat, and people are kind of like *Yeah, who gives a shit?* But stick a guy in an airport with a baby and a backpack, and flight attendants and passersby will fall all over themselves to make his life easier. But even without the kind assistance of others, we now had a routine: we cuddled up together in the window seat during takeoffs and tried to nap all the way until the landings. (Usually. When Madeline was fussy I apologized to our seatmates, often offering to buy them drinks.) We made it to Minneapolis without incident, and after I picked up a lemonade at the French Meadow in concourse F near Gate 3, we headed to Candee and Tom's to meet up with the rest of the grandparents.

A few days later I was standing in the wet grass, feeling a little nervous. Running is not my favorite activity, but more than the fear of having a heart attack, it was the location of the run that was getting to me. Lake Calhoun was the obvious and, for everyone else, ideal spot. Minneapolis residents regularly converged upon it in the summer, making parking nearly impossible, though the struggle was always considered worth it, and the paved road around the lake was just about 5K. Liz's childhood home was on Lake Calhoun.

The day of the run was absolutely gorgeous. It felt like everyone had shown up—guys I'd known since fifth grade, friends from college, even my mom's hairdresser. We gathered near the volleyball courts, and when we were confident that pretty much everyone had arrived, I stood in front of the crowd to thank them for coming. Minutes later people started moving in groups around the lake.

I had A.J. by my side and Maddy fitted securely into her new jogging stroller, and with my best friend and my best gal, I started to run. The sky was blue, without even a hint of clouds. The sun glinted off the lake. I made it about a quarter of a mile before the running became comically difficult for me. My knees ached and my heart felt as though it were trying to escape my chest, but I pushed on, trying to make it at least halfway around the lake before starting to walk. It should have been muggy, but it wasn't—it was perfect. A perfect day to remember Liz.

The Calhoun Beach Club was now directly ahead of me, the beautiful brick building that contained so many of my most cherished memories. This was the place that caused me to break down when I was in Minnesota for Liz's second funeral. All I could think was that she had not reached her thirty-first birthday. I knew I would be seeing this building today, but still I was unprepared. I was trying to combat the emotions I was feeling at the same time I was trying to manage the physical pain I was inflicting upon my body. I tried to focus on breathing, but the pain in my chest made it almost impossible. I tried to focus on the pain in both knees as they absorbed the shock of my feet hitting the pavement below. I tried to focus on anything but the emotional cloud that had begun to engulf me, hoping that the physical pain I felt would distract me from thinking of Liz. I tightened my grip on the stroller and finally slowed to a walk. Fuck it, I thought. I nodded and smiled at my fellow runners to try to let them know that I wasn't going to drop dead.

I didn't really see them, though. I couldn't focus on anything but the Beach Club. As we rounded the northwest corner of the lake, we passed that spot where Liz and I had stared into each other's eyes, unaware of the photographer taking another close-up shot of us. I felt like I was looking through a window at something that had happened three years before. I saw Liz and me; I saw how happy and how in love we were. I saw how much hope we had for our future.

Then I started jogging again, moving back into the present where Liz was not. But all of these people were here with me running because they cared about my wife, about my daughter and me. I steadied myself with this thought and completed my trip around the lake.

After the run we all hung around for a while. A number of people, friends and strangers, shared their own stories with me. A woman from Florida was telling me that she had come up to see her son, Bob, who lived in Central Minnesota. His wife had died in childbirth.

"He has completely shut down," she confided. "I don't know what to do. He lost his job. He won't leave the house. He doesn't want to talk to anybody." She reached out and gripped my arm. "Would you talk to him?" she asked.

In the past months, I'd had many requests to reach out to grieving individuals. I was comfortable giving them my phone number or my e-mail address, but I wasn't going to knock on anybody's door and force them to hear my point of view. I'm a guy, not a guru.

"Of course," I told her. "Of course. I'll give you my information and you can pass it along to him. Tell him he can call anytime." I was curious about this man, and sympathetic. I hadn't encountered that many widowers—there were definitely more women reaching out and getting involved, and many of them were in straits much more dire than mine. Confronting my past on this run brought me back to my own sadness, and now, hearing the stories of others who had faced similarly shitty circumstances, I felt their sadness, too.

As people began moving off toward their cars, I looked back toward the club. I could still see the faint trace of me and Liz, all dressed up for the party she had always wanted. I may have missed her birthday last year, and that was something I was never going to forget. But I had been able to give her the wedding of her dreams, and that counted for something.

Madeline and I had been back in LA for a couple of weeks, enjoying our usual routine of hanging out, when we got a call from Rachel.

"Are you ready to hear how much we made?" she asked.

"Yes," I said. "I'm ready."

"Four thousand four hundred and ten dollars," she said. "For you guys to use. However you want."

As soon as Rachel told me the number, I thought of Bob. And I thought of Jackie, whose husband died on the exact same day as Liz, from the exact same thing. I thought of Kim, whose husband died and left her with two young children. I thought of Jen, whose house burned down a few months after her husband died, leaving her a homeless, single mother. Here I was, with Liz's life insurance payout in the bank for emergencies, my own job at Yahoo! poised to start up again shortly, monthly Social Security checks coming in to help with raising Madeline, and, if worse came to worst, supportive and generous family members. I could afford food. I could afford everything Maddy needed. I could afford records and beer.

So many other people that I had encountered did not have what I did—some of them didn't even have the basics.

When we started organizing the 5K—when we asked people to donate seven dollars—I hadn't really thought about the fact that seven dollars times hundreds of people would become a quantifiable amount of money that could be exchanged for goods, services, or whatever else someone in need may require.

I neglected to realize that I was actually going to get a check after the event. My only goal with this 5K was to honor Liz at her birthday. Now that there was a tangible (and significant) sum involved, I was floored, and frankly, I was a little uncomfortable.

"Rachel," I said, "I can't accept the money. I want to give it away."

"To who?" she asked.

I already had a couple of people in mind, I told her. And then I thought about how many more people could use some support—the support of a community as loving as the one that had erupted around me.

"Maybe we should just start a nonprofit," I said. I was surprised by how quickly the words came from my mouth. I hadn't even considered doing something like this. In fact, I was totally kidding when I suggested it.

Then Rachel said, "You know, I was thinking the exact same thing."

Fuck, I thought. I guess we're going to do this.

no one to
kiss me on the cheek
while wishing me
a good day
at work.
no one to call
on the way into
the office
with whom i could share
traffic information.
no one to deliver to
me the lunch
i've forgotten
on the counter.
shit.
this is all
hitting me and i
haven't even left the
house yet...
today should be a real
fucking treat.

Chapter 20

It was time to get my life together. Realizing that I was ready to direct all of my help and support to others through some sort of organization was just the kick in the ass I needed. Well, that and HR at Yahoo! was beginning to wonder when I was coming back to work.

I could have stayed out longer with a physician's note declaring me mentally unfit to be in an office environment; the doctor I visited said she would prescribe me antidepressants, and whether or not I chose to take them, a diagnosis would be on my record. Diagnosis? What was there to diagnose besides "dead wife"? There's absolutely nothing wrong with any sort of help, but I didn't think I would benefit from it. Even if I did take Zoloft or Paxil or anything else, I was sure that I would still feel the grief just as keenly when I eventually went off the medication. I intended to go into therapy with Madeline when the time was right for her, but for me, right now, the best way to handle my situation was head-on. I needed to feel it.

So I admitted that I wasn't really mentally unfit for an office environment. And frankly, I felt curious about what life as a functioning member of society would be like. After seven months with my daughter as a permanent sidekick, spending her days sitting in her pink bouncy chair near my desk while I wrote and listened to music at home, or strapped to my chest as we explored the city, I was ready to welcome responsibilities beyond feeding her and putting her down for naps. It was time for my return to the world I never expected to leave, time to make good on my promise to provide Madeline with the kind of life that Liz and I wanted her to have.

But before I left the bubble that had become mine and Madeline's world, I realized I could no longer put off the list of to-dos that had been building up. I would have to do them; I would have to be the responsible parent. Liz's death hadn't just completely changed my life—it had changed my perspective on how tenuous my grasp on life was. Before, I might have driven around without a seat belt or put myself in the middle of a riot to get the perfect photo (Bangalore, 2006). But now I hesitated to even rush out of the shower, fearful that I might slip and crack my skull open, my brain spilling out onto the wet tiles. I spent a lot of time considering all the ways that I could die and leave Maddy completely parentless: a heart attack brought on by years of unhealthy eating; getting crushed by an avalanche of records; tripping into and drowning in the pond in our backyard.

While Liz had a certain amount of life insurance provided to her as part of her employment at Disney, we hadn't taken out an additional policy—early death hadn't really been an option

for us. We assumed it would come at the end, only after we had
finished with the important business of raising our daughter
together, of growing old together. And though we had decided
that A.J. and Sonja would be Madeline's guardians if the shit
really hit the fan, they'd need some sort of financial recourse as
well. No matter how much you love a baby, it cannot grow up
on hugs and encouragement alone.

So here we were. Tom put me in touch with a friend of
his in Minneapolis who sold life insurance, and the guy sent
somebody over to the house to collect samples from me—in my
backyard....

My backyard was lovely. It really was. Big and lush with
a giant eucalyptus tree in the far corner, and a koi pond full
of fat, orange goldfish that did nothing but swim in circles all
day. It was a big part of why Liz and I wanted this house: so
our children could run around in this backyard, and we could
host big parties for all of our friends and family. One thing
I never imagined happening in our backyard was a woman
coming over to take my blood and collect a urine sample.
(Okay, that wasn't technically collected out back, but it *was*
where I handed over the warm jar of piss.) Then the lady and
her mobile unit drove away with the bodily fluids that would
hopefully prove I was worth more dead than alive. At least if I
was going to die, I was going to die responsibly.

My reentry into the real world also meant that I obviously
needed to find somewhere for Madeline to spend her days while
I spent mine in an office. The idea that people could just leave
their kids somewhere all day was crazy to me, but I knew I had
to do it. The place I wanted for her was clear in my mind, but
more elusive in reality—somewhere incredible. The most gentle, safe, healthy, loving day care on the entire planet.

Liz had been adamant about returning to work after she had
the baby. "I cannot be a stay-at-home mom" was a familiar re-

frain, which hadn't surprised me—she had always worked her ass off, focused on and determined to do well at her job, to move up. I have no doubt that she would have been a VP by the time she was thirty-two while raising our child at the same time. So when I started thinking about what it would be like to leave Maddy at day care, it helped to know that Liz would have been all for it.

But finding the place for our daughter without my wife's input meant a lot of research and a lot of legwork. Luckily, one of Liz's best friends, Elizabeth, stepped in to help me with the search. She had been one of Liz's colleagues and supporters at her first job out of college, and later they had been reunited at Disney. When Liz died, Elizabeth generously incorporated us into her life, bringing her three little girls over so they could play with Maddy. Well, by *playing,* I mean looking and poking—she was just an infant.

I had also posted on the blog about my search. One reader sent a note that said, "I just moved to Portland recently, and the thing I miss most about LA is this day care." My first reaction was that this e-mail was incredibly weird. I mean, if I left LA, the list of things I'd miss would include the Tiki Ti and Amoeba Records, but probably not the place my kid hung out without me all day. But my second thought was that this was the most ringing endorsement I had ever heard for a day care.

After we looked at somewhere between fifteen and twenty facilities, I actually ended up picking that one. My choice was based on a mixture of research, recommendation, and gut feelings. Usually, when Elizabeth and I went to check out a space, something would turn me off immediately, like the way the staff talked in baby voices to the infants, or the surplus of baby books about Jesus. But at this place, I was charmed. The school was in a house with a calm, friendly, earthy vibe that I immediately connected to, even though I'm the last person you would find in the parking lot at a Phish show. There were toys everywhere, the schedule seemed less rigidly structured than at some of the other places, and their philosophy included talking to children like adults. I was never a goo-goo ga-ga kind of dad—I'd rather just explain to my six-month-old that the Silver Jews were never a Pavement side project. As soon as I saw the garden out back where the older kids grew vegetables and flowers, I knew it would be a good place for Madeline.

On the morning of Madeline's first day, I spent twenty minutes thinking about how Liz would have dressed her, and none at all thinking about how her father would be presenting himself. She was in a brand-new, pink long-sleeved onesie with flowers, and I in my usual outfit: a plaid shirt with pearl snap buttons, jeans, and a pair of vintage Nikes. I was stylish in certain parts of Los Angeles, but next to the parents of the other children, I probably looked like a college student.

When we arrived, I sat in the car for fifteen minutes, alternating between sobbing and thoughts of just taking Madeline back to the house. Shit. Could I kidnap my own kid? For the first time in a long time, the tears were not about Liz's absence. They felt different. They felt more normal, more common—the kind of sadness natural to parents abandoning their young. Which was exactly what I felt like I was doing.

When I handed Madeline over, she went to her teacher without a fight, which made leaving her there even more difficult. We had developed an incredible bond, and I was worried that by leaving my daughter with someone new, we would somehow lose that. I finally understood Liz's fear that she wouldn't be as close to Madeline because I'd been the one to change her diaper and feed her first. I tried to tell myself that I was being ridiculous and that this day care would be the best place for her while I was working—the only place for her—but leaving her that first day felt almost impossible. I walked out and closed the door behind me, crying like a motherfucker.

Walking through the familiar doors of my office gave me anxiety, too. When I arrived there a little while later, my head started pounding and my heart was pumping so hard that a doctor would have been able to check my pulse in even the smallest artery in my body. I had imagined work as a place that wouldn't—couldn't—change in my absence; I was looking forward to a reintroduction into what I remembered as a bustling office with jokes between colleagues who acted casually but managed to complete their assignments somewhat professionally, balancing sneakers-and-jeans attire with a secretly impressive work ethic. My family life may have imploded, but in my mind, the desks at Yahoo! were still organized in the same configuration, the same friendly faces occupying the spaces above them. I thought I would walk in to a bunch of back slaps, a couple of hugs, maybe a few congenial nods. Three *I'm sorry*s, two *Welcome back*s, and one or two *Hey, Matt*s.

I could not have been more wrong. I realized almost immediately that things at Yahoo! had gone on without me—everything here was business as usual. It was like I had been transported to the days before Madeline was born and Liz died, when the only thing I should have been worried about was what to eat for lunch that day.

Some facts about my job had stayed the same: my salary, which building I would be in, my phone number. But everything else had changed: my old responsibilities had been reassigned to somebody else, which I knew, since somebody had to manage the outsourcing while I was at home. There had been a slew of layoffs, turning what had been a social, busy space into a decimated department with rows of empty cubicles. My desk had been relegated to a desolate corner, where I sat alone.

Every day after I handed my daughter over, I sat in the corner of the room at work waiting for someone to give me something to do. My coworkers had been amazing and understanding during my time off, but now that I was back here, some of my colleagues were less sure how to handle the potential awkwardness of my situation. They had sent me kind e-mails when I was away at home, and now it felt like they were ignoring me. They weren't doing it to be cruel—for all I knew, it was the way they thought they could be the kindest.

Sure, I was never a "big man on campus" type, but I'd never been a social pariah, either. It was like my identity had been reassigned. Instead of The Guy Who Loves Music, or The Guy Who Worked in India for All Those Months, I was somebody else—somebody weird and unfamiliar. I hadn't even had a chance to be The Guy with the Baby; I was just The Guy with the Dead Wife. I felt as though some of my coworkers were treating me like death was somehow contagious. And I couldn't blame them, really—I probably would have reacted the exact same way.

Even the phone's silence drove me crazy. I watched the light at the top stay dark all day. Liz had been the only one to call me on that line—as an Internet company, we almost exclusively used online messaging and e-mail to communicate. I would come back from lunch and see that red rectangle lit up, excited to have a voice mail from Liz, however mundane her message would be. Now I dreaded I would never see that light again—or worse, I would, but the message wouldn't be from her.

I spent my first few days back sorting through e-mails. I moved all of the messages that had come during my leave to a folder called Before. But first, I sorted everything by sender and moved all the e-mails from my wife to a separate folder called Liz. I had thousands of them from her, but I simply wasn't ready to look through them yet. I wanted to preserve them, though, so that if I ever felt ready to revisit her words, I'd be able to.

I did read two of them, but not on purpose. The e-mails were sorted by date received, the most recent e-mail at the top. There it was: the last e-mail she ever sent to me.

> from: liz
> to: matt
> sent: sun 3/23/2008 5:48 PM
> subject: I gained weight.
>   Probably from cookies and crap but when I stand up
>   I feel bigger ... can't wait to show u!

I remembered that day. It was the day before Madeline had been born. I went to pick up dinner for us, and while Liz waited for me, she got a visit from one of the nurses, who told her that she had finally gained some weight—something she had been struggling to do through her entire pregnancy. It was a sign that the bed rest was working.

Looking at the e-mail reminded me of how fucking great we had felt on March 23. We'd had no idea that Madeline would make her appearance the next morning and that twenty-seven hours after that, Liz would be dead.

I saw one other e-mail that same day, and it sent me into a conference room for longer than I care to admit.

> from: liz
> to: matt
> sent: fri 3/21/2008 1:13 PM
> subject: I love u
>   And I'm excited to have a baby that looks like u :)

Fuck.

And my response:

from: matt
to: liz
sent: fri 3/21/2008 1:22 PM
subject: re: I love u
    Let's hope she looks more like you...

Double fuck.

When I finally stopped crying, I returned to my desk. The empty, gray walls of the cubicle were a stark reminder of just how empty my life had become. Everything that had been in my old cube, including the one framed photo of Liz that I had kept there, was still packed in the boxes under my desk, and I wasn't ready to confront any of it yet.

I spent the next hour printing out enough photos of Madeline to completely cover the walls of my cubicle.

as much as i never
expected to,
i love shopping
with madeline:
i try to buy
clothes that
liz
would choose,
but every once
in a while, i get
something that
she would have
rolled her eyes at,
just so madeline
gets both perspectives.

Chapter 21

Before Madeline was born, Liz and I had many conversations about what our lives with her would—and should—be like. Of course, they never included the possibility of a future without me there, or without her there. We figured our biggest challenges would be whether or not our daughter needed braces, if we liked her boyfriends, or where she should go to school. But we firmly agreed that she would not absorb our entire selves.

"This baby is not going to change our lives," Liz would say.

"This baby is not going to change our lives," I would agree.

We knew our lives *would* change in a good way, but even with the middle-of-the-night feedings that our friends talked about and the sleepless nights we were primed for, it was our intention to maintain who we were and what we had become together. Liz would still decorate the house, worrying over curtains and votive candles, and she would continue hitting boutiques all over Los Angeles, spending a shitload of money on a purse or another pair of shoes; I wouldn't stop going to concerts whenever a decent band came through town, and I would keep getting up early on Saturdays to wander the streets of Los Angeles, taking photos with Ben. Most important to both of us, we agreed, our regular date nights would continue. Liz knew that if we were happy, our kid would be happy, and neither of us wanted to be a slave to a baby.

She had always planned on working, and while I joked about giving up my job to be a househusband, it was never something I could really bring myself to do. Of course, I had been slightly mistaken—now I would have given up every hour at that office to spend more time at home with Madeline. But my daughter and I got used to the shift in our routine, obeying an actual schedule instead of moving through our day at a leisurely pace. We kind of had to find ourselves a new rhythm.

I would leave work early, which was easy since there was nothing much for me to do there, and even though I could have left Maddy at day care until six o'clock while I did my own thing for a little while, I would pick her up immediately. With the time we were spending apart, it became even more important to have her with me as much as I could. I wanted to do the things I knew I'd be doing if Liz were still alive, but I didn't want more time away from my daughter. Bringing Madeline with me on my adventures was exactly what Liz and I had meant when we said we weren't going to be changed by our child. We'd instead incorporate her into the activities we both loved so much, each of us influencing her in our own way. But now I had a much heftier responsibility than just keeping our baby happy—I had to preserve and cultivate both of our interests so that Madeline would have an equal amount of influence from both parents. I knew that Liz would have fucking loved that.

Even when Maddy was just a blurry picture on an ultrasound screen, Liz started fantasizing about taking our baby girl to the spa and dressing her up. I didn't give a shit about that stuff—I just wanted to teach her to appreciate music. I could practically see her on my shoulders, a mini-Liz chirping excitedly, helping me pick out records as I walked through the aisles of Amoeba, my favorite record store.

Tuesdays had always been the best day of the week—the day the new releases arrived at the record store. But since Liz died, Tuesdays had become the designated slot for me to torture myself again and again with thoughts of how many weeks she had been gone. And I was still living from Tuesday to Tuesday. I felt that by counting them, by anchoring the scurry of time into weeks, I somehow tethered Liz to me, keeping a line to the last time I saw her alive.

These weekly trips to Amoeba helped me escape the awfulness that came with waking up to another week gone by without Liz. I knew that no matter how shitty the day started, I'd at least be able to escape some of it with a bag full of new records. Like most other weeks, on what happened to be the thirty-third Tuesday since Liz had died, I left work early and picked Madeline up from day care. I parked in the lot behind the shop, where the walls are covered with years' worth of caked-on graffiti, and walked into the store with my baby hanging off my arm in her car seat. You should have seen the looks the hipsters gave me as I squeezed through the vinyl aisles, digging for records by Ariel Pink's Haunted Graffiti and Swearing at Motorists. They believed what I had believed before Liz was pregnant: that all people become lame when they

become parents. But lame is one thing I am not, and I dreamed
of a confrontation that would end with my inviting some asshole to my house for a look at my record collection and a couple
of beers. As we wandered the store, I explained my selections to
Maddy carefully, even though I knew she wasn't yet old enough
to understand the difference between Bon Iver and Bon Jovi.

I rolled up to the counter to check out with the reissue
of Pavement's *Brighten the Corners* and Mark Kozelek's *The Finally LP*, but before we left Amoeba, there was one stop for
us to make—a photo I had been meaning to take. Near the
shop's entrance was an elevator that nobody ever used. There
were fewer than twenty steps between the store and the parking lot, so I had never even looked inside it until I had to
get a baby and stroller up the stairs. I felt as though I had
discovered some secret art space. The elevator was just filled
with graffiti. I mean, literally, floor to ceiling, covered in graffiti. I grew up in Minnesota. I didn't go to record stores with
my parents. We didn't really go anywhere that had graffiti. It
thrilled me to share my tastes with Madeline and to give her
a different—though not necessarily better—childhood than I
had. The elevator was so fucking cool-looking, and I thought
it would make a great photo, just a little baby in this room full
of the scrawls of thousands of unidentified people. I took her
out of her stroller, placed her on the floor, and backed into the
opposite corner to click the shutter a few times. The resulting
photos were great. Madeline looked like she was completely
alone in a place where a child shouldn't be at all. I knew she
was going to love to see it someday.

Instead of going straight home, I stopped in Los Feliz to
take Madeline on the kind of shopping trip her mom would
have taken her on—a venture I would have stayed completely
out of if Liz had been around. I couldn't help but worry that
with me as her only parental influence, Madeline would be

missing out on all the things her mom loved and planned to do with her, so I tried to keep it on my mind all the time. I didn't think, How should I dress Madeline? I probably would have had a kid wearing hand-me-down flannel shirts fashioned into onesies. Instead, I thought, If Liz were here, how would she dress Madeline?

There was a great little boutique there that had gorgeous clothes for girls. The prices were astronomical, but I didn't really care. If Liz had ever bought an expensive dress for Madeline, I would have lost my shit. Kids grow fast and every move they make creates a mess, so to spend any more than five dollars on an outfit seemed outrageous to me. But doing so would have made Liz really happy—not so much because she was spending a lot of money on our child, but because she was doting on her.

I loved that I had discovered this place on my own, without a recommendation from a friend, a blog reader, or even from Liz. I likely wouldn't have even noticed a kid store if Liz were alive, but now I shopped at this place all the time. On this particular day, I saw an absolutely beautiful dress in the store. It was khaki colored, with jewel-like buttons and an ornate circular pattern running up and down the seams and around the arm and neck holes. Absolutely gorgeous. I knew that Liz would have loved it, would have bought it, no matter what. So there I was, a bearded man who looked like he should have been on line to buy tickets for the National, standing in a fancy children's clothing store shopping for dresses with a little blonde-haired, blue-eyed cherub.

"This is beautiful," I told the woman behind the counter.

"It's Chloe," she said.

I almost said, "I'm Matt and this is Madeline," but then I realized she was gesturing at the label.

"Of course," I said, like I had known that already. In my head, the sarcasm was rampant. Who gives a fuck if this is a

Chloe dress? Who the fuck is Chloe, anyway? I'm wearing a Sears shirt for which I paid six dollars eight years ago at a thrift store in Chicago.

But I knew that Liz would have cared. And to be honest, now I cared. I wanted to do for Madeline what her mother couldn't do for her, but I also felt that if I could dress my daughter properly, if I could show the people around us that I could match her outfits, the bows and the shoes and the socks, they would know that I was spending time with her, focusing all my attention on her, and that she was going to be okay. So like a good daddy, I handed over my credit card—I figured it was good practice for when my daughter would be demanding designer clothes for her first day of junior high. And then I asked how much it was.

"Two hundred dollars," she said.

I briefly considered fleeing, but I saw the bitchy look on the salesgirl's face as I tried to comprehend a baby dress that cost more than my entire wardrobe, and its lace trim caught my eye. I looked at Maddy sleeping in her stroller, and I bought the dress.

For two hundred fucking dollars.

With my credit card still smarting from the purchase, I put her and our new cargo into the car. When it was me and Liz, I was thinking, I knew how things would go. I would have followed her lead at the beginning and, as I got more and more comfortable, played an increasingly bigger role in raising our daughter, even doing the little things like making sure her outfits matched. But I had to learn how to care about all the girly things I didn't grow up with without Liz's help. I had to close my eyes and imagine how she would have done things, because few things were more important to me than making sure I channeled her influence in Madeline's life.

* * *

Before Madeline was born, I had talked to Liz about buying a rug for our living room. It wasn't that I was interested in helping redecorate our house or anything—that was her thing—but I was worried that the wood floors would hurt our baby's little knees when she eventually learned to crawl.

"What? She'll be fine on the wood floors."

"Liz, she's going to hurt her knees if she starts crawling on these floors."

"She'll be fine."

I was adamant. "What's going to happen when she collapses facefirst on the floor? She's going to have a broken nose, and I'm pretty sure no doctor would perform a nose job on a baby."

"Seriously, Matt. She'll be fine."

"Have you ever crawled across a wood floor when you were drunk? I have, and that shit hurts."

Her head tilted, her beautiful long eyelashes waving at me as if to tell me to go away.

"Our daughter is going to be a late crawler if we don't do this," I said.

She laughed. "Okay, we'll get a rug. But only if you shut your mouth."

Now I watched as Madeline used her arms to lift up her tiny body—a definite sign that she would soon start crawling. I thought back to that conversation with Liz. I had to go get a rug. And soon.

That same afternoon I took photos of the living room and I went to the Pottery Barn in Beverly Hills. I walked in and, as usual, felt out of place. I waited patiently, watching as the salespeople went from yuppie couple to yuppie couple, ignoring the mountain man with the baby growing from his chest. I decided that I would probably be getting better service if I were cleanly shaven and had a white cable-knit sweater tied around my neck. And they'd certainly be paying more attention to me if there were a woman standing beside me.

I wasn't going to shave for these fuckers, and the sweater was way out of the question. And my wife was dead. How would Liz have handled being ignored when all she wanted to do was give a store a bunch of her money? She definitely would not be standing quietly in the back of the place just waiting for someone to help her like I was. I decided to take matters into my own hands. I approached one of the saleswomen and the buttoned-up couple she was with and said I needed her help, telling her to come toward the sound of the babbling baby when she was finished with the folks she was talking to. I didn't deliver the message with the sort of sternness Liz would have, but I did channel the annoyed smile she would have been wearing.

When the saleswoman finally came over to me, I pulled my camera from Madeline's diaper bag and held the display in front of her face. "Okay," I said. "What rug would match this living room?"

Within a few minutes the woman found the perfect rug. I knew it was perfect because she told me so. Frankly, I didn't give a shit what the rug looked like. All I wanted was something soft for my daughter to crawl on. But Liz would have spent weeks shopping for the perfect rug, making sure it matched the rest of the room. I couldn't go quite that far, but I knew that she would be proud—and relieved—that I'd thought to bring photos in so someone with better taste could help me.

i miss a lot of
things about the
woman i love,
but it's her
voice that
i miss the most.
i know i can
still hear it
if i want
to, but right now,
i don't think
i can handle it.

Chapter 22

I have a video of Liz that I shot in the hospital when she was being wheeled away to the delivery room. Now it was October, and I still hadn't watched it. It was still too soon for me to sit there and hear her voice, to see her smile, to listen to her talking and laughing. I wasn't ready, and I didn't know if I would ever be. But I had to save it for Madeline, because I was sure that she'd someday want to know what her mom's voice sounded like. I missed that voice so much, but I was still actively avoiding it. I hadn't cleared the messages from our answering machine, and I also once inadvertently hit the speed-dial key that connected me to her cell phone. When I figured out that the faint female voice in the room was coming from my phone, I held it to my ear, realized what I had done, and immediately disconnected.

But a few of Liz's friends were in the habit of calling her cell phone and listening to her outgoing message again and again. This was unthinkable to me. I could not handle the familiar rise and fall of her voice, how her sentences began and ended, or the way she whispered over the vowel sounds. I was afraid that hearing her speak would make her seem alive again. And I would have lost my shit.

One afternoon her phone rang while I was in the middle of doing some laundry. I ran into the living room, hoping to silence it before the ringing woke Madeline. The number was blocked, and I paused, taking a deep breath before answering another call from another person who hadn't yet heard the terrible news.

I cringed every time it rang; there had been too many instances since her death when I'd answered it and had to confirm what some distant friend thought was a horrendous rumor, or break the news to a professional contact who had heard nothing of the awful truth. Every time I had to tell someone else, it was like entering some kind of sadistic time machine, sending me back to that very moment in which I realized she was dead.

"Hello?"

"This is Detective Berryman from the LAPD. Are you missing a BlackBerry?"

"Uh, I don't think so."

"Well, the number I just dialed was at one point associated with the phone I'm holding in my hand."

I told him I was on my way and hung up without saying goodbye. When our house had been robbed, there had been so much chaos—and so many more important things taken—that we had never even realized that Liz's old BlackBerry had been stolen. The detective had called about a phone, but I was hoping there was more. I would have liked nothing better than to dig through a pile of unclaimed items and discover Liz's missing jewelry.

I headed to the police station just a few miles from my house. When I arrived, I immediately started crying, fucking destroyed that Liz wouldn't see the jewelry I was about to recover. I was not what a roomful of manly men in ties and suspenders needed or expected to see when they were busy doing their work in one of the worst parts of Los Angeles.

"I got a call about a stolen BlackBerry," I said through my sobs.

A uniformed man behind the desk gave me a confused look and silently got up from his desk to escort me through the station. I thought for sure that he would call me something nasty under his breath, but I think—more than anything—that he was bewildered into silence.

I calmed myself down by concentrating on my breathing. In the back room, at the same evidence table where I had stood with Liz last January, I immediately recognized the detective who had helped us then. He handed me the phone and I thanked him; I also asked about the jewelry that was still missing. Months had passed since the break-in, and maybe, just maybe those pieces were here. I knew Liz would want them back with me. With Madeline.

"We've got this," he said, "but there was nothing else." My front crumbled and I started crying harder than Maddy with a wet diaper. The detective just looked confused. I could see him wondering how the loss of a few trinkets could break down a grown man like this.

"My wife," I explained, "who I was with last time. She died."

He looked stricken. I took the phone and went home, without Liz's jewelry. Without Liz.

For a long time keeping Liz's cell phone on felt like the right thing to do, continuing to pay the bill every month just to keep active the number that I knew by heart. It allowed me a real attachment to her, but after this incident I wanted to cancel her phone service—it just seemed like the right time. I was worried that if I did, though, I would be losing another piece of her—that I would be erasing more from my memory by essentially deleting this from my life, and I would lose that opportunity to hear her voice should I ever want to.

But it wasn't the phone number that helped keep me connected to Liz. I thought about her and talked about her all the time. I wrote about her daily and continued to live in the house we bought together. She was still a part of almost every move I made. Those were things that mattered. Besides, she would surely call me an idiot for paying sixty-five dollars a month for the privilege of preserving an outgoing voice-mail greeting that I never even listened to.

Turning off her phone helped me realize that it was time for me to move through this mess in other tangible ways. I had yet to do *so* much in this regard. Liz's clothes still hung in her closet, and there were still two baskets of crumpled clothes inside (one to be washed, one to be sent to the dry cleaners). Her jewelry and perfume were still atop the dresser that was still filled with her neatly folded clothes. Her razor still sat on the ledge in the shower, right next to her shampoo bottles. These things were so small and I was so used to them that I could overlook them, like they blended into the scenery or something.

But her car was still parked out front, and that big hunk of salmon-colored metal was difficult to ignore. I hadn't really been driving it, and sometimes my parents or Tom and Candee would use it when they were in town, but it caught my eye each and every time I looked out the giant picture window in our living room, and it assaulted me every time I pulled up to the house. I hated seeing it. Before she died, Liz's car was the one definitive sign that she was home; now each time I saw it I had an instant reaction, thinking this was all a fucking nightmare. I wasn't actively changing anything inside or outside the house—I just wasn't ready. But the idea of letting Liz's car go actually came from a total stranger.

During one visit from Liz's family, I noticed a man in the street through my living room window. We were all hanging out, and suddenly I saw some sketchy dude peering into Liz's car out front. He was walking around it, trying to open the doors, and kicking the tires.

I walked outside, and said, "Can I help you?" Pleasant words, aggressive tone. This guy smiled back at me, totally harmless, and said, "Is this car for sale?" I was confused. I didn't expect those words from his mouth. And I certainly didn't have an answer prepared. I kind of felt like an asshole—I came at him like a man whose car was about to be stolen, and he couldn't have been nicer.

Finally some words came to me. "I'm not sure," I said, trying to hide my fluster. "I don't think so. I mean, maybe." Not articulate, but words nonetheless.

"I'll give you two thousand dollars. Cash."

I took his number and went back inside. I was still confused. I really hadn't planned to sell Liz's car, maybe ever, but I was planning to get rid of mine. In fact, I had been to the dealership with Tom that very morning. Bending over to put Madeline into my little old Honda Accord was starting to hurt my back—it was time to suck it up and get a "dad car." I felt so fucking old.

When I told Candee and Tom that somebody wanted to buy the car, I spun it like it was a terrible idea, like there was no way I would sell it—no reason to.

"Really?" said Tom. "What else are you going to do with it? Are you going to drive it?"

"No," I said.

"Wouldn't it help pay for your new car?" asked Candee. "That you need for Maddy?"

"Well, yes," I said. But I didn't know if I could really do it. Fuck, I thought. Maybe I should keep it for Madeline or something, so that she can drive her mom's car when she's finally old enough to get her driver's license. When I said this out loud, the suggestion was met with uproarious laughter.

Well, okay then. As much as I wanted to hang on to this relic of Liz's, I knew that the car was not serving much purpose beyond acting as a scenic obstruction to my front yard. I'd only used it back in July when my car was in the shop.

That had been fucking awful.

Maddy and I were on our way back from a playgroup and were driving down the freeway when someone smashed into us, causing my car to completely spin out. We wound up facing forward, and luckily we weren't hit by any oncoming traffic. The other driver sped off. My car was a mess, but we were okay, and I called the cops so I could obtain a police report for insurance purposes.

When they came, one of them said, "Why didn't you follow the woman who hit you?"

"Excuse me?"

The officer repeated her question, and I just couldn't believe it. With a baby in my back seat? Who am I, Steve McQueen? Admittedly, a few years prior, I would have done exactly that—stepped on the gas and chased that fucker down. But now, my kid's safety was more important than being a vigilante.

After I dropped off my beat-up sedan for repair a few days later, I decided to walk back to the house with Maddy. It was close enough and no one was around to give us a ride. I didn't think it was worth getting a rental car, since I didn't really need to leave the house. Besides, Liz's car was sitting out front in case I did.

The first time I drove it was to Casita del Campo for dinner and a drink with friends; Madeline was set to spend the evening with Anya. I managed to ignore the familiar feeling of sitting in the car until I dropped Maddy off, but when I pulled away I could not help but freak out. It was just so fucking weird to be alone in Liz's car. She and I had made so many memories in the ugly piece of shit. They raced through my head, each bringing my heart up to my throat in a fresh way.

This was the car Liz's uncle had shipped out to LA from Minneapolis when she finished college. We rode in it nearly every weekend to Runyon Canyon to hike. It had taken us to that party in Hermosa Beach where she met my oldest friend, Alex, and she had dragged me in it to that horrifying Jessica Simpson concert at Universal Amphitheater. She brought this car to Dr. Nelson's office to get the ultrasound that confirmed she was pregnant. Liz had driven this roller skate for seven years. She'd even named it "the Little Zipper." What a stupid-ass name.

Being in the car now was making me crazy. It was the first time I'd been in the driver's seat since before Liz died, and there were physical reminders of her everywhere. Her fine blonde hairs were still on the cloth upholstery, and her favorite Top 40 stations were still programmed on the radio. It hit me hard that she had sat in this seat, used this seat belt, looked in these mirrors, operated this gearshift, and pressed her small feet against this brake and this accelerator. In the house, I had finally acclimated to our stuff so that I no longer thought *She used this apple corer* every time I wanted to cut up a piece of fruit. But here, it was impossible not to pay attention because it was all around me. I was literally inside of it.

When I was adjusting Maddy's car seat, I saw an opened can of Diet Coke in the backseat beverage holder. Liz had loved Diet Coke. It was her drink of choice—no coffee, just that goddamned diet "pop" all of the time. (She was a good Midwesterner.) Seeing the red and silver thing just sitting there shook me—Liz drank from this can; she held it in her hand and put her mouth on it. I wrote about it on the blog, how it had messed with my mind.

After that, Tom called to tell me that it was his soda—he had left it there. He waited for my reaction, and when I started laughing, he laughed with me.

On a trip to the grocery store that week, the odometer caught my eye. I looked down at a red light for no particular reason, but I would have been blind to miss it: I caught it at 77,777 miles. Liz's favorite number, five in a row. That hit me hard. If I had looked at the next light, the number would not have been nearly as jarring. I didn't think this moment had some grandiose meaning, but I wondered how someone else might interpret it. Many would say that this was a sign from Liz, that she was still with me even though she was dead. I thought that kind of thing was utter bullshit; I knew it was just a random coincidence and that my mind was trying to assign meaning to it. But sign or not, it was definitely fucking weird.

It was time. I had to get rid of Liz's car—it was the right decision. I called the guy up and told him that two thousand dollars was a fair price, and that he needed to pick the car up immediately. He came over the next day to drop off a check and get the keys, but he said that he'd pick it up in a few days.

"I'm going to New York in three days," I told him. "I need it gone by the time I get back."

As the lone soul who had wanted the car to remain, I now felt strangely insistent that it disappear as soon as possible. I'd made the decision to sell it, and I wanted it gone before I found a reason to change my mind.

I knew the morning we set out for New York was the last time I would see Liz's car. Before we left for LAX at five o'clock, I stood on my quiet, empty street with Maddy asleep in my arms, just staring at it. If any of my neighbors had seen me, they probably would have thought I was out of my fucking mind. It was bad enough that I had left this ugly, goddamned thing just sitting outside my house for the past seven months, taking up a precious parking spot. I waved at the car, and headed out to the airport. I wasn't sad. I was mostly mad at myself for acting like a jackass and waving at an inanimate object.

When we got home from New York a few days later, it was after midnight and the street was just as quiet as when we had left. The car was gone. I looked at the inscriptions on my inner wrists—it was as if Liz had scribbled on me just that morning with a Sharpie. I had decided to get the numbers that represented the two most important dates of my life inscribed on my skin a few months earlier: 24 on the left, 25 on the right. I hadn't even pondered it for very long; it was a random idea that felt so right that I headed out to get them almost immediately. When I walked outside and saw Liz's car parked behind mine that day, the idea crystallized in my mind, and I realized that the numbers had to be in Liz's handwriting.

I found a sheet of paper in the drawer of her bedside table with equations she had scribbled, trying to calculate how long she could make her maternity leave last. I scanned the page and found crisp examples of a 2, a 4, and a 5, with her distinctive and elegantly looping cursive. They were the two most significant dates in my life, and they were the very first symbols that ever meant enough for me to have etched onto my body.

Even though I was beginning to let go of these tangible objects, I knew that I would never lose my connection to Liz. Sometimes I had to let logic overrule emotion—it didn't make any sense to hang on to a rusty razor or a shirt she had given me that no longer fit. But I had memories, and I had Madeline. And thanks to these tattoos, I had a permanent reminder of my wife.

we were excited to
show off the small
bump she had
and to visit
with friends and family.
we talked about
how fun it
would be to go
back to the mn
for future holidays
with our kid.
here i was,
one year later
with that kid we
were so fucking
excited to show off,
but it was
two of us rather
than three
getting on the plane.

Chapter 23

Time was passing so much more quickly than I had anticipated. I found myself constantly flashing back to what Liz
and I had been doing exactly a year earlier—it was impossible
not to. As much as I loved thinking about the trips we'd taken
and the fun we'd had together during our time together, it hurt
so much more to remember what it had been like just the year
before: our *last* vacation, birthday, whatever, together, and without our knowing. It was shitty to think about how happy and
full of hope we had been. Now the holiday season approached,
and I knew I was about to enter a minefield of memories.

Minnesota during the holidays had always been a pain in
the ass. Liz and I had to run from my dad's house to my mom's
house to her parents' house—it was exhausting. But this year,
our first year without Liz, our holidays would become a true

family affair. We were all going to gather together: my dad and his wife, and my mom and my stepdad—they would all come over to Tom and Candee's to mix with their huge families. It made my life a hell of a lot easier because I wouldn't have to run around with an eight-month-old. Everyone excited to see—and spoil—Madeline would be in one place. Everyone but Liz.

In the present, I kept thinking that everything had been perfect when we were eighteen, but I hadn't known it. Sure, there had been big challenges facing us, but they were like a Brat Pack movie: where to go to college, what to wear to prom, and how to deal with the idiots at Liz's preppy high school who didn't like the kid with the beat-up truck coming by to pick up their princess and drive her to the other side of the tracks every day. Really, we usually just went back to Liz's.

After school we would tumble out of my truck and into the kitchen, grabbing some food and drinks to take into the living room, just doing mundane shit. I had a memory of Liz asking me to help her hang up the giant photo collage we had put together for her graduation party in her bedroom. After pounding a few nails into the drywall, the board was up and we stood back to admire it. It was like a testament to her life so far, with pictures of her with her friends and photos of us, all pinned to a corkboard. There was a photo of two of her high school friends making out on the trampoline in someone's backyard, and another of Josh and me out at his cousin's farm, standing near the ostrich pen. And my favorite, sweet little Liz and her huge smile, holding a rifle and a winner's certificate—turns out the prissy girl from the suburbs was one hell of a shot.

Those times seemed so far away now. Since we had been teenagers hanging out poolside in her parents' backyard, I had experienced so much of the world. When I was growing up, the people around me were all from Minnesota and tended to stay in Minnesota. Liz encouraged me to cast my glance across the country—across the oceans. She encouraged me to make my world larger, and she did so with me. I wondered now what it would be like to go back to our hometown for a holiday with our families, but without her.

When we arrived at the Goodmans' house, I felt hyperaware that Liz was dead. There had been so many of these holiday events during our twelve years together, and she was by my side during every single one of them. I felt like I was going to sink without her.

I wanted her memory to be present, even if she couldn't be. Not in any sort of creepy way—we didn't set aside a plate of food or a spot at the table for her—but I made sure to talk about her and to let our families know that I wanted them to feel comfortable talking about her. Sure, it was for my own sanity, but it was also for Maddy's sake, and it was something I did all the time. When we would pass by Blush Salon, and I would tell my baby that it had been her mom's favorite. I would dress her in something blue and tell her that her mom had looked beautiful in that color. I would point at the photos hanging on the wall, and tell Madeline stories about what Liz was doing in each scene. I didn't think my daughter really had any comprehension at this point, but soon she would. And I wanted her earliest memories to include stories of her mom; I wanted her to feel close to Liz even though they'd never really met.

Tom grabbed our luggage from the car and ushered us into the house. "We set Liz's old room up for you and Maddy," he said. Liz and I always stayed in there on our visits.

We walked in to set our stuff down, and my heart sank into my shoes. Everything was different. The walls were still light brown, but all of the furniture—save a foldout couch—had been removed to make space for a crib. The collage that Liz and I had hung up was gone. The closet door was open, displaying not Liz's old clothes but new clothes for our baby. The bookshelves that once held the dried corsages and awkward photos from our prom were now filled with diapers, wipes, and toys.

Reeling, I handed Maddy to Tom and headed for Candee, who was in the kitchen.

"The room," I said to her. I was crying by now, and I expected her to do what she always did: to be the rock, to tell me it was going to be okay, to hold me. Instead, her face crumpled, too, and she started to sob. I had seen Candee cry before, but in their house, I had thought of Tom as the softy. He could always be counted on to tear up when it came to his girls, especially when he was happy or proud of them. Until I had my own daughter, I never understood it. But Candee—she was the strong one. She was the one who held everybody else up, who kept her back straight even when she wanted to fall apart. The only time I had really seen her lose it was in the moment after Liz died and during her funerals.

In Banff, her silence and composure had confused me. I hadn't realized that these nonactions were the lid on the pressure cooker, a thin piece of steel holding a deluge of emotion in place. Now, her anguish pierced the surface, and I caught just a glimpse of the mother whose child had died.

Candee and I stood there and held each other for a long time, grieving openly—finally. Grieving together. And this time, I was the one who said, "It's going to be okay."

That experience moved me like few others had. Instead of feeling like I was the only one who missed Liz, I was now certain that I was mourning with somebody, somebody who truly felt her absence as keenly as I did. I knew that everyone was hurting, but sometimes I needed to watch somebody else completely break down to really feel it. As fucked up as it may sound, seeing Candee like this gave me a lot of hope. I could now see a future that had us—all of us—sharing our stories and emotions with Madeline, keeping Liz's memory alive. And it helped me believe that I'd be able to make it through this holiday without completely losing my shit.

Thursday afternoon, the entire extended family—close to one hundred people—gathered to share a twenty-pound, deep-fried turkey, Auntie Penny's hash brown potatoes, Nana's gravy, Auntie Pam's sweet potatoes with marshmallows and brown sugar on top, and a million other dishes. My mom helped me situate Madeline in her high chair, and my dad brought over a small plate of food. She ate some of Auntie Mary's vegetable medley and drank a cup of milk. Always thinking about the awesome photo op, I grabbed a turkey leg from the platter, handed it to her, and started snapping pictures. The rest of the family made their way into the kitchen, and we all laughed together as Madeline hit herself in the face a couple of times trying to get the thing into her mouth. I looked over at Candee and gave her a wink. Just yesterday we had stood in this same spot, crying about what was missing from our lives. And today, well, today we were thankful for what we had.

The weekend following the holiday, I had plans to meet up with Rachel so that we could make another donation from the money that had been raised for Madeline and me during the 5K. I had already sent a two-thousand-dollar check to Jackie and given one thousand in cash to the receptionist at Dr. Nelson's office, whose boyfriend died when she was a few months pregnant. Giving the money away provided me with an enormous sense of pride and convinced me that we could do so much more to help people in situations similar to mine—worse than mine. Liz would have been proud and happy to know what was being done that weekend in her memory, but honestly, she would have been in disbelief that I was the one behind it. She'd be more than a little surprised that I was not only doing a bang-up job of taking care of our kid, but that I was taking time to help others as well.

I picked Rachel up on Saturday morning, and we drove into the Minnesota countryside with Maddy asleep in the back. We were having a rare moment of quiet, though I was sure that as soon as she opened her eyes, we would once again be treated to a steady stream of baby babble. I was actually excited. We were on our way to see Bob, whose mother had approached me at the 5K a few months earlier. We wanted to fulfill the promise I had made to her: that I would help however I could.

Driving toward his home in the small town of Albertville, Minnesota, I had no idea how he would react to our visit or to the fact that we were bringing him a check for one thousand dollars, no strings attached. I knew he could use the money, but still, I didn't know whether he would be okay with a pair of strangers stopping by his house. It might be completely fucking awkward for all of us, but I felt confident that the good we were trying to do would be recognized and welcomed.

When we arrived, Bob's mother-in-law answered the door; he was standing behind her. As soon as Rachel and I introduced ourselves, this woman's anger became obvious—not just about her daughter's death, but about everything. She went on and on about the hospital and the doctors who "killed" her daughter, saying there was "nothing good in the world" now that her daughter was dead. I wanted to point out that she had a grandson who was proof that there was some good in the world, but I'm not one to lecture anyone on how they should feel pain. Their situation was different than mine, and since I didn't have all the details, I just nodded in agreement and attempted to talk to Bob. Besides, I had definitely learned since Liz died that everyone grieves differently.

When I got Bob away from her, his entire demeanor changed. He went from quiet and withdrawn to talking vivaciously about the woman he loved who had died not long after giving birth to their child. Our kids played in his living room, and he walked me around his house, showing me photos of his wife, telling me bittersweet stories of their time together, and talking lovingly about his son. He was so much different than I had pictured him after meeting his mother in September. I assumed he'd be sullen and angry, but despite his circumstances he actually seemed pretty happy. And he was unabashedly grateful for the money that we brought to him. He thanked us, and as he walked us out he offered to help us in any way that he could in getting the foundation off the ground.

I felt pretty fucking good as we drove away from Bob's house. "This is your mother's legacy," I would be able to tell Maddy later. "This is how we will honor her."

Madeline was asleep when we arrived at the house. After an emotional Thanksgiving trip home and now a late-night arrival, I was thrilled to finally be back in Los Angeles. I gently placed her on the floor next to the couch and did my usual inspection. I went from room to room, checking out the cleaning our friend Elizabeth had done while we were away. I walked into Madeline's room and saw three huge plastic bags filled with clothes that no longer fit her. More donations, I thought. I couldn't believe how big my kid was getting. There was a time when I thought she'd never outgrow her clothes—never grow *into* them—but here I was, reminded of the fact that life goes on, whether or not we expect it to.

I stood in her doorway, staring down the hallway at the photos of my life with Liz that lined the wall to my right. I looked to my left. This wall was completely empty; I was waiting to paint it before I started covering it with memories, too. The door to my bedroom was closed, just as it had been for the past five and a half months. I'd managed to almost completely avoid stepping foot inside since returning from our trip to Minnesota in June. I looked down at the multicolored paper

cranes that had been hanging from a string on the doorknob
since the day of Liz's funeral, and I decided that tonight was
the night. It was time to move from the couch; it was time to
go back to my bed.

Holding my breath and closing my eyes, I opened the door
to the bedroom. I breathed the room in for the first time in
months, smelling the mixture of Liz's perfumes. The individual
scents of Beautiful by Estée Lauder, Glamorous by Ralph Lau-
ren, and that Marc Jacobs perfume without the name. I opened
my eyes, and the room was just as I'd left it five months ago.
Her closet door was cracked open, but I avoided looking inside,
unwilling to lay my eyes on her piles of dirty laundry or the
bags of clothes back from the dry cleaners waiting for her to
jump into them.

I looked at the wall on my side of the bed. Hanging there
was a photo from our high school days that Deb had given us
as a wedding gift back in 2005. We were sitting on the dock
at the Goodmans' cabin, and I was demonstrating to Liz how
she should put a worm on the hook at the end of the fishing
line. I was laughing; she was squirming. It was such a perfect
representation of our life together.

I looked around at the furniture, a bunch of rickety used
shit we got from one of Liz's coworkers. We both hated it and
had vowed to replace it as soon as we had the money and time
to do so. It would be my next redecorating project.

I could see a note on her dresser, the one I had written to her
promising a new necklace from Tiffany's for Valentine's Day.
I'd been so busy with work and with taking care of her that I
hadn't been able to pick one up in time. Liz understood, and
she was just grateful to have me around to wait on her during
her bed rest. But she sure as hell would have collected on that
as soon as our life had stabilized.

Everything in the room was so familiar, yet it felt then

that I'd discovered a set of ancient ruins after hacking my way through the thickest of jungle plants.

I looked at the bed. Damn, that thing looked comfortable, especially after so many months on the couch. We had been so happy to finally have a king-sized bed after years of sleeping together in the full bed I purchased back in grad school. I used to imagine us, the three of us, watching Saturday morning cartoons in this bed, but not *Pokémon* and all that other modern anime shit, no. I wanted Madeline exposed to the cartoons I watched as a kid: *The Jetsons*, *The Smurfs*, *Woody Woodpecker*, and of course, the good old-fashioned violence of *Tom and Jerry*. I sat down on the edge of the bed and let the numbness overcome me. I wasn't sad, and I wasn't crying. I sort of felt relieved that I had finally walked back in here.

I brought Madeline's bassinet in from the living room and placed it next to what was my side of the bed. My side of the bed now was what used to be Liz's side of the bed. Without waking Maddy, I moved her from the car seat to the bassinet and covered her with the blanket my mom had given her. The ceiling fan was spinning fast enough to distract me from the silence; I lay there, doing my best to count the revolutions.

I couldn't help but feel proud. Over the past week I'd managed to survive the barrage of memories that came with Thanksgiving and another trip back to Minnesota. I had given away a big chunk of money to help someone else. I had once again traveled alone with my child. And now, I was finally back in our bed. As I drifted off to sleep, my phone rang, scaring the shit out of me. I looked at the clock before I answered. It was 1:25 a.m.—no one ever called me that late. But it was A.J., letting me know that Sonja had just given birth to a beautiful baby girl, Emilia. I congratulated him and told him I'd call him in the morning. I hung up smiling, knowing the happiness that had just entered their lives.

but these two days,
they may be the worst.
why?
i have no idea.
fuck...
i'm trying
and i'm sorry,
but it just
doesn't feel like
christmas without
her.

Chapter 24

One of my favorite photos of Liz is from just before our last Christmas together. She had just started showing, and she looked so goddamned gorgeous, tiny and blonde and just a little bit pregnant, standing on the steps outside my friend Nate's house and smiling down at me from the top stair. Just after I took it, she waved good-bye and left me there to have fun with my old friends while she went back to her parents' house to get some sleep. She picked me up, still in the throes of my Christmas Eve hangover, the next morning.

Liz thought Christmas was amazing.

"Matt." I could almost hear her voice, a mixture of plaintive and bossy. It was the same thing every year. "We will hang Christmas lights."

"Fuck that," I would say, resorting to the sort of persuasion that never worked, adding an equally convincing groan or eye roll.

Christmas in Los Angeles felt fake enough, especially for a Midwestern native used to snow starting in November and lasting all the way through spring. With its always-blooming flowers and ever-blue sky, Southern California just never felt like the right place to have pine needles on the floor. It was weird to wear shorts to pick up a tree. Besides, we headed to Minnesota for Christmas every year—we wouldn't even be around for the actual days requiring the tree. This was my most valid argument.

"Matt," she would say again—she was fond of using my name when making a point—"Matt, we will hang Christmas lights. We will have a tree. It is Christmas. I don't care that we are going to Minneapolis. I want a tree."

And so we found ourselves, every year, in the lot at Target buying a tree that (1) was fucking annoying to drag home, (2) would shed its needles all over the house, and (3) definitely would not be seen on Christmas. But this was just another example of us. Yes, Liz could be cynical, but when it came to the holidays, she was 100 percent sincere. She went crazy for that shit, using her own brand of merry peppiness to counteract my Grinch-like attitude.

"We can hire someone to put the lights up," she had said just a year ago.

"And we'll have to hire someone to take them down again," I responded. "Liz! We don't need lights!" I could also use her name to make a point.

Now here I was, a year later, looking at our bare roof by myself and I could not believe that I had been such an ass as to deny my pregnant wife some fucking lights on her *last Christmas*. Fuck, I thought. What was wrong with me? What would have been the harm in letting someone decorate our house? I wouldn't have had to do any work, and Liz would have paid for it. Why did I put up such a fight?

The year before that, though, I had been in Bangalore during the holidays, and Liz had flown out to see me. It was our first Christmas away from our families, and I wanted her to be her usual happy holiday self. I decided to surprise her because I felt bad about taking us so far away during her favorite time of the year. I went out in the city and bought a shitload of decorations. I got a little tiny Christmas tree, maybe a foot high, sparse branches—it was fucking ugly, with a wooden base that was painted yellow, red, and green, like some Rastafarian Charlie Brown Christmas tree—and these gorgeous cardboard stars that folded out with holes so light could shine through. They were all over the city at this time of the year. My tiny apartment on this noisy street in Bangalore was about as far away from snowy suburban Minnesota as we could get.

I picked Liz up from the airport and brought her through the raucous calling of car horns, through the thick smell of diesel smoke, into a place that was completely unfamiliar at a time of year when we were used to going home. When she opened the door and saw the fully decorated room, she started crying, dropped her purse on the ground, and jumped into my arms. The only thing that might've surprised her more would've been seeing her entire family waiting inside.

Now, just two years later, I was in Los Angeles on a block with Spanish-style houses and palm trees, staring at an empty roof. I wished I could go back in time and cover it so thickly with lights that Liz would have been able to see it all the way from the plane to Minneapolis. I wished I hadn't been such an ass about it.

A week before Christmas, I dressed Maddy in a red and white striped onesie and brought her to the parking lot of the

Target in Eagle Rock to buy a tree. Even though it was a pain in the ass to drag home by myself, especially with a baby in tow, even though there would be pine needles all over the floor that I would have to clean up, and even though we weren't going to be there on Christmas Day, I wanted Madeline's first Christmas to be as much like it would have been with Liz around. My kid looked like a fucking candy cane, but I knew her mom would have loved it.

As happy as I tried to be for Madeline, the shopping trip was excruciating. There were dads and moms and kids everywhere, pointing and running and laughing, and my heart was just...broken. Obliterated. Ground up into a fine paste. Their Christmases would be perfect, their families intact. They may not have appreciated that, and I daydreamed about telling them that they should. I wanted to give up on the holiday, to just say fuck it and drive home. Maddy wouldn't remember this Christmas anyway, and besides, we'd be in Minnesota in a few days.

But I stayed. I chose a tree and dragged it over to the car, because none of this was for me. All I could think about was how I had always given Liz shit about loving Christmas. Why the hell couldn't I just let my wife enjoy the holidays? I mean, I still hated this shit—I wasn't suddenly going to go out caroling for the neighbors. This was for Madeline; this was what Liz would have done.

As I struggled to get the immensely cumbersome thing into the living room, the needles scattering everywhere, I heard her: "Matt, of course we're going to get a tree. It's for Madeline! She needs to know about Santa Claus."

So I bought the goddamned tree, and I told Madeline about jolly St. Nick. And a couple of days later we were on our way to the airport.

* * *

Every Christmas Eve when we got back to Minneapolis, Liz's parents picked us up from the airport, we stopped over for a snack, and then she and I headed over to Nate's. Going to his place was a big part of our end-of-December tradition, and when I got to his front steps this year, I froze. I saw Liz standing at the top of them, looking at me as she did when I snapped that photo of her with the Polaroid camera she bought me for my thirtieth birthday. Flushed, glowing, happy. It was one of those eerie time-machine moments where everything was wrong, but I couldn't fix it. Everything at Nate's was the same as it had always been, but all without Liz. And so the most basic action, something I had done hundreds of times before—just bounding up those stairs—felt impossible.

I had expected the family stuff to be difficult. I had expected it to be impossible to sit in my mother's living room exchanging gifts, imagining that Liz was sitting on the couch while everyone cooed over our daughter and gave her enough presents for the next ten Christmases. I had not expected it to break my heart to walk up to Nate's porch on Christmas Eve.

What the hell could I do? I went inside. I had a couple of beers. I cracked some jokes. I did what we had done every year. I needed my friends to talk to me like it was okay, and like I was okay. I didn't want sympathy. I just wanted to laugh.

When it was my turn to get more beer, I went to the refrigerator and on the door, I saw a picture of Liz smiling and pointing at her pregnant belly in our backyard. Just below the photo were two dates separated by a hyphen. It was the program from her funeral, and it was the last thing I needed to see right then. I grabbed the beers and went back out to the living room, the sounds of vintage Paul Westerberg crackling

through Nate's shitty bookshelf stereo speakers. I clanked bottles with the guys, and sat down without a word.

This gathering was without question my favorite part of
Christmas—no decorations, no overzealous happiness. Just
good conversation and drinking with friends. When I was
there, I didn't feel different. Sure, things were different, but I
was somehow the same. The night before I descended into the
maelstrom of family, my child was safe with her grandparents,
and I was safe in the circle of my friends.

I remembered how Liz would roll her eyes when she hung
out here with us, hearing the same stories a thousand times.
I loved that. She would get tired early and want to get home
while the rest of us reverted to our college selves. And I'd keep
saying, "Just a few more minutes, just a few more minutes,"
until she'd really had enough and left me there to sleep on the
couch, summoning me the next morning at eight with a phone
call or a text message, ready to drag me into the day of Christmas festivities.

Just like last year, I woke up on the couch. Just like last
year, I woke up to a phone ringing a bit too early for my liking.
And though I knew that it was my mom calling and not Liz,
I felt ready to join my family and to spend my daughter's first
Christmas with the spirit my wife would have wanted me to
have.

Chapter 25

I had been joining the Goodman family on their yearly vacations to Mexico since I was nineteen years old. To me, back then, they were a revelation. My family didn't travel this way. We'd go up north sometimes with my mom to my grandpa's cabin on Lake Mille Lacs, or canoeing in the boundary waters with my dad, but there were no group outings to Mexico. We didn't explore the ruins of ancient civilizations or swim in the Gulf. We'd had our own kinds of adventures, like shooting cans with BB guns and catching crayfish, but traveling outside the country was just never in our playbook.

This annual trip was an incredibly important tradition for Liz's family. Candee's side was mostly based in Minnesota, so it was easy for them to gather together for holidays and reunions, but Tom's was scattered all around the country, east, west, and north. The yearly trip to Akumal was how they stayed connected and close. Once it was clear that Liz and I were in love, I became part of the family—and thus part of the family trip. Every year, thirty of us would fly down, hang out together on the beach, and relax.

Now we were here, but Liz was not. I had spent plenty of time with her parents and her sister many times over the years, but this was really the first time I would be with Tom's extended family since the funeral, and it shook me. Knowing I'd see these familiar faces without Liz was difficult to comprehend. Being in Mexico at all felt like a really big deal. I had learned how to navigate Minnesota and Los Angeles, but this trip was my first attempt at visiting the places we shared abroad. If I could do this, I knew, I could do anything.

So much had changed since Liz died. It was fucking insane, really. Now, on this trip, two important things were happening simultaneously, and I was doing both in her honor. The first was that I was here with Maddy, sharing more things and places that her mother had cherished. The second was that we were about to officially launch the Liz Logelin Foundation. After Rachel and I decided to really go through with the non-profit, we organized a board of directors to get it off the ground and keep it running: me, her, Liz's parents, Anya, Elizabeth, Jackie, A.J., and a few blog readers. Even though one-fourth of the board was in Mexico, business had to happen anyway.

If Maddy was my first priority, the foundation was now the clear second. This meant that not even the lure of the sparkling blue waters or the temptation of a cold Pacifico on the beach could keep me off the phone when work needed to be done. Maddy played in the sun with Deb while I ducked off to the corner to discuss website details with A.J.

"It's launched," said A.J.

"I can't see it," I said.

"Shit, you should be able to see it now!" The trip was nearing its end, and A.J. had been busy in the States making sure the site was going to go live on time. He had been working diligently for the past few hours while I sat on the beach watching my daughter try to decide if she liked the taste of sand.

"I can't see it because there's no Internet access," I said. "Don't forget I'm in Mexico, fucker."

"Funny," he said.

"Thank you so much, A.J." My tone was serious now, as was I. We never would have gotten the site up in time if it weren't for that guy. If it hadn't launched that week, we would have missed out on a ton of important media attention that would help shine a light on the cause we were working so hard to illuminate.

"What now?"

"Now we wait and see," I said. I was eager to find out what kind of traffic we would get, and if people would embrace our new nonprofit. But there was nothing I could do about it from that beach in Mexico, so I was determined to make the rest of our vacation exactly that: a vacation.

We gathered up the family, strapped Maddy into her car seat, gave her a bottle of bottled water, and drove south to Tulum. We stopped along the way, posing for ridiculous photos at the side of the road, like one of Maddy perched in front of a huge mural depicting a woman in a yellow bikini and a monkey in a striped baseball cap holding beer bottles.

Now we were taking Madeline to another one of the geographical markers on the mental map of my life with Liz. And just like everywhere else, in Tulum, time had moved on without us. The town had exploded. There were more tourist stalls than I ever remembered, many more, and a whole new slew of restaurants with every kind of cuisine imaginable.

This part of the trip wasn't for me. We drove down here so I could show Maddy the incredible, ancient ruins full of bloody history and legions of untold stories that her mother and I had explored together. Back before they were fenced in, we would climb up the steps of the main temple and walk into the great palace—and to a Midwestern kid, well, that was just incredible. I was a teenager, I was in love, and I was learning how much I enjoyed things like travel and discovering other cultures, which, until I met Liz, I hadn't even thought about at all. When I was nineteen, the puzzle that was my world was just being assembled. At age thirty, it had been blown apart, and now I was trying to fit everything back together smoothly.

I unbuckled the car seat and carried my daughter into an open-air restaurant, asking the hostess for a seat in the shade. Maddy was playing with a new toy that Tom and Candee had brought for her, a little hammer that said "ouch" when you hit it against something. She gripped it in her palm and pounded me lightly on the shoulder while the waiter set up a high chair.

Settling in, we ordered guacamole and chips while Maddy's strange little anthropomorphic hammer looked at me with its big eyes, saying "ouch, ouch" over and over again. Maddy laughed and I laughed with her. I thought of how Liz would have loved to sit there with us, would have loved to laugh with me at the tourists with their money belts and fanny packs, and then laugh harder about how we were tourists judging other people for being tourists.

The chips came, and we ate them while Maddy gummed the mesh bag with the mashed-up banana I had packed for her. I could feel Liz in Tulum, but I was solidly in this moment, sharing with our daughter this place that we had loved together.

Sitting there, I was suddenly cast into the past. I recalled it being hot, too hot to hold hands, but I couldn't pinpoint exactly what I was remembering. I could feel the memory's roundness, how our palms were too damp to cling, but I'd misplaced the latitude and the longitude. I couldn't give it a date or affix it firmly to any specific trip we'd taken here before.

I knew that I had been here with her, but I didn't know when. The when became bigger and more important the longer we sat there waiting for our lunch, and even though I was chatting, even though I was answering and asking questions, even though I was feeding Maddy, my mind couldn't stop asking the question over and over again.

When?

I was smiling, but I was sad and I was angry. What the fuck was I going to do when Maddy asked me questions about her mom? I couldn't place this moment. What else would I forget? What else had I already forgotten? A shit pile of memories lost to time and buried by new ones without her in them. I felt as though my brain had a limited capacity to remember.

When Liz had been alive, it was limitless.

Or maybe it just seemed that way. Back then, I just hadn't felt like I needed to remember the small details of every experience, because we would have forever together and a lifetime more of them. But now, I had to remember everything to be the keeper of the past for our daughter. I wished I had recorded it all so that those stories I didn't think to preserve would have been waiting for me—waiting for Madeline. I was terrified they were all gone.

I tried to tell myself that was why I was sitting here with Maddy, because a place and the company can hold the memories, too. But I felt like I was losing Liz more with every breath that took me further away from her last.

We were eating chips and an array of red and green salsas,

laughing at Maddy as she hit her blue hammer against the table. The sun was bright in the blue sky, my daughter beating a staccato rhythm, but I was lost in what was missing, in this vague idea of *not being able to hold hands because it was too hot.* My palms were slippery now.

If Liz were here, I would make her hold my hand, even if the sweat dripped off of them like we had just emerged from the ocean.

A few days later we were on our way to the lagoon, and Liz's voice popped into my head. *Don't be such a pussy.* It then added, *Don't be such a bitch.*

Liz had loved this lagoon, especially for snorkeling. The saltwater from the ocean mixed with the freshwater streaming out of the nearby jungle, providing a bounty of creatures we could spy on until our eyes bugged out behind our plastic goggles or until the skin on our backs was red and raw from the strong sun—whichever came first.

I held Maddy in my arms as we approached, smoothing a bit of sunscreen that hadn't absorbed into her tiny white shoulders. Usually on these journeys, Liz would be looking out for me, making sure that I had remembered the SPF 15. Now I had to make sure I wouldn't burn, and I was responsible for keeping Maddy as covered up as possible, too. I was using SPF 65, just to be safe.

On the path to the water, I felt dulled without Liz's excitement, her bubbling laughter as she skipped ahead. More changes were all around me, unexpected changes, like the tacky sculptures placed at odd intervals among the plants, making it look more like a mall with a jungle theme than a place of natural beauty.

Candee found a spot for us to drop our bags and held out her arms for Maddy. I handed my daughter over and then stood there in the sunlight and silence, thinking about the difficulty of being there without Liz. What Tom must be thinking. What Candee must be thinking as our baby squirmed and chattered in her arms. What Deb must be thinking as we prepared to enter the water. How could we be here without her? How could any of this exist without her? Why are we not all crying every second of the day?

I knew how fucking useless these questions were, because I knew what the answers were. Taking trips together, eating at the restaurants we loved, swimming in the lagoon, giggling with Maddy, finding ways to smile when all we wanted to do was break down and wail. I knew already that these were not coping mechanisms; they were survival techniques. Without them, I might not have made it to this point. I would have just stayed in my house, like many of the widows I knew, losing weight until I was more skeleton than human, moping around until I was just an outline of the person I had been before Liz died.

I stepped carefully down the stairs that hadn't been there two years ago and shivered as my legs slid into the cold water. I put the fins on, standing awkwardly on one foot and then the other, then picked up my snorkel and mask, fitting it over my head easily and securely.

It felt simple and natural, exactly the opposite of the first time I had gone snorkeling with Liz so many years ago. She was an old hand at the sport, while I was just a simple guy more used to catching fish on a frozen lake than dressing like an alien in order to peer at them below the water's surface. I remembered being in the lagoon with her, and while she'd floated, peaceful and steady, I had been flustered, anxious, uncoordinated, and completely unable to breathe through the mouthpiece. Water got into my goggles and into my lungs, and I came up spluttering repeatedly, the taste of saltwater making me gag.

Liz had lifted her head up. Bobbing in the waves, she pulled off the breathing apparatus and looked at me with her big blue eyes.

"What the fuck?" she'd said. She was laughing and I was trying to breathe again. "You suck at snorkeling?"

"I have no idea what I am doing," I'd said. "I think something's wrong with mine."

She had taken it and looked it over. "There's nothing wrong with it. Toughen up!" It was such a Liz thing to say. "I've been doing this since I was a child," she'd added for good measure.

As soon as she'd said it, the mental picture had come: a little blonde mermaid zipping around scaring the fish. I rolled my eyes at her, and she rolled hers at me in response, placing the strange device back into my wet palm and pulling her mask down over her face.

Now, I pulled my own mask over my face, partly because I wanted to jump in, and partly so that Liz's family wouldn't see my face tightening like I was about to start bawling, although crying in the water actually made a lot of sense if I wanted to keep my feelings to myself.

Liz was always on me to learn how to do things and to push myself in new and unfamiliar ways. She was my guide into a world I had never been in, sometimes literally in locations, other times figuratively when it came to activities that I had never even considered before I met her. As I thought about her, I rubbed the scar that ran down the inside of my left ring finger. It was a faint reminder that she never hesitated to tell me to "take off the skirt" if she thought it was warranted.

It was exactly the kind of memory I wanted to hold on to forever, and I knew that even if I ended up a doddering old fool in a nursing home with all of my brain cells compressed and inactive, the scar would remind me of how much fun we had together, and of how much I had grown during the years she shared and shaped my life.

Just a few years before we were married, we had been swimming and playing around in the ocean with a football on another of these annual trips to Mexico.

She had tossed the ball to me, and it wobbled through the sky, haloed by the sun against the azure Akumal skies. I'd reached up to catch it like a valiant wide receiver in the last seconds of the game, but I fell backward into a jagged bunch of coral. The football flew over me, my hands flew back behind me, and I very painfully cut my finger. I mean, that shit fucking *hurt*. The saltwater rushed over the fresh wound, terrorizing my newly severed nerve endings. It was a clean slice, and it was bleeding like crazy.

"Fuck," I'd hollered, holding on to my finger like it was going to fall off. "Fuck!"

I'd jumped up and down as if on fire. Liz had not been impressed by my performance. "Don't be such a pussy." She'd said it straight out. It had been one of those moments. It wasn't that she didn't care when I was hurt—nobody worried about me more than Liz—but she was a smart woman. She had known it wasn't so bad. She had known it could have been a lot worse. At the time, I had thought it was the worst thing that had ever happened to me, like Maddy did now when she was tired or wet or hungry.

I'd looked down again. The scar was about an inch long, starting in the middle of my finger, and stopping just above the platinum ring that bound me to my wife.

"Toughen up," she had said to me then.

I thought about her words, and then I dove in and swam to the middle of the lagoon.

I could hear her family entering the water at the shore, but I didn't wait for them. I knew Madeline would be safe with

Candee. Treading water, I spit into my snorkel mask, rubbing the little white bubbles around and around on the inside of the lens, a trick that Liz taught me to keep the plastic from fogging over. I rinsed the mask and placed it over my face, tightening the straps until I could feel them digging into the sides of my head, and took off toward the ocean.

I swam and swam, remembering the unofficial races we used to have here. They had silent starts—Liz would swim past me, stirring up what little competitiveness I had in my body. Jesus, she was so much better at this than I am. She had been a swimmer in high school and college, whereas I had been out of shape since at least 1996. I glided through the water now, kicking my flippered feet, and here in this place, with so many memories, with quiet, clear water enveloping me, and the song "In the Aeroplane over the Sea" running through my head, I felt an incredible peace—a peace I hadn't felt since last March.

In the next few seconds, I learned that no matter how pure one's sudden inner calmness, and no matter how much spit one smears on the plastic, it's absolutely impossible to see anything while weeping inside a snorkeling mask.

I resurfaced, slipped it off my face, and used my salty, wet hands to wipe my eyes. Then I swam back toward where Madeline was splashing around with Tom and Deb. Candee was sitting on a towel at the shore, beaming from behind her over-sized sunglasses.

I swam up to Deb and held out my arms to Maddy. "Oooooooooh," she called, reaching toward me.

She came to me, slippery and squealing, my little blonde mermaid.

that sunset-
sunrise cycle is so
emblematic of this
whole fucking mess.
sadness about
the darkness, the loss of light,
but happiness about
the return of
the light...
then the sun
sets again and
we're left with
the darkness that
invades our world
every night.
and then the sunlight,
oh that sunlight.
it is so
fucking beautiful.

Chapter 26

I was determined that March 24 would be a day of celebration. Few things were more important to me than making sure that Madeline's birth date and Liz's death date were separated in my mind and in the minds of everyone who interacted with her. I knew this would become more important as my daughter got older. No child should be deprived of something as special as a birthday, especially after being deprived of her mother.

Just as I'd had to get away for what would have been our third anniversary, I knew I had to get away for this, too. From the day that Liz died, I had been great about sharing Madeline with our friends and family, trying to ensure that she was around to help them with their grieving processes. But for Madeline's first birthday and the one-year anniversary of Liz's death, I had to do it alone. I wanted to be the one who made her first birthday as amazing as possible; I wanted to be the one who made the decisions about how it would be celebrated.

Well, sort of alone. I talked to A.J., asking if he, Sonja, and Emilia would like to join us in our travels. Liz and I had been talking to them about a trip like this for years, but we had never gotten around to going. There was always next year, soon, or someday, but now we all knew that the future was not guaranteed. So instead of their usual spring ski trip with A.J.'s family, we all went back to where Maddy and I had been just a few months earlier. Back to Akumal.

The truth was, we could have gone anywhere in the world to celebrate my daughter's birthday—we could have gone to Egypt to see the pyramids or to Moscow to see Red Square. A.J. was on spring break from his job as a technology coordinator at a school in Minneapolis; Sonja could take time off from her gig as a pediatrician; I had made some money from putting ads on my blog; and Maddy and Emilia were just babies without any prior engagements. Nothing was keeping us from trekking through the Himalayas or sampling the local fare in Cambodia or any of the other numerous and pleasurable things that one can do when one has time, friends whose company is a joy, and available cash.

But after a year spent retracing Liz's steps through Minneapolis, through Los Angeles, and, recently, along the coast of Mexico, I had discovered that it was in the place where we vacationed with her family every year that I felt her spirit the most keenly, the most purely. So back to Mexico we went. Maddy wasn't quite a year old, not yet, but this was her second trip abroad in just a few months. In her short life so far, she had already accumulated almost ten thousand frequent-flier miles, which meant that she would be better traveled by her first birthday than I had been at age twenty.

It was hot and humid the day we arrived, and we stood there for a moment, blinking in the sun outside the airport, a ragtag group consisting of two boys masquerading as grown men, two actual babies, and one beautiful woman. That poor woman, passersby must have thought, imagining that she would have to spend her vacation taking care of all of us.

But I wasn't going to be coddled and catered to like I had been on every single trip to Mexico with Liz's family. When you travel with a group like theirs, things just happen magically—well, because someone else manages all of the arrangements and shoulders the hassles. On this trip, I didn't just want to go along for the ride. I appointed myself the driver, the travel agent, the financier, and even sometimes the babysitter.

"Who needs water?" I asked, making myself useful from the moment we arrived. I put Maddy's passport and mine in the safest place in my backpack, and settled my friends in the shade.

"I'm going to get the car," I announced. There was no way I was going to make them suffer in the shuttle to the place where our rental was parked. I hoisted Maddy up, holding her securely with my right arm. I could just bring her car seat, I had decided while the plane taxied, and drive back with her to pick up the rest of the group.

"Leave her with us," said Sonja in her best let's-be-reasonable voice. "Why should she have to take the shuttle?"

"She's going to go nuts when I leave. And you guys have your own kid to worry about," I said, even though I knew Sonja was right. This was not how my SuperDad routine was supposed to progress. If I could have pulled it off without looking like a crazy car seat juggler, I would have insisted that Emilia come with me, too, sending Sonja and A.J. to have a margarita and meet us at the condo later.

But Sonja's plan prevailed, and the four of them waited for me at the airport while I argued with the rental officials at a location that felt a thousand miles from the airport. It took two hours to get the car, an hour and a half to drive to our condo in Akumal, and another hour to settle the kids down, change out of our sweaty travel garb, and unpack our suitcases.

I had remembered almost everything we needed for Madeline to have a great birthday: the sunscreen, her cute little bathing suits, bathing suit cover-ups, and even her hat with the extra-broad, extra-floppy brim. But I had forgotten to bring a box of cake mix so I could bake her a birthday cake in Akumal, an omission that clashed sorely with my desire to be the perfect father to my baby as she turned one. Disappointed that I'd forgotten this integral detail, I gave up on unpacking.

We got settled in as quickly as possible and made our way to the white lounge chairs on the beach to stare out at the ocean, at least half a day of sun still ahead of us. That night, as our babies fell asleep in our arms and the sun started to set, I looked around at my friends, and I felt . . . good. I felt like an adult. Like I was taking care of things. By recognizing when I needed help, and by being able to ask for it. By inviting others to go away with me instead of always accepting invitations to go away with others. By remembering on my own to pack the SPF 65. Now I really felt like I was following Liz's lead by not following anyone's lead at all.

Sonja kept trying to give me time alone with A.J., but I didn't need a best-friend comfort zone. I needed to feel capable—to feel in charge. I had spent the past year being worried about and catered to, and now I wanted to spend some time thinking about someone else.

"Come on, guys," she said in the mornings, while we idled over café con leche and freshly cut mango. "Go explore the village. Go hang out. I've got the girls."

"No, no," I would retort. "You guys go. I've got them. I want to do some writing, anyway."

On March 24, Sonja baked a cake for Maddy's birthday. It had white frosting, rainbow-colored sprinkles, and a Winnie-the-Pooh–adorned candle in the shape of the number one. She had brought all of the supplies with her from Minnesota—I had no idea she'd planned anything at all. It was like she knew I was going to forget this detail. I stared at the candle. My baby wasn't five or seven or eleven months anymore, I thought to myself. She was one. One whole year old. It didn't seem possible. She was no longer the fragile creature I had worried over, the tiny baby behind glass with tubes and electrodes protruding from her body. She was a hearty, healthy, happy child. I thought about the year that had just gone by, and I couldn't even begin to fathom how we had gotten here. I mean, most of the details were clear, but for the first time I wondered how the fuck we actually did it. We made it here together, but I felt like Madeline had done all the hard work. She'd had to eat, grow, and build new synapses—she'd had to be my everything through the most difficult year of my life.

I smiled through the tears as we sang "Happy Birthday." I couldn't help it—my mind drifted to Liz. I kept thinking that Maddy should be hearing her mom sing this song to her. I shook the thoughts from my head and helped her blow out her candle. Then I hung back and let Madeline tear into her birthday cake—the one I forgot, the one that Sonja remembered. In the process, she somehow wound up sitting on it; I shook my head with mock disgust, but I couldn't be angry because my daughter had just tasted cake for the first time and was wearing one of the biggest smiles I'd ever seen on her face. Looking at her at that moment, I remembered what my mom used to say when she was trying to convince me and Liz to give her a grandkid. "You'll never feel love like the love you have for your child."

After Madeline had gone down for the evening and everyone else had said good night and gone to bed, I wandered out to the patio to enjoy a Pacifico and looked up, searching the sky for anything familiar. I rubbed my ring finger, tracing my scar where I knew it was, even though it was too dark to see it. And then I went to sleep, thinking of Liz, thinking of what I had lost, and thinking of what I had gained.

When I woke up the next morning, it, of course, was March 25. Fifty-two weeks since Liz died. Three hundred sixty-five days since my world imploded. I didn't know how I should have felt as I lay in bed, watching the ceiling fan make the brightly colored tapestry flap against the wall. I felt numb again. How strange that an accumulation of days and weeks could somehow add up to one year since my beautiful wife died, one year since my beautiful daughter was born. Madeline was still asleep, but I picked her up from the twin bed next to mine anyway. She remained sleeping as I held her close to my chest and lay back down in my bed. I needed my baby.

I woke up to her hungry whines. I wasn't sure how long I'd fallen back asleep for, but it felt like years. I got up and walked out to the kitchen to boil some milk for Madeline. A.J. and Sonja were drinking their coffee on the couch with Emilia, and the scent of eggs and onions was in the air.

The five of us sat on the patio enjoying the breakfast they had made. It felt weird to think of us as an odd-numbered group. I couldn't get it out of my mind that there should have been six of us at the table as I filled another tortilla with the egg concoction. We said nothing, letting the clanging of silverware against the plates and the crashing of the waves on the beach do all of the talking. Everyone seemed to be waiting for someone else to speak first. I hadn't thought much about what we should do on this day, but sitting there bouncing Madeline on my knee, I knew we had to go to the lagoon.

We carried our daughters to the place where we'd spend the afternoon, finding a spot to set up our stuff. We took turns looking after Maddy and Emilia so that each of us had ample time to swim in the gorgeous, clear waters. It was just as pleasant to sit near the trees and watch the babies coo at the birds in the trees above them, or to try to engage them in conversation even though all they could do was babble.

While Emilia slept on a towel in the shade, I held Maddy in my arms, telling her about her mom even though I knew she had no clue what the hell I was saying. I told her how Liz had walked through these trees and that her feet had touched the dirt upon which we now sat. I told her about the time we swam through a crack in that huge rock, discovering a part of the lagoon where there were no other humans. We had a physical connection to this place; now, with every breath I took, I felt closer to Liz, not further away.

That night we had a nice dinner together, talking mostly about Liz. It felt good to be here with my best friend and his family. When we got back to the condo, Sonja suggested that A.J. and I take a walk to the bar down the street. She would watch the sleeping girls so we could have a drink or two. I submitted only because it was the twenty-fifth and I could really use a walk.

We headed over and sat down at a long wooden table on the beach, hoping to have a quiet night and a couple of beers. Instead, we were assaulted by the sounds of high school kids on spring break singing awful karaoke versions of shit songs like "Don't Stop Believin'" and "Livin' on a Prayer." But it was actually perfect. We'd been quiet most of the day, and we both needed the distraction.

I ordered a beer and A.J. a margarita, and we laughed, watching eighteen-year-olds trying to sneak drinks when their parents weren't looking. As the alcohol flowed, the singing got louder and so did our laughter. Karaoke is supposed to be bad, but this shit was aggravating. I have absolutely no patience for crappy music, so after an hour of ear abuse, I was ready to go.

When we stood up A.J. said, "Hey, remember that New Year's Eve when we played Karaoke Revolution?"

"Liz loved that fucking game."

"She even got you to sing," he said, with a devious look in his eyes and a smirk on his face.

I knew where he was going with this. "Well, I'd had a few more drinks that night. You know damn well that you'll never hear me sing again."

"I'm going up there. With or without you."

"Without me. Wait. You're not even drunk?"

"I have no shame."

He went to the front of the place and started in with his standard karaoke song: "Bust a Move." This had been Liz's favorite bar in the entire world. She loved sitting on the swings, gripping a Corona Light in one hand, her bare feet not even close to touching the sand below her. I never saw her have more than one beer at a bar, my dainty little lady with the mouth of a truck driver. We'd talk about coming down here with the children we didn't yet have, and if things worked out well for us, someday retiring here. Fuck, I thought, those dreams evaporated one year ago today. A.J. finished off one of the most horrifically awesome versions of the Young MC song, and it was officially time to get out of there.

I stacked our luggage neatly in the back of the rental car, strapped Madeline securely into her car seat, and climbed into the driver's seat to wait for my friends. It was time to get back to our real lives. Mexico had been the right place to come. Here, Liz and I had learned that our relationship was not just grounded in Minneapolis, not just caught up in our high school years, not just based on our homegrown, hometown crushes.

Over the past few weeks, as this anniversary had approached, I had noticed some kind of resolution creeping into the voices of the people I talked to every day. Like we had made it to the end of the race, or that everything would now be better. Well, I could confirm that everything was just as it had been before the twenty-fifth. I was never going to not miss Liz, but during this trip I had realized that there was a way to hang on and let go at the same time. That I could retain all of the positive parts of my love for Liz without gripping so tightly to her memory that I cut off the oxygen flow to other parts of me.

In the five minutes it took for A.J. and Sonja to find Emilia's missing pacifier, I figured out that I would mourn Liz for the rest of my life. I figured out that it would get easier to mourn her. I figured out that the unending anguish I felt would gradually become less intolerable. It would get more comfortable, this memory that I carried. It would fold itself into my blood, into my cells, into my DNA. My heart would pump it and my veins would carry it, every moment, all the time.

In my head I apologized to Liz for forgetting Maddy's cake, and promised her that I would never do that again. Then I promised her that I would never move on. And right there in the rental car in the driveway of the condo, I switched my wedding band from my left hand to my right, where it will remain until the day I die, and I promised her that I would keep on learning how to move through. For her. For me. For Madeline.

i'm dreaming of soap,
warm water and
a wash cloth
as some asshole
hands madeline
a cupcake with
green frosting.
it was something
she had no
intention of eating,
and i knew it.

Chapter 27

Madeline deserved a day that was just about her. I had to keep those two landmarks entirely separate, and the trip to Mexico had really been for Liz and for me, too. The proximity of Madeline's birthday to her mother's death was something she would be dealing with for the rest of her life, but I didn't want her to ever feel overshadowed when we commemorated her life and her accomplishments.

I also felt a bit guilty for taking Maddy away to celebrate her birthday in Mexico, so having a second party at our house seemed like the best way to make it up to all of our friends and family. Even before we had purchased the plane tickets, I knew that I would want to celebrate her first birthday at our house in a major way when we returned. Actually, that's an understatement—I wanted to make sure my daughter had the best fucking party we could possibly throw.

All the grandparents came out from Minnesota, and Deb came down from San Francisco. There was a fair amount of preparation to be done in order to properly entertain a house and yard full of people, and everyone was excited to be involved in planning out the details. The grandfathers were great about finding projects around the house that I'd long neglected. On this trip they decided that I should have a new dishwasher, stove, and tankless water heater installed, and they planned to have everything done in under two days. It sounded impossible, but my dad had been a contractor since the 1970s, and I swear he could build an entire house in a week. Whenever he came to visit, especially with my stepdad and Liz's dad, too, I was ready to have my house turned into a construction zone. Deb and the grandmothers decided that the first task was cleaning up and reorganizing my house, and by the time they were done, I could see the floor in my dining room for the first time in almost a year.

As for the party itself, there was going to be ice cream, cake, party favors, and pink and blue balloons, and goldfish. Yep, live goldfish.

But the ice cream never came because the shop we ordered it from had a power outage and everything melted. The woman who was supposed to deliver Madeline's birthday cake got into a (minor) car accident on the way to my house and never made the delivery. And the goldfish? When they arrived, they already seemed to be struggling. Of course, one expects a party favor goldfish to die eventually—but at the party? Unconscionable.

Deb saved the day by picking up two cakes and a couple of buckets of ice cream from the local grocery store, and my dad grabbed a straw and blew bubbles into each of the fishbowls,

literally breathing new life into the struggling fish. I couldn't
believe it worked.

At most children's birthday parties, there are many more
adults than kids, and this one was no different. My friends,
Liz's friends, and new friends I had met through the blog were
all clustered in the backyard. There were a significant number
of children, though—enough for at least one mom to comment
that she'd never seen so many children at a one-year-old's birthday party. I thought that was pretty awesome.

It was like almost every other day in Los Angeles—sunny
and hot—and people were standing and sitting wherever they
could find some shade. The kids old enough to walk made their
way along the short trails that wound around my yard, flipping
over rocks to find lizards and throwing stones into my koi pond
when their parents weren't paying attention. The older guests
sipped beer and wine while my dad flipped burgers and bacon
and pineapple sausages on the grill. I played the good host,
walking from group to group and stopping to make a few jokes
or hold a baby. When everyone had had their fill of grilled meat
and conversation, it was finally time for cake. Remembering
how much Madeline had loved it in Mexico, I half-hoped she'd
end up on top of the cake again. The other half of me—the
clean freak half—hoped she wouldn't get her outfit dirty.

My daughter sat atop the table in her pretty denim dress,
waiting patiently as the party guests sang "Happy Birthday."
She had no idea what she was waiting for, but she knew that
she had everyone's undivided attention, and that was enough
to keep her from making any sudden moves. I looked around
at all of the people who'd assembled in our backyard, everyone
who came to share in my family's joy, and then it hit me: there
hadn't been this many people in the backyard since Liz's wake.
It was like déjà vu, but with a twist. Many of the faces sur-
rounding me had been here just a year ago—but now they

were here for a far different purpose, not dressed in dark funeral clothes, not crying. As I brought myself back to the present, a few tears flowed from my eyes.

I was crying for Liz, who would never see this birthday or any that would follow; I was crying for Madeline, who would never meet the woman I loved, the mother who had wanted to meet her so badly. I tried to shake the thoughts from my head, working hard to keep my promise of focusing today on Madeline's happiness rather than on my own sadness. But it was hard. The reminders of Liz were everywhere, and I wanted nothing more at that moment than to be our family of three.

When it came time to blow out the candle in the middle of the cake, Maddy stared at the flame, not sure what to do. She reached out, aiming her little fingers at the flickering light, and I quickly blew it out before she had a chance to learn what a second-degree burn felt like. Everyone clapped and cheered, eliciting a huge, largely toothless smile from Madeline.

In addition to constant hand washing, part of my pre-baby OCD included an aversion to messy little kids with dirty little faces. I used to get sick to my stomach when I saw a kid licking the mixture of snot and accumulated dirt from his upper lip while trying to suck the steady stream of mucus back up into his nose. Madeline had cured me of this disgust for the most part, but now I was beginning to cringe. I was fucking dreading the whole first-birthday rite-of-passage thing in which parents allow their children to purposefully smash cake in their faces and smear frosting all over everything. But I knew I had to be a fun and carefree father. I'd learned.

It began slowly. Madeline grabbed the candle, getting a little frosting on her arm. Okay, I thought, maybe she'll be satisfied with that. But she suddenly tossed it aside and started grabbing fistfuls of cake, like a bank robber trying to pick up the cash spilling from his bag as he fled the scene of the crime. She was squealing with delight as the frosting gushed through her fingers and flew in every direction while she waved her hands with excitement. Within seconds we were both absolutely covered in cake. And for a few minutes, I completely forgot about everything but Madeline's happiness.

She looked so damn proud of herself after the destruction, and truth be told, I was pretty proud of her, too. To see that smile, and to think just how far we had both come—that was enough.

The food and drinks disappeared and the sun began to set, signaling bedtime for the littlest guests at the party. After everyone was gone, the grandparents were back in their hotel rooms, and Madeline was fast asleep in her crib, I flopped down on my couch and picked up my BlackBerry for the first time in hours. There were two texts from my friend Katie. The first one read, "Buying fish food at Petco right now. Husband cursing your name as we speak. Great party. Thanks for having us." The second one, also from Katie, one hour and thirty-seven minutes later, said, "Fish is dead. Back to Petco to return food."

It's a momentous occasion in any parent's life when your child makes it through the first year, and now it was finally time to stop counting in weeks and months. My daughter was one year old, but so too was my pain. It was the first time I had thought about things on such a large scale—time had been filled with hours, days, weeks, and months, all counting back to Madeline's birth and Liz's death. It wasn't like I suddenly decided to stop marking time in small increments—before the first year of anything, there's no other way to count the passage of time. Mondays reminded me just how amazing my life was, and when the sun rose on Tuesdays, I was instantly transported to that twenty-fifth day in March when the only woman I'd ever loved died right in front of me. Each week that passed was excruciating, and each month that I confronted was yet another kick to the balls.

Yes, Maddy and I had made it through a year without Liz. But really, a year is nothing. It felt like such an arbitrary measure, especially when it was used to quantify the time since sadness had entered my life. Of course, it had also been a year since Madeline—and the happiness that only she could bring—had entered my life. I had never ever imagined I would be in the position I was in, and I wished like hell that I would someday wake from some sort of deep coma to find Liz and Madeline sitting next to me, telling me that it had all been an awful dream. But I knew that would never happen. We had officially made it through the worst fucking year of our lives. I took comfort in the fact that Madeline wouldn't really remember a goddamned thing about it. I wish I could say the same for myself, but I knew I would remember every second of it. But with a year now behind us, maybe—just maybe—we could begin to look to the future.

Restlessness suddenly got the best of me, so I walked back outside, the lights directly below the pitch of the roof illuminating the entire area. I stood in the wet grass, looking at the disaster that was my backyard. Only one thing had been missing from this party.

I closed my eyes and remembered the day we first saw this house, how Liz squeezed my hand and looked at me with eyes that told me that this was the house where we would soon start our family. I remembered the photos I took of her, standing right on those stairs—beaming with the kind of glow that only an expectant mother could have—just days before she would walk out of our house for the very last time. I remembered the look of relief on her face when she saw Madeline for the first and only time. Before I let myself remember what she looked like just after she died, I opened my eyes to emptiness.

I went back inside and headed straight for Madeline's room. I quietly opened her door, and just like I'd done every night since the day she was born, I kissed the tips of my fingers twice and touched her forehead. One kiss from me, and one from your mother. One for what could have been, and one for what will be.

Dear Madeline

It's been three years since you first changed everything. Without you in my life, I wouldn't have one at all.

You're the one who has gotten me through...
Through my darkest hours.
Through my most difficult moments.
Through the times I miss your mom the most.

Because of you I've been able to confront a lifetime of memories.

Together we've walked where she walked in Los Angeles, New York, Minneapolis, Vancouver, Akumal, Paris, Singapore, Kathmandu, Agra, and so many other places. And so many more to come, too.
I've hugged you close as I stood in the place where I met her.
I've floated with you in the same waters where I swam with her.
I've squeezed your hand as you walked the steps where I asked her to marry me.
I've held you tightly while standing where I vowed to love her forever.
I've cradled you in my arms in the place where she died.

* * *

Because of you I can wake up in the morning.
Because of you I can smile.
Because of you I am.

And when I look at you, I see so many things.
Happiness.
Hope.
A future.
And though you only met her once, I see so much of your mom
in you:

> The way you put your left hand on your hip while scolding
> me and pointing at me with your right.
> The way you say "nuh nuh nuh nuh nuh no" when I ask
> you to do something you don't want to do.
> The way you clap your hands together under your chin
> when you get excited about a cupcake.
> The blonde hair she paid so much to have.
> Your smile.
> The look in your big blue eyes when you say, "I love you
> too, daddy."

That's your mom.
You're of her.
She's in you.

And it's through this book, our travels, the memories, and the
photos that I hope you learn about the woman who loved you
more than you will ever know.

* * *

I'd give anything in the world to have her back here with us. I'd give everything. Everything but you.

Here's to a lifetime of joy.
Love,
Dad

P.S. You were a great baby. You better be an even better teenager.

This letter was originally published in 2010 for the occasion of Madeline's third bithrday.

Reading Group Guide

1. Matt tells the story of his wife's death and the first year of his life with Madeline with searing pain and a dry sense of humor. Can you think of comparable memoirs that mix emotions in a similar way? What distinguishes this book from others like it?

2. Liz and Matt spend a great deal of their relationship living apart. How do you think the physical distance during times in their relationship affected Matt in dealing with Liz's death?

3. Matt seemed ambivalent or even hostile at the thought of having a doula after bringing Madeline home from the hospital. What does that say about Matt as a person? Would you welcome the help?

4. When describing the community of people that rallied around him after Liz died, Matt draws on his background in sociology. Do you think his experiences helped him embrace these strangers as friends?

5. Matt uses a significant amount of profanity throughout the book in order to convey his feelings and to give the reader an honest view of what he was thinking at each moment. Do you think it adds to or detracts from the story? Why?

6. Gender plays a positive and a negative role in the assumptions people had when they saw Matt alone with Madeline.

How do you feel about the reactions he received? What would you think if you saw a man alone with a baby?

7. Matt had a strong reaction to Windy's assumption that Deb was Madeline's mother. What do you think of how Matt responded to the situation? What would you have done?

8. Matt travels with Madeline to many of the places he had been with Liz, but on their wedding anniversary he chooses to be in a place the two had never visited. Why do you think Matt made that decision?

9. What do you think about the way Matt handled his emotions on the night of his third wedding anniversary in Banff? How would you react in such a situation?

10. Do you think writing this book was a cathartic process for Matt, or do you think it kept him mired in sadness? Do you ever use writing as an emotional release? When?

11. As he tells this story, Matt focuses much attention on his relationship with Liz's family. Why do you think he chooses to write about them so much?

12. How would you describe this book to someone who hasn't read it? A book on grief? A parenting book? A memoir of catharsis? Is it all—or none—of these things?

13. Matt talks a lot about music. How did these details help you gain additional understanding about how Matt dealt with the tough moments in his life? To what or whom do you turn for comfort in times of distress?

14. How do you think Madeline will feel about Matt's blog and this book when she is older? Will she be happy that her father's memories exist in such a public way, or will she wish they had been kept private?

15. How would you hope your spouse or partner would react if you passed away? Did Matt succeed in building Liz her Taj Mahal?

How We Got Here
...and What Followed

It was within a month of Liz's death that the idea of writing a book first came up. I didn't feel ready at the time, but considered that maybe someday I would be. Then, I was concentrating solely on taking care of Madeline and keeping myself from completely breaking down—the last thing on my mind was writing a book. The only way to survive without Liz was to pour all of my time, energy, anguish, joy—everything—into Maddy. I made her my singular focus, not only because I knew that's what Liz would have wanted, but also because Madeline truly *was* my whole world: my only care after Liz died. We went everywhere together, exploring the city I'd known only with her mom by my side. The numbness brought on by Liz's death was somehow alleviated with Maddy in my arms; I needed her as much as she needed me.

Although I'd written blog entries that people found extremely personal and revelatory, the truth is, I was always holding back. I couldn't bear to confront many of the thoughts and memories swirling around inside my head and I certainly wasn't ready to have my deep feelings criticized, whether by readers or by an editor. Besides, the idea that I could become an author was tantamount to thinking that I could become a plumber or a physicist simply because somebody had suggested it.

As I settled into my role as a widowed father, and as more and more folks approached me about it, I began to consider the crazy idea that I should—and could—actually turn my experiences into a book. But if I was going to act on the opportunity and really write a memoir, I wanted to do it for Madeline. I wanted Maddy to know the emotions I carried with me on a daily basis, how I reacted to them, and how I loved her throughout, no matter how shitty I felt. *This* is the book I set out to write: a book for my daughter.

I quickly realized that in order to undertake this task, I had to get as far away from my everyday life as possible. And because it's almost impossible to fully escape anything these days, I was unequivocally positive that the only way would be to go to the other side of the globe. Literally. Not only were there a ton of physical distractions in my house, but I needed a new setting; somehow, someplace less familiar would make the memories fresher, more recent. I had to be back in a place I had visited with Liz, but a place I didn't think about or pass by on a daily basis. I was used to seeing Liz's clothes in my bedroom every day, but now it was time to go back where I hadn't been since before she died. I couldn't run away from our special moments all over the world anymore; instead, I had to run *to* them. After all, they were everywhere: elephant rides at the palace in Mysore, sitting by the pool at the hotel in Delhi, and having lunch at the outdoor cafes of Paris. I had to return to a place that held the kinds of memories I thought I'd wanted to avoid—to confront them head-on.

So on October 1, 2009, I worked my last day at Yahoo!, moving forward with the insane notion that I would now define myself as a full-time writer. Five days later, Maddy and I were on a flight to Bangalore, India, joined by a woman named Rachel whom I'd met while sitting at the bar at the Troubadour in Los Angeles during an Iron & Wine concert in May. Soon after that evening, I convinced her to leave her job at a Santa Monica art museum so she could act as a nanny for my child while I spent my days writing. Clearly, she was blinded by Maddy's cuteness.

Within a few days of our arrival in Bangalore, Maddy and Rachel were off exploring the city and I found myself hunkered down in a booth of the open-air bar at the Oberoi Hotel on M.G. Road, alternating my stare between the bright white glare of the empty Word document in front of me and the jungle-like plants dripping with humidity in the courtyard. I wanted nothing more than to be with Maddy while she experienced life in a foreign country, but all I could hear was the voice of my editor sternly reprimanding me for missing yet another deadline. With my fingers hovering just a few centimeters above the keyboard, I wondered how one actually goes about writing a book.

Not one word landed on my screen that first day. Zero. The first draft was already late and I hadn't even begun writing. I was deep within my head, wracked with self-doubt over whether or not I, a (now former) middle manager at an Internet company, had the ability to write a memoir. Fuck. I didn't even know how to start what I'd traveled half way around the world to finish. Over the sound of the cricket match playing on the television behind the bar, a cacophony of voices—friends, family, and blog readers, all in my head—promised that I'd find some sort of profound release through an intimate exploration of my feelings. But I was worried, almost convinced, that trying so hard to remember the best moments of my previous life would somehow suck me back into the state of supreme grief that had buried me just after Liz died. And even though the last thing I wanted was to be steered even deeper into the near-constant heartbreak I still felt, I hoped that chasing these joyful memories would cultivate the kind of catharsis that would help me find some level of contentment with a life I couldn't change. I was afraid to remember, but I was also afraid not to.

But as much as I wanted to distance myself from all of the awful shit that happened on March 25, I knew I was holding on to the memories of that day as tightly as I possibly could for fear of losing them forever. If I forgot those moments—and the pain that came with them—I'd be doing a disservice to Maddy, and worse, to Liz. Our last few minutes together were in my head at almost all times, but especially at night. No matter how hard I tried to banish the images from my mind, the last scene my brain conjured before I fell asleep each night was Liz lying lifeless in that hospital bed, and it was that same image that assailed me when I woke up each morning. I was reliving her death over and over again, and as a result, I hadn't had a decent night of sleep since even before Liz had entered the hospital. As more time passed, many of the happiest memories of our twelve-plus years together had faded into the recesses of my mind, only to be recalled through immense effort during moments of near total isolation. It was as if that one awful day was clouding all the others.

Sitting there in the same soft, green-vinyl booth on my second day of writing (or of trying to write), inside my calm oasis in the middle of the loud and bustling city, I thought about the three or four times I had sat here with Liz, drinking tea, taking in the scent of the fake jasmine pumped in by the hotel to cover up the awful chemical smell used to keep the mosquitoes at bay. Everything seemed the same. It was as if I had been suddenly transported three years into the past, but the mirage of my old life evaporated the moment the waitress placed a few packets of Liz's favorite non-sugar sweetener next to my cup of tea. They were yet another reminder that I would never see her, never hold her again, and that if I didn't record these memories now, I may forever lose them. They were the spark that started my writing, and within minutes of their arrival on my table, I typed the following:

"i love coming here!"
that's what
she said each time
we sat down
for tea.
it wasn't the respite
from the noise
of the city
that this place provided.
it wasn't the
beautiful surroundings.
it wasn't the time
alone with me.
it wasn't even
the quality of the tea.
it was the sweetener
in the yellow packets.
"this is the only place i've seen it in india!"
she'd say
as she quietly slipped
packet after packet into
her purse.
i used to laugh
at her, calling her
"thief,"
"junkie,"
and countless other

words that
would have been less than
flattering if they'd
been overheard by
anyone around us.
but to her,
to us,
these words
were the way we
showed love.
it was the teasing
that made us smile,
because between us,
we both knew
that me calling her a
no-calorie sweetener junkie
or a yellow packet thief
meant that i
noticed the little things,
that i knew
her better than
anyone else in the world.
i'm thankful for
those moments,
because as i sit
in the exact same spot
we used to sit,
writing about her,
drinking my tea,
happy that something
as mundane as
little yellow packets
filled with

dextrose, maltodextrin, and sucralose
can elicit the kind
of emotions usually
reserved for the
the music, movies, words, and places
of our past.
yes.
it's the little things
that make all of
this hard,
but it's also the little things
that make all of
this so.

When I finally typed that last period, I knew that I had
broken the impasse; the memories would flood back and the
words would flow forth faster than I expected. By the time the
grounds crew started spraying for mosquitoes at dusk, I had
written 7,000 words. Six days later, I had completed a first
draft of Part I.

As momentous as it was for me to finish that first third of
my book, what followed was even greater: I slept soundly for
the first time in more than eighteen months. After being held
captive by my sorrow, I was finally able to escape from its grip.
I was so scared to think of Liz dying, but I didn't want to let go
of the memory either, and now that I had moved the thoughts
from my mind to my computer, I was freed from the burden
of having to remember them. They were now preserved for the
future—for Madeline.

After exhausting my memories in Bangalore and writing as
much as I possibly could, it was time to face more of my past
to keep the words flowing. We headed to Northern India and
Nepal, where Maddy ambled along (and was sometimes car-

ried) in the places her mother visited. She wandered through the oppressive heat of Fatehpur Sikri, used the Taj Mahal as her playground for a few hours, and held my hand outside the temple where I asked Liz to marry me. With all but one of the hotels in Kathmandu filled to capacity, we ended up in the very place where Liz and I had excitedly called our families to tell them about our engagement, and thanks to nothing but chance, my daughter and I slept in the exact same room I had shared with her mother just five years earlier. Every night we were there the pigeons on the ledge outside the room kept me awake, just like they had then. In each location I told Maddy the stories of my time there with Liz, and embraced my daughter as tightly as I grasped the moments that defined my life with her mother. Though just eighteen months old and completely unaware of the places we were or why they were significant, I was giving Madeline a physical connection to Liz in the only way that I knew how. We didn't have a gravesite or any sort of memorial to visit, so we went where Liz had been. More important, we were creating our own reasons to return that now had just as much to do with *our* past as they did with my past with Liz.

Maddy and I haven't stopped traveling since that trip, visiting places I went with Liz as well as cities that we never made it together. Travel has been a constant in my adult life, and I want it to be a huge part of Maddy's life to ensure that she has the kind of worldly perspective I didn't gain until I was in college. We spent Madeline's second birthday in Paris, and her third birthday in Puerto Vallarta. We've been to and explored ten U.S. states, two Canadian provinces, three Mexican states, and six countries—over ninety round-trip flights together in her first four years of life. I didn't take my first plane trip until I was twelve.

There are still several places in the world I want to bring

Madeline, so many memories yet to confront, and a lifetime of memories yet to create. I can't help but smile, thinking about how proud Liz would be of the life I've built for our daughter.

Many years before 2008, Liz had said, "If I die before you, I want you to find someone who makes you happy." I just stared back at her, in total disbelief at the words that had just come from her mouth. She had never before spoken so frankly about death and in fact, used to recoil at any discussion of the subject. But thanks in part to some stupid episode of *Grey's Anatomy* she was watching as I tried to read one night, I was suddenly confronted with the notion that someday I'd live a life without her in it. "Promise me," she said, as I nodded back in silence.

I was just as uncomfortable with the idea as she was, so I placed the book down on the couch, gently reached for her hands and did the only thing I knew how to do: I made a terrible joke. "If I die before you, you better mourn me 'til the day you die." She looked at me with the kind of knowing glare I got from her several times each day and before she could say anything I added, "Really though, I'd want the same for you. I'd want you to be happy."

As we sat there in a now sort of awkward silence, I tried to figure out what living without her would really mean, wondering why the hell I'd even want to attempt to find love again at age eighty-nine or ninety-five or whatever.

Of course, I hadn't imagined the scenario would come at age thirty.

The last thing on my mind when Liz died was when, how, or even if I'd be able to fulfill that promise to her. I was too busy mourning her, wishing that she were there with Maddy and me, hoping that I alone could provide the kind of life our daughter should have. But the time spent away from my real life in Los Angeles in India and Nepal, and the writing I had done while I was away had a significant, profound, and unexpected effect on my life. It afforded me the opportunity to keep moving through in a way I hadn't considered: meeting someone I could fall in love with.

It was on a night a few days after what would have been Liz's thirty-second birthday, in the same building where we were married, that I met the woman who would eventually become my future. I was in Minneapolis to participate in some fundraising events for the Liz Logelin Foundation; Brooke was a volunteer, lending her time to a cause that had touched her only because of her compassion for others. She had never suffered the kind of tragedy that the foundation aimed to alleviate, yet she was as devoted to the cause as anyone else I knew. Brooke worked so selflessly and completely under the radar that I didn't even know who she was until that night. She didn't need anyone to notice her, but I did anyway. I left for India a few weeks after our initial meeting, and while I was away, we exchanged a grand total of two e-mails about Brooke running into my cousin in a Minneapolis skyway.

Upon my return from India, Brooke and I went out for the first time, meeting at a local Minneapolis dive bar called Liquor Lyle's for a couple of drinks and some fried food. I thought she was way too cool for me when she walked in wearing a T-shirt with skulls on it, and I loved that she was open to going somewhere that many women would never consider stepping inside on what amounted to an unintended first date. It was nearly impossible for me to believe, but within just a few days it became obvious to me that Brooke was the woman with whom I wanted to spend my new life and more important, the woman I wanted in my daughter's life. I hadn't realized it then, but it was the trip to India; the revisiting of my past and the writing I did while there gave me the ability to open myself up to love again.

At some point, I knew, I would have to introduce Brooke

to the people in my world, and I knew exactly who should come first: Madeline. Maddy was too young to really care or even realize that she was meeting the woman I was dating—mostly she was just thrilled to chase Brooke's cat, Leo, around her apartment (a sure sign of success). After that, I didn't waver when considering who would be next: Liz's parents. As I thought about the actual moment in which they would meet Brooke, I tried to imagine the emotions that would be coursing through their bodies and how they would handle the news. Their reaction would be my gauge for how others would accept my decision; if they were okay with our relationship, then everyone else in the world should be as well, I thought. Truthfully, I expected nothing less from them. Since Liz had died, Tom and Candee had only been supportive of the decisions I had made, and of me. They encouraged me to write, to travel, to do whatever it was that I needed to find my way through my grief, because they knew if I was okay, then Maddy would follow my lead. And when they met Brooke, they really were happy for me, and especially thrilled for Maddy. I think they were sort of excited about the fact that Madeline would now have a female influence in her life; a woman in our lives meant that Maddy might learn about the world of fashion beyond how to style plaid shirts. And I had been right: When I told the rest of my family and friends about my new relationship, they were just as supportive as Tom and Candee.

When I wrote about Brooke on my blog, the response was overwhelming. Most people were happy for me and were able to understand things from my perspective, congratulating me for finding a new kind of contentment and for choosing not to stay mired in my sadness. Others judged me harshly: "She's a replacement" and "Wow, you moved on fast!" were common refrains. It was difficult to put my feelings into words while I tried my best to defend Brooke's role in our lives, as I wasn't really concerned with what people thought about me or my decision. These critical strangers didn't truly know us; I alone would determine what was right for Maddy and me. But I worried about losing Brooke: I didn't want her to read the comments these strangers left on the blog and think that I felt the way they did. I tried to tell people that there could never be a "replacement," that "moving on" is an impossible thing for any widow or widower to do, and that there is no such thing as "too fast." Anyone who has experienced the death of a partner knows that the love for that person never diminishes and certainly the capacity to love does not die with him or her. But I wasn't really explaining this to all of these blog commenters—I was writing it out for Brooke.

In the time since I announced our relationship, things have not been perfect. It's with the best intentions that we communicate and understand each other's feelings. I sometimes struggle to fully grasp how difficult it is for her to be the woman in my present while I write and speak about my past so often. Brooke struggles to play the role of a motherly figure in Maddy's life without actually being her mom, doing her best to not step on any toes or upset my family and friends. I struggle to explain my ability to love two women at once. And Brooke struggles to shake the feeling that she's living in Liz's shadow.

But we do it all with grace (though she's far more graceful than I am).

And through it all, we love each other.

Relationships are complicated, and this one is no different. But I'm confident that the decision I made is the right one, and that Brooke is the right person for us to make new memories with.

Besides, I know that Liz would want someone like Brooke in our lives.

And so does Maddy.

* * *

It's been four years since Liz died. I still think about her constantly, but I've found peace with the amazing memories of our time together, to the point where I can wonder about mundane things like how she would handle the situations I find myself in. I rely on my memories of our time together and all that she taught me—whether or not I recognized the teachable moments at the time—to make many of my daily decisions. She's the voice scolding me when I forget to put my seatbelt on or when I go a few too many days without eating a salad, and the one cheering me on as I accomplish each new goal I set out to achieve. I no longer work a nine-to-five job. Instead, I'm a published author who regularly speaks to groups about my life (but please don't call me a motivational speaker). I'm also the president of a nonprofit foundation that has helped over one hundred families with financial assistance after the death of a partner and parent. It's almost unimaginable for me to believe the turns my life has taken in such a short time.

Madeline is now four years old. It's impossible to know just by looking at her what she's been through in her short life. The effects of her having been born seven weeks early have all but disappeared. She's as tall as her peers and her language skills are far above average. Her ever-present smile is a sure sign of her happiness.

Liz's parents can't help but see the similarities between the daughter they raised and the granddaughter they now watch grow up. I believe I know the kind of woman Madeline will become because I was lucky enough to spend over twelve years with her mother. Like Liz, she can be obstinate, loud, and frustrating, but more often, she is fun, gentle, and empathetic. With each day that passes, Maddy looks more and more like her mom. Her long blonde hair pulled back in a ponytail, the bangs sweeping across her face, barely covering just one of the stunning blue eyes she inherited from Liz. I can already see the resemblance between the Liz I knew and the Maddy I know so far.

Even with all of the similarities that are so obvious when we compare our memories of Liz to Madeline in front of us, I do my best to treat her as an individual, so that she doesn't spend her life trying to live up to some unrealistic idea of perfection that is often created after someone dies. I've made every attempt to ensure that Madeline's life will not be defined only by what happened the day after she was born. Yes, her mother's death will affect her forever, but I hope that when she looks back on her childhood, she will do so with the same giant grin she shows off on the playground, when she sees a squirrel running across a power line in our backyard, or when she eats a piece of chocolate.

Every time I see that smile or hear her tell me that she loves me, I can't help but think how lucky I am despite everything.

And how truly, truly happy.

*July 16, 1996—Liz and me
at a concert in Minneapolis.*

August 12, 2005—The two of us at our wedding rehearsal.

*December 31, 2006—
Celebrating New Year's Eve in
Bangalore, India.*

March 24, 2008—Liz seeing Maddy for the first and only time.

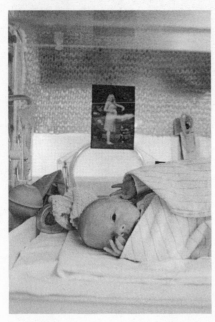

March 28, 2008—Maddy in her incubator, a photo of Liz behind her.

May 13, 2006—Liz and me at the Taj Mahal, Agra, India.

*November 5, 2009—
Maddy and me at the Taj
Mahal, Agra, India.*

May 13, 2006—Liz at the Red Fort, Agra, India.

November 5, 2009—
Maddy at the Red Fort,
Agra, India.

June 19, 2004—Liz in front of the temple where I proposed at Durbar Square, Kathmandu, Nepal.

November 9, 2009—Maddy and me in front of the same temple at Durbar Square, Kathmandu, Nepal.

August 27, 2006—Liz giving me "the look" while I teased her about her height.

August 14, 2011— Measuring Maddy, just like I used to do to Liz.

October 25, 2009—Maddy
and me bathing elephants in
South India.

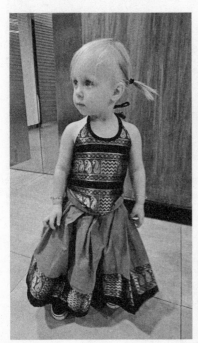

October 16, 2009—Maddy out
for dinner in Bangalore, India.

November 9, 2009—In
Durbar Square, Kathmandu,
Nepal.

*March 20, 2010—
Maddy in our hotel room
in Paris.*

March 23, 2010—Outside of Notre Dame in Paris.

March 15, 2009—In a cage at the old zoo in Griffith Park.

October 25, 2010—
Celebrating my birthday in
our backyard.

August 15, 2010—Madeline in the sky near San Simeon, California.

December 20, 2010—Catching snowflakes in Minnesota.

February 13, 2011—Looking at me the way her mom used to.

October 17, 2011—Playing in a puddle in Alaska.

February 20, 2011—At the Mayan Ruins of Coba in Mexico.

March 24, 2011—Running on the beach in Puerto Vallarta on her third birthday.

January 9, 2009—In the elevator at Amoeba in Hollywood.

July 12, 2011—In the same elevator two-and-a-half years later.

September 25, 2011—Maddy.

May 8, 2006—Liz.

Acknowledgments

Any omissions are unintentional.

Without the help of the following people, this book would not be possible: Rachel Sussman, Eve Bridburg, and the folks at Zachary Shuster Harmsworth. Special thanks to Sandra Bark for getting me to where I needed to be. Extra special thanks to my editor Amanda Englander for pushing me to get this done and for not giving up on me when I missed each and every deadline.

I'd like to thank all of my friends in Kathmandu and Bangalore, especially the Bista family, Anish Divakaran, Karthik Ramachandran, Vidushi Lath, Vinod Sankar, Shreyas Pandit, Srikant Suvvaru, Eshwari Shunmuganathan, and Scattle.

These people have been wonderful to us over the past three years: the nurses at Huntington Hospital, Dr. Sharon Nelson, Dr. Jennifer Hartstein, my blog readers and the Creeps, especially Rachel Engebretson, Kris Stutz, Darcie Gust, Nancy Reins, Laurie Henry, Gina Brown, Chris Tuttle, Kate Siegel, Christa Rokita, Michelle Moore, Ali Smith, Cara Ulm, Katie Jackson, Becky Peterson, Leigh Acevedo, Kelly McElligott, Marissa Colvin, Maureen Casey, Teal Fyrberg, Sol in Argentina, Meggin Juraska, Marcy, Piper and Bailey, Kim Barth, Tricia

Madden, Katy Epler, Danielle Ireland, and Kate Sowa, Jackie Chandler, Kim Lucio, Kay and May at Cribsheet, Kristine Lazar, Pat Pheifer, Jana Shortal, Bea Chang, Gina Lee, Briana McDonnell, Tom and Cass, Michele Neff Hernandez, the employees, HR, and management teams at CAST, Disney, and Yahoo!, and the volunteers and donors of the Liz Logelin Foundation.

I am grateful for the support of my friends, especially the Ash, Keen, Caufield, Dumper, Nuruki, Sowers, Spohr, Gay-Rose, and Jensen families, Lindsay Lewis, Chrissy Coppa, Alaina Shearer, Ken Basart, Peter Miriani, Eileen Scahill, Ben and Dana Parks, John Sherwood, Heather Stanley, Jason and Allie Beecher, Amy and Greg Cohn, Christina Vickers, Jon Wu, Melanie Larsen, Rhonda Hicks, Bob Okeefe, Anna Harris, Mark Heaney, Anthony Downs, Mark Musgjerd, Richard Peterson, Steve and Emily Broback, Biraj and Anjali Bista, Nathan and Stacey Meath, John and Andrea Kannas, Jamie and Cara Thompson, Alex and Heather Dowlin, and especially A.J. and Sonja Colianni for being there whenever I needed you.

Endless appreciation to Jeanette and Jennifer, Jasmine Payne, Aislinn Butler-Hetterman, the Valdivia family, Diane Baek, Chandra Locke-Bradley, Kathy Dixon, and especially Anya Kitashima, Maleeda Wagner-Holmes, Annie Birnie, and Ari Mayer for being the best friends a girl could have, and for promising that Madeline will know *everything* about her mother.

Thanks to Rachel Monas for not questioning my sanity and for keeping my baby girl safe from pinching fingers, sadistic children, camels, horses, and elephants.

Thanks to Kate Coyne for her psychic abilities and the Bob Ross painting.

Thanks to Wesley Siemers for the morning greetings and for keeping her updated.

Extra thanks to Brooke Gullikson for patience, love, and understanding.

For inspiration while I was writing: Derek and Kurt (for the Derek Tape), Jeff Mangum and Neutral Milk Hotel, J. Tillman, PJ Harvey, Liz Phair, The National, Ariel Pink, Bon Iver, WHY?, Silver Jews, Sun Kil Moon, Pavement, Broken Social Scene, Arcade Fire, Swearing at Motorists, Vic Chesnutt, Paul Westerberg and the Replacements, Eazy-E, Will Oldham, Jeff Tweedy and Wilco, Gil Scott-Heron, Ryan Adams, Glen Campbell, Richard Buckner, Iron & Wine, the Hold Steady, John Coltrane, Minneapolis, Los Angeles, Akumal, Kathmandu, Pashupatinath, the Bagmati River, Fatehpur Sikri, Jaipur, Agra, Paris, Robert Bingham, Charles Bukowski, John Fante, Philip Levine, Robert Lowell, John Berryman, and especially Mark Kozelek, Yoni Wolf, and David Berman for your kindness and generosity in letting me use your words.

Limitless gratitude and love to the Logelin, Shoberg, Werner, Hedstrom, Bensman, Lee, and Goodman families, Becky Werner, Ray and Pauline Logelin, Adam, Holly, and Ava Shoberg, Tina, Travis, and Trevor Metz, Heather McKinley, Alex, Taylor, and David Logelin, Nick and Molly Logelin, Josh, Jane, and Isla McKinley, Tom and Bev Logelin, Sara and Rodney Shoberg, and Tom, Candee, and Deb Goodman.

Most important, I want to thank Elizabeth Goodman-Logelin and Madeline Elizabeth Logelin for making me who I am today.

About the Author

Photo by Ben Parks.

Born and bred in Minnesota, MATT LOGELIN is the founder and president of the Liz Logelin Foundation, a nonprofit organization that aims to financially assist widows and widowers with young families. In addition, he is a public speaker and has given talks at venues ranging from the Vascular Disease Foundation to Camp Widow to the West Hollywood Book Festival.

Matt and his daughter, Madeline, live in Los Angeles, but they travel often to see as much of the world as possible. His long-term goal is to ensure that she grows up happy and listening to good music; after completing this book, achieving those things shouldn't be too difficult.

Please visit them at www.mattlogelin.com.